T0212389

Lecture Notes in Computer Science   11777

More information about this series at http://www.springer.com/series/7410

Simin Nadjm-Tehrani (Ed.)

Critical Information Infrastructures Security

14th International Conference, CRITIS 2019
Linköping, Sweden, September 23–25, 2019
Revised Selected Papers

 Springer

Editor
Simin Nadjm-Tehrani 🆔
Linköping University
Linköping, Sweden

ISSN 0302-9743   ISSN 1611-3349   (electronic)
Lecture Notes in Computer Science
ISBN 978-3-030-37669-7   ISBN 978-3-030-37670-3   (eBook)
https://doi.org/10.1007/978-3-030-37670-3

LNCS Sublibrary: SL4 – Security and Cryptology

This Springer imprint is published by the registered company Springer Nature Switzerland AG
The registered company address is: Gewerbestrasse 11, 6330 Cham, Switzerland

Preface

This volume contains the proceedings of the 14th International Conference on Critical Information Infrastructures Security (CRITIS 2019). The conference was held at Linköping University, Linköping, Sweden, during September 23–25, 2019. It was organized by the Department of Computer and Information Science with support from the national Research Centre on Resilient Information and Control Systems (RICS) financed by the Swedish Civil Contingencies Agency (MSB). The CRITIS 2019 program included five outstanding invited lectures, two from academia, two from governmental and European agencies, and one from a European Research Center, providing a wide range of insights for both academics and practitioners as follows:

- "Everything is Awesome! Or is it? Cyber Security Risks in Critical Infrastructure", by Prof. Awais Rashid, University of Bristol, UK
- "NIS Directive and the Role of ENISA", by Dr. Marianthi Theocharidou, ENISA, Greece
- "Challenges in Quantifying an Adversary's Cyber Access to Critical Infrastructures", by Prof. David Nicol, University of Illinois at Urbana-Champaign, and Director of the Information Trust Institute, USA
- "National Risk Assessments and EU/JRC Guidelines", by Dr. Ainara Casajus Valles, European Joint Research Centre (JRC), Belgium
- "Hybrid Threats Impacts on Crisis Management", by Mr. Yves Rougier, Head of Planning and Crisis Management at the Ministry for the Ecological and Inclusive Transition, France.

The organizers of the conference are grateful for the time and effort allocated by the keynote speakers and their excellent talks as a contribution to the program.

The conference followed the well-established tradition of soliciting research articles from a wide range of critical infrastructure domains, covering both theory and experimental/empirical research, as well as a special theme and topics related to disruptive technologies and their impact on critical infrastructure protection. The special theme around which a round table discussion was organized was "Cyber Ranges and Testbeds". Four distinguished researchers, Prof. Anne Remke from University of Twente, The Netherlands, and Münster University, Germany; Dr. Olaf Manuel Maennel from Center for Digital Forensics and Cyber Security at Tallinn University of Technology, Estonia; Dr. Shahid Raza from the RISE Research Institute, Sweden; and Mr. Tommy Gustavsson from Swedish Defence Research Agency (FOI), Sweden, participated in this discussion session. All in all, participants from 12 countries and 3 continents were present at the conference making a truly international atmosphere.

10 regular papers, selected among 30 submissions to the conference, and 5 short papers covering preliminary results constituted the content of the technical sessions in the program. These sessions were organized around some broad themes, e.g. Risk Management, Vulnerability Assessment, Resilience and Mitigation, as well as more

specialized application domains like Transport and Finance. The selected papers were subject to a thorough double-blind review by at least three members of the distinguished Program Committee. The authors were then given the opportunity to use the comments by the reviewers to improve their papers. The authors' revised versions appear in the proceedings with no further review, grouped under the themes of the program.

In addition, a special session on Industry and Practical experience reports consisting of four presentations was organized by two designated chairs. The work of the mediating session chair Dr. Francesco Flammini, and also Prof. Sokratis K. Katsikas, in reviewing these works is gratefully acknowledged. A white paper based on the topics presented was co-authored by all involved presenters and the two session chairs for presentation in the proceedings.

A conference is a place to meet, exchange ideas, be questioned while presenting, and get inspired while listening to others. The social events of the conference and facilities that made the whole participation a unique experience would not have been possible without generous support and dedicated help from numerous organizations and individuals. This is an attempt to bring their efforts to the forefront.

Saab AB, the Swedish aerospace and defence company, and the Swedish Grid, the responsible agency for electrical transmission in Sweden, shared their support for the conference when the program was a blank page. The 3D imaging company, Vricon, provided both a venue for the conference reception and an interesting technical presentation of the company's success story. Sectra, once a spin-off from the host university and now operating in multiple countries, with its communications division providing services to the EU and NATO, was present and generously supported the conference.

Last but not least, as a tradition at CRITIS, the Res on Network on Intelligence and Global Defence, with Professor Santarelli as the initiator, was a generous provider of prizes for the Young CRITIS Award (YCA) nominees. This year's YCA was awarded to Zack Ellerby for the presentation of the paper co-authored by Josie McCulloch, Melanie Wilson, and Christian Wagner from the University of Nottingham, UK.

In addition to the Technical Program Committee members, there were many other individuals working behind the scenes. I sincerely thank all the local organization members, coordinated by the organization chair Dr. Mikael Asplund, for the fantastic cooperation. Valuable input to the conference traditions was provided by Prof. Bernhard Hemmerli, Prof. Gregorio D'Agostino, and Dr. Inga Šarūnienė (the general chair of the last edition of the conference). Without all this support CRITIS 2019 would not have been a successful conference!

November 2019   Simin Nadjm-Tehrani

Organization

CRITIS 2019 was organized by the Department of Computer and Information Science, Linköping University, Sweden.

Executive Committee

General/Program Chair

Simin Nadjm-Tehrani   Linköping University, Sweden

Honorary Chair

Sandro Bologna   AIIC, Italy

Organization Chair

Mikael Asplund   Linköping University, Sweden

Industry Session Chairs

Francesco Flammini   Lineaus University, Sweden
Sokratis K. Katsikas   NTNU, Norway, and University of Piraeus, Greece

Publicity Chair

Magnus Almgren   Chalmers University of Technology, Sweden

Program Committee

Members

Cristina Alcaraz, Spain
Mikael Asplund, Sweden
Alberto Avritzer, USA
Fabrizio Baiardi, Italy
Emiliano Casalicchio, Sweden
Michal Choras, Poland
Kris Christmann, UK
Gregorio D'Agostino, Italy
Geert Deconinck, Belgium
Mathias Ekstedt, Sweden
Francesco Flammini, Sweden
Igor Nai Fovino, Belgium
Dimitris Gritzalis, Greece
Stefanos Gritzalis, Greece

Bernhard Haemmerli, Switzerland
Chris Hankin, UK
Grigore M. Havarneanu, France
Mikel Iturbe, Spain
Zbigniew Kalbarczyk, USA
Sokratis Katsikas, Norway/Greece
Marieke Klaver, The Netherlands
Vytis Kopustinskas, Italy
Panayiotis Kotzanikolaou, Greece
Ričardas Krikštolaitis, Lithuania
Elias Kyriakides, Cyprus
Javier Lopez, Spain
Eric Luiijf, The Netherlands
Jose Marti, Canada

Linas Martišauskas, Lithuania
Marcelo Masera, Belgium
Aditya Mathur, USA
Kieran McLaughlin, UK
Max Mühlhäuser, Germany
Gabriele Oliva, Italy
Evangelos Ouzounis, Greece
Stefano Panzieri, Italy
Ludovic Pietre-Cambacedes, France
Anne Remke, Germany/The Netherlands

Henrik Sandberg, Sweden
Inga Šarūnienė, Lithuania
Alberto Tofani, Italy
Maria Paola Scaparra, UK
Roberto Setola, Italy
Nils Ole Tippenhauer, Germany
Eugenijus Uspuras, Lithuania
Emmanouil Vasilomanolakis, Denmark
Stephen D. Wolthusen, UK/Norway
Jianying Zhou, Singapore

Sponsoring Institutions

Saab AB, Sweden
Swedish Grid, Sweden
Sectra Communications, Sweden

CRITIS Steering Committee

Chairs

Bernhard M. Hämmerli   Technical University Lucerne and ACRIS, Switzerland
Javier Lopez   University of Malaga, Spain
Stephen D. Wolthusen   Royal Holloway, University of London, UK,
                          and NTNU, Norway

Members

Robin Bloomfield, UK
Sandro Bologna, Italy
Gregorio D'Agostino, Italy
Grigore Havarneanu, France
Sokratis K. Katsikas, Norway/Greece
Elias Kyriakides, Cyprus
Eric Luiijf, The Netherlands
Marios M. Polycarpou, Cyprus

Reinhard Posch, Austria
Erich Rome, Germany
Antonio Scala, Italy
Inga Šarūnienė, Lithuania
Roberto Setola, Italy
Nils Kalstad Svendsen, Norway
Marianthi Theocharidou, Italy

Additional Reviewers

Georgios Karopoulos
Georgia Lykou
Dimitrios Papamartzivanos
Rossen Naydenov
George Stergiopoulos
Apostolos Malatras

Contents

Industry and Practical Experience Reports

Invited Papers

Everything Is Awesome! or Is It? Cyber Security Risks in Critical Infrastructure

Awais Rashid[1]([✉])[iD], Joseph Gardiner[1][iD], Benjamin Green[2][iD], and Barnaby Craggs[1][iD]

[1] Bristol Cyber Security Group, University of Bristol, Bristol, UK
{awais.rashid,barney.craggs,joe.gardiner}@bristol.ac.uk
[2] Security Lancaster Institute, Lancaster University, Lancaster, UK
b.green2@lancaster.ac.uk
http://www.bristol.ac.uk/engineering/research/cyber-security/

Abstract. Industrial Control Systems (ICS) play an important role in the monitoring, control and automation of critical infrastructure such as water, gas, oil and electricity. Recent years have seen a number of high profile cyber attacks on such infrastructure exemplified by Stuxnet and the Ukrainian Power Grid attacks. This naturally begs the question: how should we manage cyber security risks in such infrastructure on which the day-to-day functioning of societies rely? What are the complexities of managing security in a landscape shaped by the often competing demands of a variety of stakeholders, e.g., managers, control engineers, enterprise IT personnel and field site operators? What are the challenges posed by the convergence of Internet of Things (IoT) and critical infrastructure through the so-called Industrial Internet of Things (IIoT)? In this paper, we discuss insights from a multi-year programme of research investigating these issues and the challenges to addressing them.

Keywords: Cyber security · Industrial Control Systems · Critical infrastructure · Industrial IoT · Cyber risk decisions

1 Introduction

Critical infrastructure systems, e.g., water, power, etc. are increasingly being connected to other enterprise systems for a variety of reasons. These range from the need to remotely update and maintain systems, reducing the effort, time and cost of visiting remote, hard to access facilities through to the desire to gain real-time business intelligence in order to optimise processes and improve efficiencies. Consequently, the past assumption that such systems are air-gapped from wider networks, and the Internet, is increasingly being proven to no longer be valid. Unintentional connections are also an increasing issue, with poorly configured controls allowing outside connections to individual control devices. For instance, a browse though the Shodan search engine of Internet connected devices shows

---

The author conducted the work while employed by the Bristol Cyber Security Group.

© Springer Nature Switzerland AG 2020
S. Nadjm-Tehrani (Ed.): CRITIS 2019, LNCS 11777, pp. 3–17, 2020.
https://doi.org/10.1007/978-3-030-37670-3_1

a large number of programmable logic controllers (PLCs) from various manufacturers. As we note above, increasingly, these connections to external systems, and the Internet, are being introduced intentionally for remote connectivity and configuration capabilities or other business needs. This results in a number of risks to critical infrastructures as a consequence of an increased cyber-attack surface.

As we build more and more complex large, connected environments, the scale of connectivity and complexity of such enrivonments will only increase further—resulting in increased scale of attacks and impact. The problem is compounded by the fact that often critical infrastructures have multiple organisations that collectively contribute to the environment, e.g., power producers and power distribution networks are often owned by different organisations not to mention the large number of organisations that form the supply chain. The infrastructures remain in operation over a long lifespan and their make-up (devices, software, communication protocols) changes over time, often resulting in a large number of legacy and non-legacy systems working in conjunction to deliver critical services to citizens.

For instance, we are seeing the emergence of multiple products and services on the market that allow for data from industrial environments to be sent to the cloud for processing, allowing remote monitoring of processes, under the banner of Industrial Internet of Things (IIoT) and Industry 4.0. The latest push is to move onto SCADA-in-the-cloud, where more and more control functions are moved into the remote cloud environment. This transition results in ICS equipment becoming Internet-of-Things devices, with indirect connections to IT networks and the wider Internet—providing a route for attackers to gain access to these devices through compromise of the cloud environment.

Cyber security risks, therefore, need to be managed in the face of these new attack vectors and increased attack sophistication whereby highly resourced adversaries may disrupt critical services to large parts of the population. Managing such risks is, however, non-trivial for three reasons:

- Risk is a socio-technical construct—requiring not only an understanding of the technical threat landscape but also organisational and human dimensions of risk and risk decision-making.
- Risks arising from both legacy and non-legacy systems need to be understood especially those that emerge from the convergence of the two.
- Such understanding needs to be developed through direct engagement with the stakeholders and experimentation on realistic infrastructures. The former is often challenging due to the sensitive nature and confidentiality cultures within critical infrastructure organisations. The latter cannot be achieved through experimentation on production environments (as this can lead to disruption to the infrastructure), hence requiring realistic testbeds that enable modelling and experimentation of non-trival attack scenarios.

In this paper, we discuss insights from a multi-year programme of research investigating both social and technical dimensions of cyber security risks in critical infrastructures. We first summarise (Sect. 2) insights from our prior work [4,5] to discuss the human and organisational dimensions of cyber risks. We then move onto the technical aspects of the problem and particularly the risks arising from convergence of IIoT and ICS environments. We describe the Bristol Cyber Security Group (BCSG) testbed (Sect. 3) followed by detailed discussion of an attack (Sect. 4) against an ICS environment (set up using our testbed) which utilises a cloud provider. We exploit the connection from the operational network to the cloud to provide a tunnel through which we can gain access to the control equipment. Through this access we force the physical process, a water treatment plant, to enter an unsafe state by disabling a pressure alarm and increasing he speed of the primary pump.

2   Human and Organisational Dimensions of Cyber Risk

In prior work [5], we analysed a number of high profile attacks against industrial control systems (including those impacting critical infrastructures) and highlighted that perception errors play a key part in attack success. These perception errors relate to four dimensions (Fig. 1):

System qualities. Operators may have incorrect perceptions of particular qualities of the system, e.g., confidentiality, integrity, availability, resilience, etc. This may lead them to think that the system can withstand particular faults or recover gracefully when this may not be the case in reality.

System boundaries. Operators may have incorrect perceptions a system's isolation (physical or virtual) from other systems. This, in turn, may lead the operators to assume that lateral movement across systems or from less critical to mission critical systems is not possible when this may not be the case in reality.

Observability. Operators may assume that, at a particular point in time, their observation of system behaviour is accurate and complete.

Controllability. Operators may assume that, even under attack conditions, they maintain control of the system especially safety-critical components.

However, these perception errors often arise due to *latent design conditions* [9] – improper specification of system qualities, borders, observability and controllability – during conception, design, implementation or evolution. These latent design conditions are further exacerbated when the attacker *actively tampers* with the observation and control link between the operators and the system.

A number of stakeholder decisions shape security within such a system, and by consequence, may lead to latent design conditions. Previously, we designed a game, Decisions & Disruptions[1] and analysed the decision-making processes of three different stakeholder groups: managers, computer science/IT experts and security experts [4]. The game (see Fig. 2) charges a team of players to defend a hydro-electric power producer (represented by a Lego® board) against cyber attacks. Players invest in various defences over four game rounds. Attacks occur

---

[1] https://www.decisions-disruptions.org.

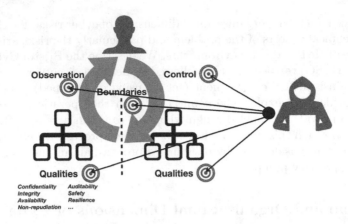

Fig. 1. Dimensions of cyber risk perception

during each round and their success depends on the defences in which the players have invested. However, the players have a limited budget in each round (unspent budget carries over to the next round) so they must prioritise and choose amongst the different types of defences. These range from basic defences such as firewalls, anti-virus and security training to more advanced network monitoring solutions. Players can also seek to gain intelligence by paying for a threat assessment and an asset audit. The game is available under a CC-BY-NC license and all the cards, a Bricklink model the Lego® and the rule book are all available on the website.

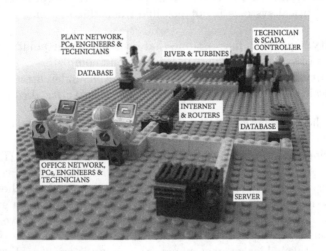

Fig. 2. An overview of the Decisions & Disruptions game board

Our analysis of twelve teams representing the three stakeholder groups: managers, computer scientists/IT personnel and security experts from academia and industry has highlighted a number of interesting patterns. We briefly summarise these below. Readers are referred to [4] for a detailed discussion:

- *Security experts* favoured advanced cyber security protection measures, e.g., the advanced network monitoring product (effectively a very expensive intrusion detection system) and often deprioritised basic protections (e.g., firewalls, anti-virus and patching) and intelligence gathering (e.g., threat assessment or asset audits). Their discussions were *scenario-driven* (e.g., what if ...) and they had *high confidence* in their decisions – even when these decisions led them to catastrophic outcomes.
- *Computer scientists*, by contrast, focused more substantially on intelligence gathering and human factors (e.g., security training) and deprioritised advanced cyber security protection measures. However, they also deprioritised data protection – a fundamental requirement for information security. They used *diverse* strategies during decision-making but expressed *low confidence* in their decisions even those that subsequently successfully deflected attacks.
- *Managers*, on the other hand, did prioritise data protection along side basic cyber security protection whilst also favouring advanced cyber security technologies. However, they paid less attention to human factors. Their decisions were very much *intuition-driven* (e.g., I like the firewall) and they too exhibited *low confidence* in their choices.

The analysis also showed that security experts did not necessarily always perform the best. There were also a number of good, bad and ugly decision-making patterns that stakeholders should look out for when making decisions about cyber security in an organisation. These are detailed in [4].

Having summarised human and organisational aspects of cyber security in critical infrastructure settings from prior work, in the rest of the paper, we discuss a concrete scenario emerging from the convergence of tranditional control systems (so-called *operational technology (OT)*) and Industrial IoT platforms and devices and demonstrate how this leads to an increased attack surface and successful attacks.

3   Testbed

Before we discuss the details of the attack, we provide a brief overview of the testbed environment that is under attack. For a more detailed discussion of the testbed we refer the reader to [6].

3.1   Physical Process

The primary physical process of the BCSG testbed, and the target of the described attack, is the Gunt CE581 water treatment plant[2], as seen in Fig. 3.

---

[2] https://www.gunt.de/en/products/process-engineering/water-treatment/ multistage-water-treatment/water-treatment-plant-1/083.58100/ce581/glct-1: pa-148:ca-255:pr-57.

The CE581 system, designed for the training of water treatment engineers, consists of a three-stage filtration, absorption and ion-exchange process. The CE581 physical aspect is largely off–the-shelf, however we had the unit customised with safety valves to release system pressure when under attack, and added a removable copper pipe between the filtration and absorption stages to allow for the easy installation and removal of additional sensors.

The CE581 initially utilised a small Eaton PLC for control. By using swappable terminal blocks, we replaced the control equipment with our own control architecture. This allows us to utilise equipment that more closely represents real-world scenarios. This architecture is discussed in Sect. 3.2. The original control equipment can be made operational with minimal effort if required for maintenance.

The system has five controllable elements: the pump and 4 electronically operated valves to control the flow of water though the three stages. The system also has a number of sensors, including a pressure alarm, differential pressure across the filtration tanks and temperature sensors.

Normal Operation. Under normal operation, the system operates with the pump set at 80% speed utilising all three stages of the treatment process. Under these conditions, the system runs with around 1.55 bar of internal pressure. If the pump speed is increased past 90%, the system pressure increases above 1.6 bar. If this occurs, the pressure sensor sends an alarm signal to the PLC, and the logic deactivates the pump. After a few seconds, the pressure will drop below 1.3 bar and the alarm will terminate, allowing the pump to restart. If the pump speed is not reduced, the system will repeatedly exceed the pressure limit, shut down and then restart.

3.2   Control Equipment

We now describe the different pieces of control equipment that control the water treatment process. The control equipment is connected via ethernet to a Westermo industrial switch, which provides communication between devices and to other services.

Programmable Logic Controllers (PLCs). The primary PLC for the water treatment plant is a modern Siemens S7-1500. This unit controls the electronic valves and pump speed, as well as receiving inputs from the various sensors on the plant. A second, much older PLC, a Siemens ET200S, is used to control the pump on-off state. This mix of older (more vulnerable) and newer devices allows us to examine the convergence of old and new devices.

Human Machine Interfaces (HMIs). The operator HMI is a wireless Siemens panel (MobilePanel 277 IWlAN V2). This is connected to the field site network over WiFi using a Mikrotik access point. The screen can be seen in Fig. 5a.

Key:
1 Input (dirty) & output (clean) water tanks
2 Filtration tanks
3 Absorption tanks
4 De-ionisation tanks
5 Wireless HMI
6 Original control panel, replaced by field site board
7 Safety bunds
8 IO cabling to field site board
9 Removable copper pipe for sensor installation

Fig. 3. Water treatment process

Remote Telemetry Unit (RTU). Telemetry is provided through a SCADA-pack32 from Schneider, which communicates with the ClearSCADA software.

3.3 Networks

An overview of the network architecture is presented in Fig. 6. The network is divided into the IT and operational (OT) networks. These are, in turn, divided into multiple subnets, with each assigned its own /24 address space. Alongside the IT and OT networks there exists an experimental network which has a primary function of allowing researchers access to the testbed for experimentation and maintenance. For example, all virtual machines have a connection to the management network to allow for easy RDP access. Subnets are mapped to VLANs for allowing access by virtual machines. Each individual field site (physical process and associated control equipment) is assigned its own field site network.

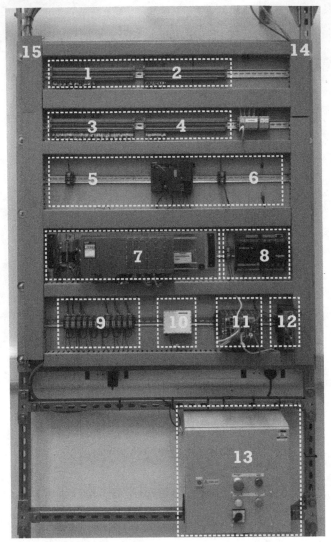

Key:
1 & 2 Digital Inputs\Outputs (32 each)
3 & 4 Analogue Inputs\Outputs (16 each)
5 & 6 Secondary PLC\RTU Housing
7   Primary Programmable Logic Controller (PLC)
8   Primary Remote Terminal/Telemetry Unit
9   24VDC Distribution
10   WiFi Access Point
11   L3 Managed Ethernet Switch
12   Firewall
13   240VAC to 24V DC Power Supplies
14   Ethernet Back-haul to Core Network Infrastructure
15   IO Cabling to Physical Process

Fig. 4. Field Site Control Board

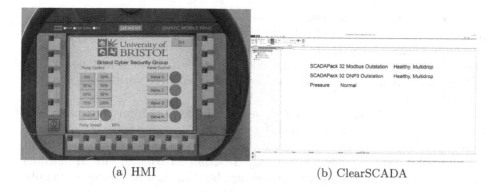

(a) HMI   (b) ClearSCADA

Fig. 5. HMI and ClearSCADA screens

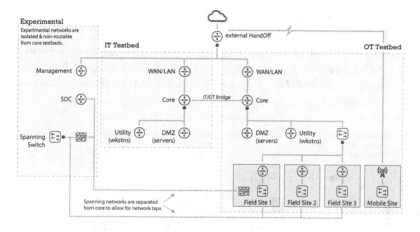

Fig. 6. Testbed network diagram

The network is configured with multiple spanning networks to allow for network captures across any of the individual subnets within the network.

3.4   Software

All software is installed within virtual machines on a single server running VMWare vSphere. Each piece of software is installed within its own virtual machine, which is, in turn, attached to an appropriate set of VLANs to insert the machine into the network architecture.

ClearSCADA from Schneider[3] is used to display telemetry data to the operations centre. ClearSCADA communicates with the Scadapack32 RTU over the Modbus and DNP3 industrial protocols and sits within the OT-Utility network. A basic example display can be seen in Fig. 5b.

---

[3] https://www.se.com/uk/en/product-range-presentation/61264-clearscada/.

KEPServerEX from Kepware[4] (henceforth referred to as Kepware) is a data historian which sits inside individual field site networks with direct access to the control hardware. It can read and write data to these devices, and send it on to higher level services, including public cloud services. Kepware is installed within a Windows 7 virtual machine with an installation deployed within each field site network.

The primary cloud service that we use is Thingworx[5] from PTC (who now also own Kepware), a cloud-based IIoT platform. Through a connection to Kepware, apps can be developed to run on the Thingworx platform with data from the control devices. Thingworx is deployed within an Ubuntu virtual machine running Tomcat 8.5, as configured by the supplier. An example Thingworx application for the water process can be seen in Fig. 8a.

4   Attack Overview

The physical process under attack is the water treatment plant as seen in Fig. 3, with the control equipment mounted onto an specially designed board, as seen in Fig. 4. The goal of the attack is to cause the water treatment process to enter into an unsafe state.

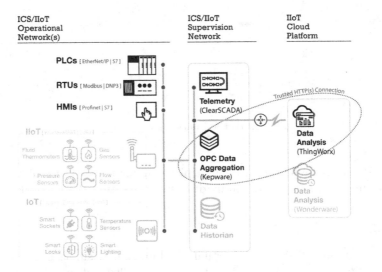

Fig. 7. Testbed environment for SecCNIoT demonstrator

The overall conceptual architecture for the attack demonstration can be seen in Fig. 7. Data aggregation from the testbed is performed by the Kepware data aggregation platform. In the deployment for the attack scenario, Kepware resides

---

[4] https://www.kepware.com/en-us/.
[5] https://www.ptc.com/en/products/iiot.

(a) Thingworx   (b) Attack script

Fig. 8. Thingworx and attack script

within a Microsoft Windows 7 VM, located within the OT DMZ network on the field site for the water treatment process, communicating directly with the devices on its related control board.

The IIoT cloud platform for the demonstrator is Thingworx, which supports the development of web-based applications utilising IIoT data. The manufacturers of Thingworx (PTC) acquired Kepware in 2016, and since have marketed Kepware and Thingworx as an IIoT solution, with Kepware providing data inputs to the Thingworx platform.

Thingworx is deployed on top of an Ubuntu virtual machine (supplied prebuilt by PTC) and uses Apache Tomcat 8.5 as its underlying platform. Our deployment operates Thingworx within a virtual cloud (i.e. inside our closed testbed environment). A trusted communication link between Kepware and Thingworx is achieved by way of a default, pre-configured, HTTP connection.

4.1 Anatomy of the Attack on the OT-IIoT Environment

We now discuss the anatomy of the attack we have implemented on this converged OT-IIoT environment as modelled within our testbed. It is an evolution of our previous work on attacks in ICS environments [7]. The flow of the attack can be seen in Fig. 9.

(1) Compromise Thingworx. The first step is to compromise the cloud machine hosting Thingworx. As mentioned, Thingworx was delivered pre-installed inside an Ubuntu virtual machine running on Tomcat 8.5. Tomcat is well known for having multiple security vulnerabilities that can be easily exploited to gain access to the host. Once access to the host is gained, through a vulnerability in Tomcat or other process, then the attacker loads a copy of the attack script onto the host. The attack script, as seen in Fig. 8b, is a simple python script utilising command line tools such as nmap and the Step7 python libraries.

(2) Terminate Thingworx. On gaining access to the machine, the attacker first takes Thingworx offline by terminating the Tomcat process. This will mean

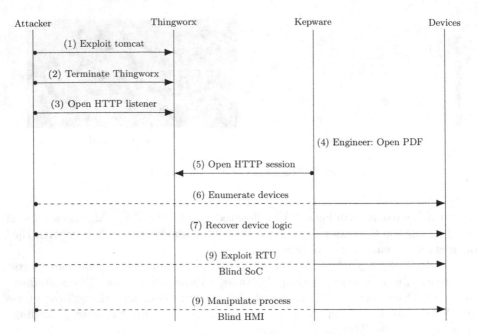

Fig. 9. Attack process. - - - indicates communication over the proxy

Kepware can no longer communicate with the Thingworx server and will display an error.

(3) Setup HTTP Listener. The attacker now starts an HTTP listener on the Thingworx host, ready for receiving a connection from within the OT network in the next step.

(4) Compromise Kepware Host. The attacker now requires an engineer to open a connection back to the Thingworx host from the Kepware host. As Kepware is now throwing error messages due to a failed connection to Thingworx, the engineer is likely to inspect the machine. Prior to the attack, the attacker would have replaced the Kepware manual, an Adobe PDF held on the Kepware host, with one which they have modified to contain a malicious payload. Whilst we take the liberty of doing this manually for the purposes of the demonstration, processes by which such a file might make it to a server, or an engineer's trusted workstation, are many and varied including USB drives, internet download, an injection into the supply chain (akin to the 2019 malware attack on Asus[6]) or a direct hack of the workstation itself.

In trying to fix the communication error, the engineer opens the malicious PDF file which, whilst appearing to open as normal for the engineer, executes the attacker's payload.

---

[6] https://www.symantec.com/blogs/threat-intelligence/asus-supply-chain-attack.

(5) Open Reverse HTTP Connection and Set up Proxy. On opening the malicious PDF, the payload opens a reverse HTTP connection back to the Thingworx host, connecting to the listener started in step (3). As Kepware already communicated with the Thingworx host over HTTP, this connection is trusted and allowed through any firewalls. The attacker then sets up a proxy connection through this HTTP link, and pipes all actions from their attack through this proxy, allowing them access to the control devices accessible from the Kepware host.

(6) Enumerate Devices. Once access has been gained to the ICS devices, the first stage is to enumerate these devices. In the first instance nmap can be used to perform a port scan across the field site network. This should give the attacker a list of devices, and open ports. From the open ports the attacker can gain some insight into the manufacturers of each device. For example, devices with port 102 open indicate Step7, which is the primary protocol in use by Siemens devices.

Specific tools can then be used to gain precise information about device hardware and software. As en example, PLCScan[7] can be used to gain details on older Step7 and modbus devices. For newer devices, there are nmap scripts as well as vulnerability scanners, e.g., [1,2], available for collecting the same information. Returned information includes the hardware and firmware versions, and device name (as set by the operator). Knowing the hardware and firmware version allows the attacker to find publicly known vulnerabilities in the devices.

At this stage the attacker could use a known exploit to carry out, for example, a denial-of-service attack. In this scenario we go further to show how an attacker could have a controlled impact on the physical process.

(7) Recover Device Logic. In order to craft attacks which can manipulate the process in a specific way, the attacker first needs to gain a copy of the logic running on the PLCs. This will allow them to know which memory addresses need to be attacked. For the Siemens ET200S, this is a simple case of directly reading a function block from the device using the Step7 protocol. This block will then need to be reverse engineered to recover the logic. For newer Siemens devices, such as the S7-1500, this no longer works. However, if the attacker has network access to the device and knows the exact hardware variant, the logic can be recovered from the device using the Siemens TIAPortal software.

Whilst reverse engineering the logic may prove difficult, especially if the attacker has no knowledge of the underlying physical process, it is possible to craft attacks using the recovered logic [8].

(8) Exploit RTU to Blind Control Room. To exploit the RTU, we developed a zero-day exploit and followed standard disclosure practices for vendor notification. Details can be found in a Schneider report [3]. Through this exploit, we load a new configuration to the device in order to change the devices IP

---

[7] https://github.com/meeas/plcscan.

address. This causes ClearSCADA to lose its connection to the device, meaning that the control room no longer has a view of the system.

(9) Manipulate Process and Blind HMI. The final step is to directly interact with the PLC to interfere with the physical process, and cause the HMI to display incorrect information. This is achieved by repeatedly writing to specific memory addresses within the PLC logic, which overwrites variables used by the logic and specific tags on the PLC. The targeted elements are the state of the pressure alarm, and the pump speed. The pump speed is increased to 95% (above the standard operation of 80%). We also overwrite the variable that is read by the HMI to display the pump speed. Writing is achieved using the S7 protocol, with packets sent repeatedly at a high rate, faster than the PLCs cycle time.

This has the effect that the pump speed increases to 90% which causes the system pressure to exceed the usual safety limit, however the pressure alarm does not trigger the safety cutoff and the pump continues to run. Meanwhile, the HMI displays no pressure alarm and continues to indicate a pump speed of 80%.

5   Conclusion

In this paper, we have discussed insights from a multi-year programme of research studying cyber security risks in critical infrastructures from a socio-technical perspective—taking into account both technical vulnerabilities and human & organisational factors. Our work, to date, has shown that effective assessment and management of such risks requires an understanding of how stakeholders make security decisions and how latent design conditions manifesting *down the line* as a consequence of these decisions impact the cyber security of such infrastructure. Our work has also shown that one must consider the complexity arising from the melting pot that represents the devices and systems that are deployed within critical infrastructures. Given their long lifespan the infrastructure is a combination of devices, platforms and protocols from diverse manufacturers. Not only so, there are a range of legacy and non-legacy devices and systems in operation in conjunction within each other. The need for business efficiencies and remote maintenance and updates is leading to the infrastructure becoming more highly connected to external systems and newer devices and platforms such as IIoT. This leads an increased attack surface that can be exploited by attackers to compromise security and hence safety as well as impact critical services to large swathes of the population. Studying such issues – from a *socio-technical perspective* – is a key part of our on-going and future work.

Acknowledgements. This work is funded by EPSRC Grant "Mumba: Multi-faceted Metrics for ICS Business Risk Analysis" (EP/M002780/1), part of the Research Institute on Trustworthy, Interconnected, Cyber-Physical Systems (RITICS) and Lloyds Register Foundation grant "Securing IoT in Critical National Infrastructure", part of the UK Research Hub on Cyber Security of IoT (PETRAS). The work is also supported by Rashid's Fellowship from the Alan Turing Institute.

References

1. Antrobus, R., Frey, S., Rashid, A., Green, B.: Simaticscan: towards a specialised vulnerability scanner for industrial control systems. In: 4th International Symposium for ICS & SCADA Cyber Security Research: ICS-CSR 2016, 23–25 August 2016, p. 2016. Queen's Belfast University, UK (2016)
2. Antrobus, R., Green, B., Frey, S., Rashid, A.: The forgotten i in iiot: a vulnerability scanner for industrial internet of things. In: IET Conference on Living in the Internet of Things. IET (2019)
3. Schceider Electric. Security Notification - Modicon Controllers and SCADA-Pack (V3.0) (2019). https://www.schneider-electric.com/en/download/document/SEVD-2017-065-01/
4. Frey, S., Rashid, A., Anthonysamy, P., Pinto-Albuquerque, M., Naqvi, S.A.: The good, the bad and the ugly: a study of security decisions in a cyber-physical systems game. IEEE Trans. Software Eng. **45**(5), 521–536 (2019)
5. Frey, S., Rashid, A., Zanutto, A., Busby, J.S., Follis, K.: On the role of latent design conditions in cyber-physical systems security. In: Proceedings of the 2nd International Workshop on Software Engineering for Smart Cyber-Physical Systems, SEsCPS@ICSE 2016, Austin, Texas, USA, May 14–22, 2016, pp. 43–46 (2016)
6. Gardiner, J., Craggs, B., Green, B., Rashid, A.: Oops I did it again: further adventures in the land of ICS security testbeds. In: ACM Workshop on Cyber-Physical Systems Security and Privacy (CPS-SPC). ACM Press (2019)
7. Green, B., Krotofil, M., Abbasi, A.: On the significance of process comprehension for conducting targeted ICS attacks. In: ACM Workshop on Cyber-Physical Systems Security and Privacy (CPS-SPC), Dallas, TX, USA, November 3, 2017, pp. 57–67 (2017)
8. McLaughlin, S., McDaniel, P.: Sabot: specification-based payload generation for programmable logic controllers. In: Proceedings of the 2012 ACM Conference on Computer and Communications Security, CCS 2012, pp. 439–449. ACM, New York (2012)
9. Reason, J.: Managing the risks of organizational accidents. Ashgate (1997)

Challenges in Quantifying an Adversary's Cyber Access to Critical Infrastructures

David M. Nicol(✉) (iD)

University of Illinois at Urbana-Champaign, Urbana, IL 61801, USA
dmnicol@illinois.edu

Abstract. We consider the problem of quantifying the potential for an adversary to move through the computer/communication network controlling a critical infrastructure. Quantification is needed to describe the risk to the critical infrastructure of cyber penetration in terms understandable to the owners/operators of the critical infrastructure. We identify several specific challenges, and conclude without having solved the problem, but having pointed the way towards some possible solutions.

Keywords: Cyber-security · Metrics · Critical infrastructures

1 Introduction

Critical infrastructures such as energy delivery systems, transportation, communications, and manufacturing are all now operated through digital control. Sensors and actuators attached to a physical system are electronically connected to controllers, operators, and data management systems. Human operators and digital controllers react to measurements of the physical system and issue commands to the actuators, which implement actions such as opening or closing a circuit breaker, starting or stopping a pump, moving a robotic arm, and so on. The dependence on digital controls makes it conceptually possible for a cyber adversary to exploit vulnerabilities or otherwise gain control access within the system to corrupt measurements, issue false commands, keep legitimate commands from reaching actuators, and obscure the state of the physical system from observation by the operators or controllers.

Assessment of risk to a critical infrastructure is of enormous interest. Owners and operators of the infrastructure need to understand the potential consequences of cyber adversaries interfering with operations. The costs of such interference needs to be expressed in terms and in units familiar to decision-makers, such as amount of power lost, lost income due to operational down time, cost of damaged equipment, even loss of life. Domain expertise is required

This material is based upon work supported by the Department of Energy under Award Number DE-OE0000780 and by the Maryland Procurement Office under Contract No. H98230-14-C-0141. The views and opinions of authors expressed herein do not necessarily state or reflect those of the United States Government or any agency thereof.

S. Nadjm-Tehrani (Ed.): CRITIS 2019, LNCS 11777, pp. 18–28, 2020.
https://doi.org/10.1007/978-3-030-37670-3_2

to identify the damage possible under specific scenarios where an adversary gains access to a set of actuators. This is an important and domain-specific part of risk assessment. Equally important is analysis that speaks to an adversary's ability to traverse the digital network and gain access to those actuators. This analysis is less dependent on details of the particular infrastructure involved, and is the focus of this paper.

Formalisms for analyzing network security have been around for at least twenty years. In 1999 Bruce Schier introduced the notion of *attack graph* [13,14], which is a means of describing how the exploits possible to an attacker can be combined to gain access to protected devices and data. Many papers on variations of attack graphs have been published. Among many of these there is a common trend. Analysis of an attack graph often leads to analysis of paths through a graph, and significant attention is often paid to the path with "least cost", usually meaning finding the sequence of exploits which among all possible sequences is easiest.

We will later speak more to the particulars of graphs and paths, but before all that note two things. The notion of a path inherently involves a single source and a single destination. If the graph nodes represent individual devices, then by itself the idea of a path won't capture access to a set of destinations (for us, actuators.) Graph nodes may represent more complex notions such as the set of all devices compromised to date in which case a path *can* speak to a set of compromised devices, but the flip-side is that those graphs are combinatorially large and correspondingly do not scale for use in modeling real (large) systems. Second, classical path analysis algorithms view the weight on an edge or node as fixed, and known. In our context it can be the case that weights enjoy neither property.

To summarize then, the challenges we face in trying to quantify an adversary's cyber-access to critical infrastructure include

- the need to consider some attacks as requiring a set of actuators, rather than just one, in a scalable data structure,
- the conceptual limitation of "shortest path" analysis in this domain because of the adversary's need to take over multiple destinations, and the need to investigate multiple potential network ingress points for the intruder,
- the underlying assumption with weighted graph path analysis that the weights are fixed, and known,
- the need to integrate the cyber analysis with cost estimates associated with the attacked physical system.

In the remainder we describe a graph that captures information about our problem, and then further discuss these challenge areas.

2   Graph Model

We employ a graph model that focuses on an intruder's lateral movement. A node in our graph represents a device. An edge directed from node n_1 to n_2

means that n_2 has an open networking connection, to which a vulnerable service is listening, that access control mechanisms (like firewalls) permit n_1 to interact with that service on n_2. The inference is that if an intruder has gained a foothold on n_1, then it *may* be able to gain a foothold on n_2 by sending a message crafted to exploit the associated vulnerability. n_1 and n_2 may be separated by one or more firewalls, but if an edge exists is it because an analysis of firewall configurations determined that is it possible for n_1 to craft and send a message which addresses the vulnerable service on n_2, and the firewalls pass that message through. In fact, the graph we describe can be exported from a commercial tools which does exactly this analysis of firewalls [2]. Note also that if n_2 offers multiple vulnerabilities to n_1 then there will be multiple edges.

In this model an actuator will normally be a node with no outbound edges. The ingress point for an adversary may be one or more particular Internet-facing nodes (for consideration of external attackers,) but may also be an interior node to capture the possibility of a network device being compromised through unspecified means, e.g., use of an infected USB stick.

We used this construction in [10], where we put weights on edges to reflect some subjective estimation of the difficulty to an adversary of exploiting the vulnerability at the endpoint. The point of *that* paper was to discuss some drawbacks of shortest path analysis, a topic we engage with again later in this paper.

3   Attacks with Multiple Compromised Actuators

Critical infrastructures are engineered to be tolerant as they can be to foreseeable natural events. For example, operators of the electric power grid are required to maintain the system in a state such that *no single failure* can impede safe operation of the system. The ability to really harm a physical system comes from combinations of compromises. For example, imagine the potential impact of a compromised firmware update for a safety device used widely in an industry. The malware could be programmed to cause all infected devices to take some deleterious action in coordination based on date and wallclock time. Imagine an attack where some actuators are compromised and take actions which can push the system into an unsafe state, and other devices are compromised to either withhold visibility into what is going on or provide a false view of what is going on—precisely one component of Stuxnet's attack on Iranian centrifuges.

An important requirement then of supporting risk assessment of critical infrastructures is to consider whether, how, and when an adversary can compromise a given set of actuators, not just individual analyses of access to individual actuators.

4   Limitations of Shortest Path Analysis

We are not the first to observe that the shortest path metric obscures information. In an analysis of a different kind of graph but one where edges encode difficulty of exploiting a vulnerability, the authors of [11] observe that the shortest path metric is insensitive to changes in the graph which do not impact the shortest path. Later work [4] makes a similar point. Later in this section we will show by example how insensitive that metric can be. But in [10] we raised other objections. There we constructed a graph with edge weights related to difficulty of exploiting the vulnerability, as a function of CVSS score [5,6,12]. We observed that the difficulty of exploiting a vulnerability can be context dependent. This arises in at least two ways. When attackers encounter a vulnerability for the first time they will invest a certain amount of effort into learning how to exploit it, or find a tool that exploits it. *Subsequent* encounters with the same vulnerability may take less time, leveraging the previously expended effort. Alternatively, if an intruder exploits a vulnerability and is detected, it might be that automated reactions implement isolation that serve to remove edges, or take other actions that make it harder for an adversary to reach and exploit a vulnerability. In both cases what occurs is the possibility that during a path traversal the weights on edges not yet traversed can be a function of the edges and node that have already been visited. In [10] we report that under these conditions we've proved that the computational complexity of finding the shortest path is NP-hard.

In Sect. 3 we argued for the importance of considering multiple destinations to capture attacks that require a set of actuators. The shortest path metric is not adequate for this. One might compute the cost of the shortest path to each of the actuators separately, and sum them, but this approach does not account for the possibility of some of those paths sharing edges. In [9] we note this problem and point out that the construct of a Minimal Steiner Tree [3] is the multi-destination analog to shortest path. There exists a multitude of trees with adversary's ingress as source, and a set of designated actuators as leaf nodes. A minimal Steiner Tree is a tree that connects source to each actuator with the property that the sum of the edge weights in the tree is minimized. However, not only do most of the problems with the shortest path metric carry over to Steiner trees, the computational cost of finding the minimum Steiner tree is intractable.

We show here graphically how the shortest path metric can significantly obscure a more holistic view of the adversary's ability to gain access to a set of actuators, and can see how the quantification shown may give more insight into possible attacker access.

To simplify the discussion (and the graphic) consider paths to a single actuator. If we now interpret the weight on an edge as the (fixed) time required to exploit the associated vulnerability, the sum of weights on a path give the total time an attacker uses to reach the actuator, call this the path's *access time*. Now we can imagine the distribution of all path access times. If we choose the edge weights to be integer value over a somewhat limited range (e.g., 1–100) we can contain the combinatorial explosion of paths, by grouping paths that have the same length. Here's how.

We call a tuple (t, c) an *access count*, where t is an integer value interpreted as time, and c is an non-negative integer interpreted as a counter. An *access count vector* is a vector of access counts $< x_1, x_2, \ldots, x_m >$ with the property that no time value of any access count is duplicated, and the access counts are sorted in increasing order of time components. We assume the graph nodes are topologically sorted, with the source being the first node in the sequence and the target actuator being the last. Each node n_i has defined for it an access node vector V_i which records the vector of access times from the source to n_i. We can build up each node's access vector using a function $merge(v_1, v_2)$, where v_1 and v_2 are both access vectors. $merge$ produces a sorted (by time value) sequence of access counts where (t, c) is in the sequence if either (t, c) is in exactly one of v_1 and v_2, or there exists (t, c_1) in v_1 and (t, c_2) in v_2, with $c = c_1 + c_2$. Likewise, every access count in v_1 and every access count in v_2 appear in the $merge$ output, except for pairs that share a time component, and have their counts summed in the $merge$ output. Another function is $shift(v, s)$, whose output is the access vector constructed from v by adding s to the time component of every access count.

Now if there are edges $e_1, e_2, \ldots, e_d$ from predecessors of n_i, if $s_1, s_2, \ldots, s_d$ are the edge weights and $V_{e_1}, V_{e_2}, \ldots V_{e_d}$ are the access count vectors of those predecessors, then we merge the predecessors' access count vectors after applying the edge weight shift to add additional delay to the time components:

$$V_i = merge(merge(merge(...merge(merge(V_{e_1} + s_1, V_{e_2} + s_2), V_{e_3} + s_3), ...).$$

The graphic we will show derives from a particular (easy to construct in a program) graph. The graph has N nodes, and a "maximum fanout" value, F. For $n = 0, 1, \ldots, N - 1$ a data structure describes the possibility of an edge directed from node n to nodes $n + 1$, $n + 2$, ..., $n + F$, of course ignoring edges which by this definition have destination node ids larger than N. Every edge has three attributes, an "existence threshold" which is uniformly sampled from $[0, 1]$, a positive weight, also randomly sampled, and a Boolean attribute of "permanent". With this construction we can compare a number of nested graphs. Given an edge threshold τ, graph $G(\tau)$ starts with the construction above and retains only edges that either have the permanent attribute, or have an existence threshold no greater than τ. For any $0 < \tau < \tau'$, if an edge exists in $G(\tau)$ then that edge necessarily exists in $G(\tau')$. An implication is that the shortest path (or minimal Steiner tree) in $G(\tau')$ is never greater than that metric in $G(\tau)$.

Now consider graphs constructed as follows. Take $\tau_1 > \tau_2 > \ldots > \tau_k$. Start with graph G, find the shortest path in $G(\tau_1)$ and then mark the edges of that path as being permanent with all other edges not permanent. Under this construction graphs $G(\tau_1), G(\tau_2), \ldots, G(\tau_k)$ will all have the same shortest path, but may differ considerably in other graph properties. For each graph we compute the actuator's access count vector, and transform it, in much the same way as a probability function is transformed into a cumulative distribution function. The ith access count of the transformed vector has the same time component as the ith access count in the original vector, but its count component is equal to the sum of the count in the ith component of the original vector and the count of the $(i - 1)^{st}$ element in the transformed vector. Thus component (t, Z) in the transformed vector says that Z is the total number of paths with lengths t or less.

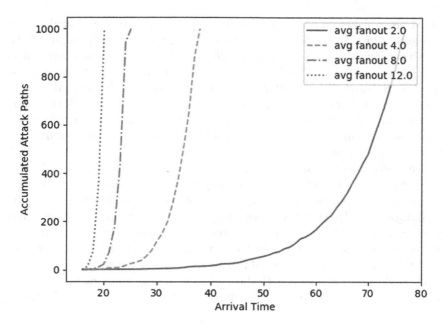

Fig. 1. Accumulating access count

On any sizeable graph the number of paths explodes. For the purposes of understanding graph attributes we don't need all that information. The plot of Fig. 1 illustrates access counts for only the first 1000 paths in each graph. For this data we created a graph with $N = 200$ nodes, with a maximum fanout $F = 20$. A graph with "average fanout X" was constructed using an existence threshold of X/F. By construction (for the purposes of illustration) each curve has the same least t value, meaning that from the point of view of minimum path length there is no difference among them. But obviously there are significant differences. In the dense graphs the shortest 1000 paths have nearly the same path length, for these perhaps minimal path length is descriptive. For the middling density graphs—fanouts of 8 and 4 the real intensity of paths does not kick in until some time later than the minimum path length, and with the average fanout of 4 we start to see some spreading of path lengths between 25 and 35 before it begins the steep climb. The curve that stands out most of course is the sparsest graph. Clearly, aside from the few paths which can connect to the shortest path, the others have to work through more edges to get to the actuator.

The take-away message from this graphic is that the short-path metric can mask some significant differences between graphs.

5   Certainty of Knowledge

Path connectivity analysis of the type described so far implicitly assumes that the existence of edges (for us, meaning the existence of vulnerabilities) is known, and that the weights on edges are known. In practice there are difficulties with both assumptions. In the former case there simply is not much empirical data on which we can develop weight models. We in [10] and others elsewhere concoct edge weights based on subjective assessments by domain experts as expressed in the CVSS scores. We transform a vector of subjectively derived unit-less metrics into a further subjectively derived description of time or effort required to exploit the vulnerability. Considerable uncertainty ought to be attached to that assessment, and yet the analytic vehicles we have do not readily admit inclusion of that uncertainty.

Better information is available about existence of vulnerabilities. Network scanners can often identify the software and its version of network services that are open on a device, and determine whether it has vulnerabilities listed in the NIST database [1]. Uncertainty arises though if only partial information is available. A scanner might determine that a port is open on a device (meaning that some software is accessible) but that the software isn't identified. Another source of uncertainty is due to the potential for the presence of as-yet-undiscovered vulnerabilities. We are faced then with the challenge of incorporating into our graph some description of our state of knowledge about the existence of a vulnerability edge.

We created means of expressing quantified vulnerability certainties in [7] and [8]. There are two elements of this work with direct bearing on the graph analysis challenge. Our approach allows one to express the relationship between vulnerability edges. Thus, if the same vulnerability exists in multiple places in the graph and we ascribe a probability of that vulnerability's existence, the existence probabilities of those edges are the same, and furthermore, in the analysis are not treated as being stochastically independent. This has ramifications on estimating the probability of an attacker being able to access a particular actuator, ramifications that we work through. A second element is that the model gives us a means of encoding our degree of certainty about the probability of an edge's existence. Based on things like analysis of device and network log data it seems feasible that we might estimate the probability of a vulnerability existing and have some basis for the certainty of that estimation (e.g. based on the number of log records that give evidence about the existence or not of a vulnerability.) The contribution of [8] beyond [7] is that edge probabilities are not single values from $[0,1]$, but are probability distributions on $[0,1]$, particularly, Beta distributions.

The work in [7] and [8] speak to estimating the probability that an adversary can reach a given actuator from a given point of ingress. Future work will engage with the problem of estimating the probability that an adversary can reach all of the members of a given set of actuators.

6   Physical System Risk Assessment

Consider the example of an owner of a shipping port who wants to understand the impact on port operations of a cyber-attack that takes over the control of loading cranes. The impact will be measured in units familiar to the owner: lost income due to breached contracts, lost income due to impeded flow of goods through the port, lost income due to damaged shipping containers, loss of life. For the purposes of this paper we assume there are two kinds of domain experts available to support the risk analysis. One kind of expert is able to forecast the deleterious results possible if a cyber-adversary is able to take control of one or more system actuators in a set $\mathcal{A}$. This is the expert who might be able to assert, for example, that there are physical constraints that keep a digital controller from being able to execute life-threatening actions, and is able to model the impact on the system of rogue actions that do get through. A second type of subject domain expert is needed to translate the findings of the first kind of expert into terms understandable by the owner or other decision makers.

Exploiting the knowledge of these experts, if a set of actuators $\mathcal{A}$ in system graph G can be compromised, we can perhaps estimate a cost $C(G, \mathcal{A})$ of all modeled attacks which are possible if all actuators in $\mathcal{A}$ are compromised. The problems with quantifying attacker behaviors and costs are expressed in [4], whose recommendation is to focus on the number (and identity) of vulnerabilities that must be patched to completely inhibit an adversary's access to a given asset. Under this restriction it might still be possible to get a handle on risk assessment. Given a node n_0 in the graph G which is assumed to be an adversary's point of ingress, we can compute $\mathcal{A}(G, n_0)$ as the set of all actuators reachable from n_0 within G. Then, given a set $\mathcal{V}$ of specific vulnerabilities, we can create G' from G by removing every edge corresponding to a vulnerability found in $\mathcal{V}$, and thereby identify $\mathcal{A}(G', n_0)$. We can estimate the reduction of the cost made possible by removing all vulnerabilities in $\mathcal{V}$ as

$$S(\mathcal{V}) = \sum_{\text{node } n \text{ in } G} C(G, \mathcal{A}(G, n)) - C(G', \mathcal{A}(G', n)).$$

One can then compare $S(\mathcal{V})$ with the cost $R(\mathcal{V})$ of removing all the vulnerabilities in $\mathcal{V}$. This places questions of investment on a basis familiar to decision-makers, the cost of investing the improvement against the gain made by doing so. While we can frame the question in such terms, it is still the case that there are many combinations of vulnerabilities one might consider removing. Furthermore, as stated, this formulation does not engage with the very real issue of lack of knowledge about existence of vulnerabilities.

However, just as the shortest path metric obscures potentially important graph information related to the adversary's ability to compromise $\mathcal{A}$ or the effort needed to do so, the approach above gives no credit to security controls that do not completely remove at least one actuator from access. This assumption flies in the face of current thinking which says we ought to assume that the adversary *can* access the network, and ask then how to impede the adversary's progress. Quantifying with higher resolution how application of controls impact adversary's access is a direction to consider, but following it necessitates making the quantitative results dependent on a number of modeling assumptions for which parameters aren't accurately known. However, so long as we use the results to compare analyses rather than to quantitative predict behavior, the approach is still useful.

Classical expression of risk is the probability of an event times the expected consequence of the event. Probability here needs to be handled carefully; while philosophically there may be the probability of an attacker attempting to breach a given system by a given time, the factors involved in that cannot be known. If we approach the question by first conditioning on the presence of the adversary with a desire to attack, then the probabilities involved can be more technical, e.g., probability that a device have a particular vulnerability, or a probability distribution of the time an attack takes to exploit a vulnerability. Within such a framework we can embed some of our earlier observations about the variability of an exploit time as a function of whether the vulnerability has already been exploited, and uncertainty about the existence of exploitable vulnerabilities. A way to connect cyber analysis with physical system cost analysis is through estimation of some sort of probabilities. For a given set of actuators $\mathcal{A}$ in a graph G, define $H(G, \mathcal{A}, n)$ to be the hitting time, or some time at which the adversary has compromised all of the actuators in $\mathcal{A}$, starting at ingress node n. Note that if the hitting time is the *first* time an adversary has compromised all nodes, we're back to the shortest path metric and the danger of important graphical information being obscured. If Fig. 1 is suggestive, it might make more sense to define the hitting time to be the time at which, say, the 100th touch on $\mathcal{A}$ occurs for which all actuators are compromised. This random variable will depend on a number of assumptions about vulnerabilities, their existence probabilities, the effort required of an attacker to exploit vulnerabilities, the resources available to an attacker, any automated reactions of the system to detection of an intruder's presence, and the attacker's strategy for avoiding detection and choosing next vulnerabilities to target. The randomness in the variable derives from stochastic assumptions about the network and the attacker's behavior. Still, given that understanding, an analysis of $H(G, \mathcal{A}, n)$ can be useful.

For a given graph G and a given set of assumptions we can use Monte Carlo simulation [15] to estimate the distribution of $H(G, \mathcal{A}, n)$ for all ingress nodes n. We can consider application of a set of security controls which lead to a new graph G', and thus to an estimate of $H(G', \mathcal{A})$. We can at a sequence of points in time $t_i = i * \delta_t$ for $i = 1, 2, \ldots$, compute the difference of probabilities

$$\Delta(G, G', \mathcal{A}, t_i) = \sum_{\text{node } n \text{ in } G} (\Pr\{H(G, \mathcal{A}, n) < t_i\} - \Pr\{H(G', \mathcal{A}, n) < t_i\}).$$

The sequence $< \Delta(G, G', \mathcal{A}, t_i) >$ for $i = 1, 2, \ldots$ gives information about the effect of applying the controls. Early in the sequence we might expect small values due to both probabilities being small—not enough time has lapsed for the adversary to reach the hitting time. Then, for a while, the sequence values will be close to one in a region where the hitting time under G is likely and the hitting time under G' is not. Eventually the hitting time of G' catches up and the difference in probabilities is again close to zero because now the probabilities are both close to one.

While this is not as clean as "invest X to eliminate vulnerabilities in $\mathcal{V}$ and see a reduction of Y in the threatened impact cost, it does give information about the cost impact of applying controls, or not. The positioning of the "bulge" in the vector can influence that decision. If the bulge is absent and the differences are mostly zero, it means that a larger (or different) set of vulnerabilities to remove has to be considered. If the bulge exists but is far in the future that means that set of controls do not especially improve G. If the bulge exists but is not far in the future, the length of the period of the bulge says something about the enduring power of the controls. All of this needs to be fleshed out of course, but the intent of the discussion is to show some direction for considering how to quantify adversary access in a way that supports risk assessment.

7   Conclusion

One of the key objectives of our work is to lay the groundwork for presenting to decision-makers information about the risk to critical infrastructures due to cyber malfeasance in terms that they understand, and to enable them to make well-informed decisions about investment in cyber security controls. To accomplish this we need to be able to integrate analysis of potential attack behavior with the costs of the impacts that behavior might have on the critical infrastructure. The point of the CRITIS 2019 keynote address (upon which this paper is based) was to point out some challenges in doing so. One of the challenges is due to the need to extend the kind of analysis usually done to this context. We echo earlier complaints about over-reliance on the metric of a shortest-path and show by example how that can significantly mask important differences that result from applying new security controls. We discuss the problem of the underlying assumption in related analyses that the existence of vulnerabilities and costs associated with them are fixed and known. Finally, we consider the end goal of integrating the analysis of attacker potential movements with costs of the potential impact on a physical critical infrastructure, and point out some directions for future consideration.

References

1. National vulnerability database. https://nvd.nist.gov/vuln-metrics/cvss. Accessed 24 Oct 2019
2. NP-View and NP-Live. https://www.network-perception.com. Accessed 24 Oct 2019
3. Du, D., Hu, X.: Steiner Tree Problems in Computer Communication Networks. World Scientific Publishing Co. Inc., River Edge (2008)
4. Idika, N., Bhargava, B.: Extending attack graph-based security metrics and aggregating their application. IEEE Trans. Dependable Secur. Comput. 9, 75–85 (2012)
5. Mell, P., Kent, K.A., Romanosky, S.: The common vulnerability scoring system (CVSS) and its applicability to federal agency systems. Citeseer (2007)
6. Mell, P., Scarfone, K., Romanosky, S.: Common vulnerability scoring system. Secur. Priv. IEEE 4(6), 85–89 (2006)

7. Nguyen, H.H., Palani, K., Nicol, D.M.: An approach to incorporating uncertainty in network security analysis. In: Proceedings of the Hot Topics in Science of Security: Symposium and Bootcamp, HoTSoS, pp. 74–84. ACM, New York (2017). https://doi.org/10.1145/3055305.3055308

8. Nguyen, H.H., Palani, K., Nicol, D.M.: Extensions of network reliability analysis. In: Proceedings of the 49th IEEE/IFIP International Conference on Dependable Systems and Networks, DSN 2019, Portland, OR, June 2019

9. Nicol, D.M.: Cyber risk of coordinated attacks in critical infrastructures. In: Proceedings of the 2018 Winter Simulation Conference, Gutenberg, Sweden, 9–12 December 2018, pp. 2759–2768 (2018)

10. Nicol, D.M., Mallapura, V.: Modeling and analysis of stepping stone attacks. In: Proceedings of the 2014 Winter Simulation Conference, Savannah, GA, USA, 7–10 December 2014, pp. 3036–3047 (2014). https://doi.org/10.1109/WSC.2014.7020142

11. Ortalo, R., Deswarte, Y., Kaaniche, M.: Experimenting with quantitative evaluation tools for monitoring operational security. IEEE Trans. Softw. Eng. **25**(5), 633–650 (1999). https://doi.org/10.1109/32.815323

12. Schiffman, M., Eschelbeck, G., Ahmad, D., Wright, A., Romanosky, S.: CVSS: a common vulnerability scoring system. National Infrastructure Advisory Council (NIAC) (2004)

13. Schneir, B.: Attack trees: modeling security threats. Dr. Dobb's J. (1999)

14. Schneir, B.: Secrets & Lies: Digital Security in a Networked World. Wiley, New York (2000)

15. Sobol, I.M.: A Primer for the Monte Carlo Method. CRC Press, Boca Raton (1994)

Risk Management

Exploring How Component Factors and Their Uncertainty Affect Judgements of Risk in Cyber-Security

Zack Ellerby[(✉)], Josie McCulloch, Melanie Wilson, and Christian Wagner

Computer Science, University of Nottingham, Nottingham, UK
{zack.ellerby,josie.mcculloch,melanie.wilson,
christian.wagner}@nottingham.ac.uk

Abstract. Subjective judgements from experts provide essential information when assessing and modelling threats in respect to cyber-physical systems. For example, the vulnerability of individual system components can be described using multiple factors, such as complexity, technological maturity, and the availability of tools to aid an attack. Such information is useful for determining attack risk, but much of it is challenging to acquire automatically and instead must be collected through expert assessments. However, most experts inherently carry some degree of uncertainty in their assessments. For example, it is impossible to be certain precisely how many tools are available to aid an attack. Traditional methods of capturing subjective judgements through choices such as *high, medium* or *low* do not enable experts to quantify their uncertainty. However, it is important to measure the range of uncertainty surrounding responses in order to appropriately inform system vulnerability analysis. We use a recently introduced interval-valued response-format to capture uncertainty in experts' judgements and employ inferential statistical approaches to analyse the data. We identify key attributes that contribute to hop vulnerability in cyber-systems and demonstrate the value of capturing the uncertainty around these attributes. We find that this uncertainty is not only predictive of uncertainty in the overall vulnerability of a given system component, but also significantly informs ratings of overall component vulnerability itself. We propose that these methods and associated insights can be employed in real world situations, including vulnerability assessments of cyber-physical systems, which are becoming increasingly complex and integrated into society, making them particularly susceptible to uncertainty in assessment.

Keywords: Cyber-security · Uncertainty · Interval-values · Intervals

1 Introduction

Cyber-security professionals play a vital role in assessing and predicting vulnerabilities within cyber-physical systems, which often form part of an organisa-

Supported by EPSRC's EP/P011918/1 grant and by the UK National Cyber Security Centre (NCSC).

© Springer Nature Switzerland AG 2020
S. Nadjm-Tehrani (Ed.): CRITIS 2019, LNCS 11777, pp. 31–42, 2020.
https://doi.org/10.1007/978-3-030-37670-3_3

tion's or state's critical digital infrastructure. As outsider threats become more prevalent and sophisticated, there is increasing pressure on experts to provide timely and comprehensive assessments within the context of the rapidly changing cyber-physical ecosystem. As cyber-systems increase in both ubiquity and complexity, methods to quantify and handle error in subjective measurements from experts need to be developed [13]. It has been demonstrated across many industry sectors that as complexity increases accurate risk assessment decreases [10]. Enabling the effective reconstruction of overall assessments from component and attribute ratings would streamline the process of updating overall system vulnerability assessments, in line with shifts in this ecosystem.

Both objective and subjective measures of risk provide useful information to aid decision making in vulnerability assessment [4,5]. Several different methods can be used to assess vulnerability and risk in a cyber-security system, such as vulnerability scanning tools [18] or the Common Vulnerability Scoring System (CVSS) [15], which gives qualitative severity ratings of *low*, *medium*, and *high*, and CVSS Version 3, which extends the ratings to include *none* and *critical* [8]. However, when using CVSS, the necessary information to complete the calculation may be missing. Hubbard and Seiersen [11] argue that assessing risk in terms of *low*, *medium*, and *high* ratings is highly subjective and open to error. It is therefore suggested that cyber-security risk should be described quantitatively. This would help quantify what areas of risk are perceived as important to cyber-security professionals and, from that, move towards how those risks might correspond to the actually enacted attacks and their success or failure.

Assessment of risk or the likelihood of an attack are inherently uncertain [1,2]. Objective measures may carry uncertainty because the measures themselves are imprecisely defined [2]. Subjective assessments (collected from experts) carry uncertainty because, for example, the experts are not familiar with the particular technology, there is inherent uncertainty caused by insufficient detail in the scenario, or due to individual personality [12,16,20].

Between-expert uncertainty is often modelled implicitly, for example, through probability distributions [7] or uncertainty measures [5]. These methods model the between-expert uncertainty, but they do not capture within-expert uncertainty. Choi et al. [4] capture within-expert uncertainty by enabling experts to express knowledge and uncertainty through terms such as *very small*, *small* and *large* and using fuzzy sets to represent the uncertainty of these words. However, this assumes that the experts share the same degree of uncertainty regarding the meanings of these terms. After capturing uncertainty, it may be modelled and handled through methods such as Dempster-Shafer evidence theory [6,9] or fuzzy logic [4,14,19].

We propose explicitly capturing uncertainty in experts' individual judgements using an interval-valued response format, as previously introduced in [17]. Experts provide ratings along a continuous scale to quantify, for example, the perceived difficulty of an attack on a component. Using an interval captures both the experts' rating (position on the axis) and the degree of uncertainty associated with the response (width of the interval). Figure 1 shows an example of a narrow rating (slightly uncertain) and a wide rating (highly uncertain). In this manner, uncertainty is captured as an integral aspect of the judgement itself, through a coherent and intuitive response-format. The novel output of this paper is to show that an interval-valued response scale can be used to effectively capture uncertainty in expert judgements, and that this can be used to better predict both the magnitude and the uncertainty of risk in vulnerability assessments.

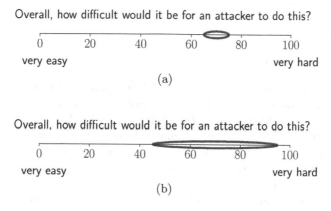

Fig. 1. Illustration of narrow (a) and wide (b) interval-valued responses capturing different degrees of uncertainty.

In this paper, we assess the importance of a variety of attributes in determining the overall vulnerability of components being attacked or evaded within a cyber-system; these include maturity of the technology and the frequency that a given attack is reported (the full set of attributes are listed in Tables 1 and 2). We also capture the overall difficulty of attacking or evading each component. Our core aim is to understand how the component attributes contribute to the overall difficulty of an attack and, equally importantly, how uncertainty in component attributes affects not only the uncertainty in the overall vulnerability of a component, but also the overall difficulty itself. For example, experts might perceive an attack as more difficult if there are *fewer* tools available to aid in this effort. However, experts might also perceive an attack as more difficult if they are *uncertain* about the availability of tools. From this, we can learn what additional insight is gained by capturing uncertainty through interval-valued responses. Specifically, we wish to answer

- how is overall vulnerability of a component affected
  - by attribute ratings?
  - by uncertainty around attribute ratings?
- how is uncertainty around overall vulnerability of a component affected
  - by attribute ratings?
  - by uncertainty around attribute ratings?

We find that although cyber-security experts only assessed attributes that were previously deemed likely to be important to component vulnerability, only some of these attributes have a significant effect. Similarly, we discover that although uncertainty around some attributes affects the uncertainty around the component as a whole, this is not consistent for all attributes. We also find that the uncertainty around some attribute ratings makes a significant contribution to overall vulnerability ratings themselves.

2   Methods

2.1   Data Collection

The data was collected from experts in CESG (Communications-Electronics Security Group), which was the information security arm of GCHQ (Government Communication Head Quarters) in the United Kingdom[1]. A total of 38 cyber-security experts at CESG assessed a range of components that are commonly encountered during a cyber-attack. They rated these on both overall difficulty to either attack or evade, as appropriate, and on several attributes that might affect this difficulty. Two types of components (also referred to as hops) were assessed, those that require an attacker to attack the component (referred to as *attack*) and those that require the attacker to bypass the component (referred to as *evade*). Examples of the hops assessed include *bypass gateway content checker* and *overcome client lockdown*, but any hop may be assessed using this method.

Tables 1 and 2 list the attack and evade attributes, respectively (variable notations are also provided, which are used in the next section). Attack hops are defined by seven attributes and evade hops by three attributes. In addition, both are described by their *overall difficulty*. Our aim is to understand how the hop attributes and the uncertainty around these attributes relate to the perceived overall difficulty of attacking/evading the hop, and to the uncertainty around this difficulty. Experts were asked to provide interval-valued ratings to enable them to coherently express the uncertainty associated with their responses; these ratings were provided on a scale from 0 to 100.

The cyber-security components chosen for this study are designed to be representative of a mainstream government system, which would include assets at Business Impact Level 3 (BIL3) – an intermediate category of impact [3]. CESG describes such a system as typically including remote site and mobile working, backed by core services and back-end office integrated systems, such as telemetry devices and associated systems used by the emergency services. Compromising assets at BIL3 might have large-scale negative effects, including but not limited to: disruption to regional power supply, key local transport systems, emergency or other important local services for up to 24 h, local loss of telecoms, risk to an individual's safety, damage to intelligence operations, hindrance to low level crime detection and prosecution, or financial loss to the UK government or a leading financial company in the order of millions (GBP) [3].

---

[1] CESG has since been replaced by the NCSC (National Cyber Security Centre).

Table 1. Attributes used to describe attack hops, the question used in the study, and the variable name used in the analysis.

Var	Attribute	Description
c	Complexity	How complex is the target component (e.g. in terms of size of code, number of sub-components)?
t	Interaction	How much does the target component process/interact with any data input?
f	Frequency	How often would you say this type of attack is reported in the public domain?
a	Availability of tool	How likely is it that there will be a publicly available tool that could help with this attack?
d	Inherent difficulty	How inherently difficult is this type of attack? (i.e. how technically demanding would it be to do from scratch, with no tools to help.)
r	Maturity	How mature is this type of technology?
g	Going unnoticed	How easy is it to carry this attack out without being noticed?
o	Overall difficulty	Overall, how difficult would it be for an attacker to do this?

Table 2. Attributes used to describe evade hops, the question used in the study, and the variable name used in the analysis.

Var	Attribute	Description
c	Complexity	How complex is the job of providing this kind of defence?
a	Availability of information	How likely is it that there will be publicly available information that could help with evading defence?
r	Maturity	How mature is this type of technology?
o	Overall difficulty	Overall, how difficult would it be for an attacker to do this?

2.2 Analysis

We use linear mixed effects modelling (an extension of linear regression) to determine the contribution of each of the hop attributes, as rated by experts, to overall hop difficulty. We also assess the contribution of the associated uncertainty in these ratings, captured through the interval-valued response-format. The midpoint (m) of the interval-valued response is used as a single-valued numeric rating of the attribute, and the width (w) of the response is used to represent the uncertainty around this rating. Note, of course, that higher widths are only possible towards the centre of the scale. That is, as the midpoint approaches the edge of the scale, a wide interval cannot exist. Also, note that while experts provided ratings in the range [0, 100], these data were standardised, through z-transformation, before entry into the model.

This approach estimates the contribution of each attribute's midpoint and width together upon the same outcome variable, in the form of β weights. These variables are entered as fixed effects. The inclusion of random intercepts also allows the model to account for potential between expert and between hop differences in baseline ratings. In addition, this technique allows us to examine the combined effects of attribute rating and uncertainty (e.g. high certainty may have an opposite effect on overall difficulty when relating to a high or low attribute rating). We model this through the inclusion of two-way interaction terms ($m \cdot w$) pertaining to the midpoint and width of each attribute.

Four separate analyses are reported. These were conducted for the dependent variables of

- attack hop overall difficulty rating (interval midpoint)
- attack hop overall uncertainty (interval width)
- evade hop overall difficulty rating (interval midpoint)
- evade hop overall uncertainty (interval width)

For each of these analyses, an initial model was created. These included fixed effects of all hop attribute ratings, all hop attribute widths and all two-way interactions, along with random intercepts for both expert and hop. Following this, a stepwise variable reduction process was applied to each model, in order to remove variables that were found not to significantly contribute to the respective outcome variable. β weights of the variables retained into the final models were then interpreted as estimates of the (significant) contribution of each of these factors to the respective outcome variable.

Table 1 lists the variables used to denote the attributes of attack hops. The sum of all simple effects for the attack hop attribute midpoints (ratings) is

$$A_m^z = \beta_1^z x_{i,j}^{cm} + \beta_2^z x_{i,j}^{tm} + \beta_3^z x_{i,j}^{fm} + \beta_4^z x_{i,j}^{am} + \beta_5^z x_{i,j}^{dm} + \beta_6^z x_{i,j}^{rm} + \beta_7^z x_{i,j}^{gm} \qquad (1)$$

where β is the coefficient, $x_{i,j}^{cm}$ is the value m (midpoint) of attribute c (complexity) for i (a given expert) and j (a given hop), and z reflects the model's outcome variable, which may be either m (midpoints) or w (widths) of the overall difficulty.

The sum of all simple effects for the attack hop attribute widths (uncertainty) is

$$A_w^z = \beta_8^z x_{i,j}^{cw} + \beta_9^z x_{i,j}^{tw} + \beta_{10}^z x_{i,j}^{fw} + \beta_{11}^z x_{i,j}^{aw} + \beta_{12}^z x_{i,j}^{dw} + \beta_{13}^z x_{i,j}^{rw} + \beta_{14}^z x_{i,j}^{gw} \qquad (2)$$

where $x_{i,j}^{cw}$ is the width w of attribute c (complexity) for i (a given expert) and j (a given hop).

The sum of the interactions between the midpoints and widths of the attack hop attributes is

$$\begin{aligned} A_{mw}^z =& \beta_{15}^z (x_{i,j}^{cm} \cdot x_{i,j}^{cw}) + \beta_{16}^z (x_{i,j}^{tm} \cdot x_{i,j}^{tw}) + \beta_{17}^z (x_{i,j}^{fm} \cdot x_{i,j}^{fw}) + \beta_{18}^z (x_{i,j}^{am} \cdot x_{i,j}^{aw}) \\ &+ \beta_{19}^z (x_{i,j}^{dm} \cdot x_{i,j}^{dw}) + \beta_{20}^z (x_{i,j}^{rm} \cdot x_{i,j}^{rw}) + \beta_{21}^z (x_{i,j}^{gm} \cdot x_{i,j}^{gw}) \end{aligned} \qquad (3)$$

Our initial model formula to explain the overall difficulty rating midpoints $(\gamma_{i,j}^{Aom})$ and widths $(\gamma_{i,j}^{Aow})$ of attack hops is then

$$\gamma_{i,j}^{Aoz} = \beta_0^z + A_m^z + A_w^z + A_{mw}^z + \mu_i^z + \mu_j^z + \epsilon_{i,j}^z \tag{4}$$

where z reflects the model's outcome variable, which may be either m (midpoints) or w (widths), for expert i on hop j; β_0 denotes the fixed intercept; μ_i and μ_j denote respective random intercepts for expert and hop; and ϵ represents the error. The remaining β terms (within A_m, A_w and A_{mw}) denote the coefficients of the fixed effects of the hop attributes.

We perform likewise calculations for the evade hops (variables listed in Table 2). The sum of effects for the midpoints of the evade hops is

$$E_m^z = \beta_1^z x_{i,j}^{cm} + \beta_2^z x_{i,j}^{am} + \beta_3^z x_{i,j}^{rm}, \tag{5}$$

for the widths is

$$E_w^z = \beta_4^z x_{i,j}^{cw} + \beta_5^z x_{i,j}^{aw} + \beta_6^z x_{i,j}^{rw}, \tag{6}$$

and for the interactions is

$$E_{mw}^z = \beta_7^z (x_{i,j}^{cm} \cdot x_{i,j}^{cw}) + \beta_8^z (x_{i,j}^{am} \cdot x_{i,j}^{aw}) + \beta_9^z (x_{i,j}^{rm} \cdot x_{i,j}^{rw}) \tag{7}$$

Our initial model formula to explain the overall difficulty ratings for midpoints $(\gamma_{i,j}^{Eom})$ and widths $(\gamma_{i,j}^{Eow})$ of evade hops is then

$$\gamma_{i,j}^{Eoz} = \beta_0^z + E_m^z + E_w^z + E_{mw}^z + \mu_i^z + \mu_j^z + \epsilon_{i,j}^z. \tag{8}$$

Each of the initial models, as presented above, was then subjected to a backwards stepwise variable elimination procedure. During this, fixed effects were iteratively assessed and those that did not significantly contribute to the overall model were removed. Specifically, this process began by selection, from the pool of all non-significant fixed effects, of the effect with the t-statistic closest to zero. This variable was then removed, and the resulting model directly compared with the preceding one, using the Theoretical Likelihood Ratio test. This was implemented through the MATLAB *fitlme* and *compare* functions. If the benefit of retaining the variable in question was calculated to be non-significant, then the model with the lower Bayesian Information Criterion (BIC) was retained into the next iteration. This procedure continued until a final model was determined, within which all fixed effects were statistically significant.

3 Results

3.1 Attack Hops

Table 3 shows all effects retained in the final model with the outcome variable of overall attack hop difficulty (midpoints), following the stepwise variable reduction process. These results indicate that a number of factors make a substantial contribution. Attacks were rated less difficult if they are frequently reported or have a large availability of tools. By contrast, attacks were rated as more difficult if they have a greater inherent difficulty or relate to more mature technologies. Attacks were also rated as more difficult when technological maturity was uncertain and, perhaps surprisingly, when easier to go unnoticed. The latter might relate to some underlying factor - for instance, some attacks may be difficult to conduct, but also difficult to detect. The significant interaction term $(m \cdot w)$ indicates a combined effect of reported tool availability and uncertainty around this. This likely reflects that a hop is rated as being more difficult to attack when experts are certain about availability being low, but less difficult when experts are certain about availability being high. Unsurprisingly, the inherent difficulty rating was found to have the most robust effect.

Table 3. Results showing significant effects of hop attribute midpoints (m), widths (w) and two-way interactions $(m \cdot w)$ on midpoints of overall attack hop difficulty ratings.

Fixed effects estimates	β	SE	t	p
Intercept: ($_0$)	.012	.066	.175	.861
Frequency m: ($x_{i,j}^{fm}$)	−.223	.044	−5.065	<.001
Availability tool m: ($x_{i,j}^{am}$)	−.201	.044	−4.574	<.001
Inherent difficulty m: ($x_{i,j}^{dm}$)	.357	.030	11.890	<.001
Maturity m: ($x_{i,j}^{rm}$)	.126	.030	4.159	<.001
Going unnoticed. m: ($x_{i,j}^{gm}$)	.142	.027	5.194	<.001
Maturity w: ($x_{i,j}^{rw}$)	.071	.027	2.612	.009
Availability tool $m \cdot w$: ($x_{i,j}^{am} \cdot x_{i,j}^{aw}$)	.077	.036	2.168	.031
Random effects estimates	μ			
Expert intercept ($_i$)	.183			
Hop intercept ($_j$)	.204			
Residual $\epsilon_{i,j}$	.502			

N = 532, DF = 524, AIC = 896.7, BIC = 943.6

Table 4 shows all effects retained in the final model with the outcome variable of uncertainty surrounding overall attack hop difficulty (widths). Even more factors were retained in this final model. Results indicated that experts were more certain about the vulnerability of hops on which attacks were reported more frequently – likely due to familiarity. They were also more certain regarding hops that relate to mature technologies or when tool availability is low. By contrast, overall uncertainty significantly increased in line with attribute uncertainty for reported attack frequency, tool availability, inherent difficulty, and ease of going unnoticed. Two interaction terms were also retained, indicating that the effects of uncertainty around these attributes on overall uncertainty were significantly modulated by attribute rating, or vice versa. These can be interpreted together with main effects, depending upon direction. For example, in the case of ease of going unnoticed, there is a relatively large positive main effect of attribute uncertainty and a smaller, but significant, negative interaction term. This indicates that overall ratings were most uncertain when going unnoticed was considered difficult but uncertain. However, overall ratings were most certain when going unnoticed was considered difficult with certainty. The effect of attribute uncertainty was reduced, though still substantial, around hops rated as easier to go unnoticed when attacking. For maturity, however, there is a negative main effect of attribute rating and a negative interaction term, of comparable size. This indicates that overall uncertainty was greatest when maturity was rated low but uncertain. Also, while an increase in maturity rating tended to increase the certainty of overall ratings, this effect was driven by cases in which maturity was itself uncertain. Of all effects in this analysis, uncertainty surrounding the inherent difficulty rating was found to be the most robust.

Table 4. Results showing significant effects of hop attribute midpoints (m), widths (w) and two-way interactions ($m \cdot w$) on widths of overall attack hop difficulty ratings.

Fixed effects estimates	β	SE	t	p
Intercept: $(_0)$	$-.031$	.036	$-.857$	.392
Frequency m: $(x_{i,j}^{fm})$	$-.116$	.045	-2.614	.009
Availability tool m: $(x_{i,j}^{am})$	.131	.045	2.934	.003
Maturity m: $(x_{i,j}^{rm})$	$-.093$	.031	-3.013	.003
Frequency w: $(x_{i,j}^{fw})$	.141	.035	4.034	$<.001$
Availability tool w: $(x_{i,j}^{aw})$	.095	.039	2.420	.016
Inherent difficulty w: $(x_{i,j}^{dw})$	.406	.037	10.959	$<.001$
Going unnoticed w: $(x_{i,j}^{gw})$	.268	.036	7.399	$<.001$
Maturity $m \cdot w$: $(x_{i,j}^{rm} \cdot x_{i,j}^{rw})$	$-.122$	.035	-3.484	$<.001$
Going unnoticed $m \cdot w$: $(x_{i,j}^{gm} \cdot x_{i,j}^{gw})$	$-.080$	.035	-2.270	.024
Random effects estimates	μ			
Expert intercept $(_i)$	.127			
Hop intercept $(_j)$	.000			
Residual $\epsilon_{i,j}$	.609			

N = 532, DF = 522, AIC = 1066.3, BIC = 1121.7

3.2   Evade Hops

Table 5 shows all effects retained in the final model with the outcome variable of overall evade hop difficulty (midpoints). Four fixed effects were retained. Experts rated a hop as less difficult to evade when more information is available to aid with this, but more difficult to evade when they were uncertain about the availability of such information. Overall evasion difficulty was also higher for hops relating to more mature technologies. A negative interaction term was evident for ratings of hop complexity, with certainty around a more complex hop being associated with it being more difficult to evade, but certainty around a hop being less complex associated with it being easier to evade. The availability of information was found to be have the most robust effect.

Table 5. Results showing significant effects of hop attribute midpoints (m), widths (w) and two-way interactions $(m \cdot w)$ on midpoints of overall evade hop difficulty ratings.

Fixed effects estimates	β	SE	t	p
Intercept: $(_0)$	$-.023$	.133	$-.173$	.863
Availability information m: $(x_{i,j}^{am})$	$-.240$	.049	-4.895	$<.001$
Maturity m: $(x_{i,j}^{rm})$	.177	.051	3.459	$<.001$
Availability information w: $(x_{i,j}^{aw})$	.142	.049	2.878	.004
Complexity $m \cdot w$: $(x_{i,j}^{cm} \cdot x_{i,j}^{cw})$	$-.105$	.053	-1.993	.047
Random effects estimates	μ			
Expert intercept $(_i)$	.457			
Hop intercept $(_j)$	.340			
Residual $\epsilon_{i,j}$	.772			

N = 418, DF = 413, AIC = 1081.8, BIC = 1114.0

Table 6. Results showing significant effects of hop attribute midpoints (m), widths (w) and two-way interactions $(m \cdot w)$ on widths of overall evade hop difficulty ratings.

Fixed effects estimates	β	SE	t	p
Intercept: $(_0)$	$-.000$	.058	$-.000$	$>.999$
Complexity w: $(x_{i,j}^{cw})$	.241	.046	5.200	$<.001$
Availability information w: $(x_{i,j}^{aw})$	.440	.045	9.683	$<.001$
Maturity w: $(x_{i,j}^{rw})$	.134	.045	2.982	.003
Random effects estimates	μ			
Expert intercept $(_i)$	.070			
Hop intercept $(_j)$	.159			
Residual $\epsilon_{i,j}$	.643			

N = 418, DF = 414, AIC = 863.0, BIC = 891.2

Table 6 shows all effects retained in the final model with the outcome variable of uncertainty surrounding overall evade hop difficulty (widths). These results show that experts were more uncertain in their overall hop rating when they were more uncertain about each of the three attributes of a given hop: complexity, information availability, or maturity. However, no significant main effects of attribute rating position, nor any interaction terms were found. Uncertainty surrounding information availability was found to have the most robust effect.

4   Conclusions

We analyse ratings provided by cyber-security experts that pertain to a range of potentially important component (hop) attributes, previously identified as commonly occurring within attack vectors of mainstream government cyber-systems. Importantly, these ratings were obtained through interval-valued responses, which enable experts to indicate both their rating and the uncertainty associated with this rating in a single, integrated response.

Our analyses provide a 'proof of concept' for interval-valued data capture applied to the field of cyber-security. We identify key factors that contribute to both component vulnerability and uncertainty, depending on whether a hop requires compromising or only bypassing. For example, the availability of information has the largest impact on the overall difficulty of evading a component, while uncertainty around the inherent difficulty of an attack has the largest impact on its overall uncertainty.

Uncertainty in experts' attribute ratings is found to be valuable in determining not only overall uncertainty, but also overall hop vulnerability. In a number of specific cases, this information explained variance over and above the discrete midpoints of attribute ratings. For instance, when predicting the overall difficulty of attack hops, uncertainty around the maturity of technology of a given hop was associated with a significant increase in difficulty rating for that hop. In other cases, we found that in order to best explain overall difficulty ratings it was necessary to consider an interaction effect, between the position and width of responses. Sometimes, the combination of both factors provided a better predictor than either did alone. It was the novel use of an interval-valued response format that made it possible to coherently capture this uncertainty, alongside traditional ratings.

This study provides initial empirical evidence for the potential added-value offered by capturing interval-valued responses to model expert uncertainty. This is demonstrated in the case of modelling vulnerabilities within cyber-systems comprising multiple components, each with varying attributes, as is characteristic of cyber-physical systems. The benefit of using interval-valued responses was found using a comparatively low-complexity linear modelling approach. While such an approach is unsuited to capturing varying effects of responses along the response scale (for instance, it cannot account for a tendency for responses to saturate towards the extremities), its simplicity facilitates interpretation of the results. In future work, we will investigate the use of generalised additive models, within which the relationships between independent and dependent variables may be non-linear. Additionally, we are pursuing an ongoing programme of research to demonstrate the efficacy of interval-valued responses, both in terms of capturing uncertainty and improving predictive power, with reference to real-world ground-truth.

References

1. Aven, T., Renn, O.: On risk defined as an event where the outcome is uncertain. J. Risk Res. **12**(1), 1–11 (2009)
2. Black, P.E., Scarfone, K., Souppaya, M.: Cyber security metrics and measures. In: Wiley Handbook of Science and Technology for Homeland Security, pp. 1–15 (2008)
3. CESG: Extract from HMG IA Standard No. 1 Business Impact Level Tables. CESG (2009)
4. Choi, H.H., Cho, H.N., Seo, J.W.: Risk assessment methodology for underground construction projects. J. Constr. Eng. Manag. **130**(2), 258–272 (2004)
5. Duan, Y., Cai, Y., Wang, Z., Deng, X.: A novel network security risk assessment approach by combining subjective and objective weights under uncertainty. Appl. Sci. **8**(3) (2018). https://doi.org/10.3390/app8030428, http://www.mdpi.com/2076-3417/8/3/428
6. Feng, N., Li, M.: An information systems security risk assessment model under uncertain environment. Appl. Soft Comput. **11**(7), 4332–4340 (2011)
7. Fielder, A., Konig, S., Panaousis, E., Schauer, S., Rass, S.: Uncertainty in cyber security investments. arXiv preprint arXiv:1712.05893 (2017)
8. FIRST: Cvss v3.0 specification document. https://www.first.org/cvss/specification-document
9. Gao, H., Zhu, J., Li, C.: The analysis of uncertainty of network security risk assessment using Dempster-Shafer theory. In: 2008 12th International Conference on Computer Supported Cooperative Work in Design, pp. 754–759. IEEE (2008)
10. Gardner, D.: Risk: The Science and Politics of Fear. Random House, New York (2009)
11. Hubbard, D.W., Seiersen, R.: How to Measure Anything in Cybersecurity Risk. Wiley, New York (2016)
12. Kahneman, D., Slovic, S.P., Slovic, P., Tversky, A.: Judgment Under Uncertainty: Heuristics and Biases. Cambridge University Press, Cambridge (1982)
13. Koubatis, A., Schonberger, J.Y.: Risk management of complex critical systems. Int. J. Crit. Infrastruct. **1**(2–3), 195–215 (2005)
14. Linda, O., Manic, M., Vollmer, T., Wright, J.: Fuzzy logic based anomaly detection for embedded network security cyber sensor. In: 2011 IEEE Symposium on Computational Intelligence in Cyber Security (CICS), pp. 202–209. IEEE (2011)
15. Mell, P., Scarfone, K., Romanosky, S.: A complete guide to the common vulnerability scoring system version 2.0. In: Published by FIRST-Forum of Incident Response and Security Teams, vol. 1, p. 23 (2007)
16. Miller, S., Appleby, S., Garibaldi, J.M., Aickelin, U.: Towards a more systematic approach to secure systems design and analysis. Int. J. Secur. Softw. Eng. (IJSSE) **4**(1), 11–30 (2013)
17. Miller, S., Wagner, C., Aickelin, U., Garibaldi, J.M.: Modelling cyber-security experts' decision making processes using aggregation operators. Comput. Secur. **62**, 229–245 (2016)
18. Munir, R., Disso, J.P., Awan, I., Mufti, M.R.: A quantitative measure of the security risk level of enterprise networks. In: 2013 Eighth International Conference on Broadband and Wireless Computing, Communication and Applications, pp. 437–442. IEEE (2013)
19. Sikos, L.F.: Handling uncertainty and vagueness in network knowledge representation for cyberthreat intelligence. In: 2018 IEEE International Conference on Fuzzy Systems (FUZZ-IEEE), pp. 1–6. IEEE (2018)
20. Slovic, P.: The Perception of Risk. Routledge, Abingdon (2016)

Estimating Cascading Effects
in Cyber-Physical Critical Infrastructures

Stefan Schauer[1]([✉]) [iD], Thomas Grafenauer[1] [iD], Sandra König[1] [iD],
Manuel Warum[1] [iD], and Stefan Rass[2] [iD]

[1] AIT Austrian Institute of Technology GmbH, Vienna, Austria
{stefan.schauer,thomas.grafenauer,sandra.koenig,
manuel.warum}@ait.ac.at
[2] Alpen-Adria-Universität Klagenfurt, Klagenfurt, Austria
stefan.rass@aau.at

Abstract. Nowadays, critical infrastructures operate a large number of highly interdependent, cyber-physical systems. Thus, incidents can have far-reaching cascading effects throughout the entire infrastructure, which need to be identified and estimated to realize a proper risk management. In this paper, we present a formal model to describe the propagation of a threat through the various physical and cyber assets within a critical infrastructure and the cascading effects this has on the entire infrastructure. We further show, how this model can be implemented into a prototypical tool, which allows to efficiently simulate the cascading effects of a given incident on the entire network of the infrastructure's cyber-physical assets. The functionalities of the tool are demonstrated using a small demo set-up of a maritime port infrastructure. In this set-up, four incident scenarios both from the physical and cyber domain are simulated and the results are discussed.

Keywords: Threat propagation · Cascading effects · Simulation
framework · Risk estimation

1 Introduction

Due to the ongoing digitalization in the industrial sector, the interconnections and interdependencies among the physical and cyber systems within today's critical infrastructures (CIs) have increased drastically. A large number of the systems required for the delivery of the CI's service are connected to, controlled by or operated by cyber systems for reasons of efficiency and convenience. Hence, a clear distinction between physical systems and cyber systems, or rather between the Operation Technology (OT) network and the Information and Communication Technology (ICT) network is no longer possible. It has been shown in the past years, that these extensive interconnections give malicious parties and cyber criminals the opportunity to hack and compromise crucial systems without big technological or financial effort. Moreover, the impairment of such a

S. Nadjm-Tehrani (Ed.): CRITIS 2019, LNCS 11777, pp. 43–56, 2020.
https://doi.org/10.1007/978-3-030-37670-3_4

system has wide-spreading effects within the CI itself but also for other CIs and the society as a whole due to these interconnections and interdependencies. For example, the Ukrainian power provider has been hacked twice in 2015 and 2016 [7,8]. The main entry point for the hackers was manipulated Word documents [8] and as a result, large areas of the country have been without power for several hours. In 2017, the WannaCry and (Not-)Petya malware have infected millions of systems in various sectors, e.g., in hospitals [2] or in maritime port infrastructures [25], with an impact of over 300 million dollars for the logistics company Moeller-Maersk alone [6]. In this case, one of the starting points for the infection was a malicious update of an accounting software in the Ukraine [6]. These are just a few examples which show, how easily a compromised or malfunctioning system can have large cascading effects on the connected infrastructure. In this paper, we present a prototypical tool, which allows to identify and estimate the potential cascading effects an incident at some system within an organization can have on the overall infrastructure. The tool is part of a larger system, which implements the concept of a Hybrid Situational Awareness (HSA) [29] and builds upon a stochastic process modelling the dependencies among the various systems within a CI. The main advantage of this approach (and thus also of the tool presented here) is that no difference is made between the physical and the cyber domain, i.e., between the ICT and the OT network. Therefore, the tool is able to indicate the effects of a physical incident on the cyber domain and vice versa. The stochastic process used in the approach models each system within the CI as a probabilistic Mealy automaton [15]. In this way, the different operational states as well as the non-deterministic nature of the spreading of an attack can be modelled. The tool as well as the mathematical approach have been developed as part of the H2020 project SAURON with a focus on critical port infrastructures; however, both can be applied analogously on any other type of CIs.

2   Related Work

Among the first models of cascading effects was the Cross Impact Analysis (CIA) [9] that allows describing how dependencies between events affect future events. An extension is the Cross Impact Analysis and Interpretative Structural Model (CIA-ISM) [1] which applies in emergency management to analyze the effects between critical events and to obtain a view on future consequences. These models can be seen as predecessors of contemporary stochastic models.

Cascading effects are of particular interest in the context of security of CIs as first introduced by [18] due to their high importance for society [17,21]. Cascading effects can occur both in a network of interconnected CIs [14,22] and inside a complex CI that contains several subsystems as, for example, in power systems [10]. A general overview and a detailed comparison of different methods is given in [22]. Due to recent incidents already mentioned in the Introduction, research also focuses on targeted attacks on CIs, e.g., on power systems [3,13].

Cascading effects in interconnected networks (sometimes called "network of networks") have been investigated based on Bayesian networks to model and analyze dependencies [4] as well as physical models such as percolation [5,16] to evaluate the propagation of failures or on topological properties and network analysis [23]. In our work presented here, we apply a model that extends the existing percolation approach by taking into account the dynamics inside a single component [15]. Generally, cascading effects are not exactly predictable due to the many factors that come into play which makes exact models infeasible. Further, consequences of incidents are often influenced by human actions (in particular for targeted attacks such as malware attacks), which further increases the uncertainty. Based on this insight, a large number of stochastic models has been developed.

Classical Markov models hinge on a high complexity of the state space and ask for specification of many transitions probabilities. One way to handle the complexity of Markov models is to use an abstract state space whose states only contain information relevant for the system dynamics [28]. The approach is extended by the Interdependent Markov Chain (IDMC) model [27] that allows describing cascading failures in interdependent infrastructures. Therein, each system is described by a discrete-time Markov chain and the chains are coupled to capture the interdependencies between them.

Markov chains with a memory are used in [33] to describe situations where the transition probabilities do not only depend on the current state but also on the past ones. A conditional Markov transition model has been applied to describe cascading failures in electric power grids [32] and the transition probabilities are derived from a stochastic for flow redistribution. Moreover, time-dependent Markov chains have been used to model system behaviour and account for dynamic aspects of attack strategies to quantify risks to data assets [31]. These phenomena are also captured by our model since the (probabilistic) automata describing a component can be seen as a representation of Markov chains and transitions may be time-dependent. However, our model explicitly allows for reactions to input signals, which is not possible for Markov chain models that update their states at fixed time intervals. Another probabilistic approach to model cascading effects in CIs is application of branching processes that are typically used to describe growth of a population. The applicability of branching processes on modeling cascading effects is investigated in [26].

A necessary input to all spreading models is a complete identification of dependencies. This is a challenge on its own as many dependencies are not visible at first sight. Interconnections between infrastructures are investigated with a probabilistic model in [19] and empirical findings are presented in [20]. An overview on existing modeling approaches and open research questions concerning CI interdependencies in urban areas is given in [11]. A method to identify and describe service failure interdependencies is introduced in [30].

3   Threat Propagation Model

The model we are using to describe the propagation of a threat through the various assets within a CI and the cascading effects it has on this infrastructure applies concepts from graph theory, automaton theory and stochastic processes. It is part of a larger project, i.e., the SAURON framework [29], which provides comprehensive situational awareness for the physical and the cyber parts of a critical port infrastructure to its operators. Therefore, the SAURON framework integrates a Physical Situational Awareness (PSA), a Cyber Situational Awareness (CSA) and a Hybrid Situational Awareness (HSA) system. Whereas the PSA and the CSA are more or less standard components which are building upon existing tools and frameworks tailored to the requirements of port infrastructures, the HSA is developed from scratch integrating the threat propagation model and represents the main innovation in the project. In detail, the HSA works on events detected and alarms triggered by both the PSA and the CSA upon incidents happening in the respective domains. In this way, the HSA connects the information coming from the PSA and the CSA and brings together the two usually separated domains.

The establishment of such a hybrid view on an infrastructure's asset architecture is achieved by using two main modules, i.e., the Event Correlation Engine (ECE) and the Threat Propagation Engine (TPE). As the name already indicates, the ECE focuses exclusively on events, i.e., general occurrences, detected by the PSA and the CSA with the main goal to identify inconsistencies among those events. The TPE deals with alarms, i.e., critical incidents, and is responsible for the identification of the potential cascading effects of such incidents. To achieve that, the TPE builds upon a graph representation of all the assets, physical and cyber, given in the infrastructure. The assets are represented by the nodes of this graph, whereas each node can be in one of several operational states (cf. Sect. 4.1 for further details). The edges in this graph represent the different dependencies between the various assets.

As already mentioned above, the TPE processes the alarms triggered by the PSA or the CSA. An alarm usually involves one specific asset and, depending on the type of incident, changes the operational state of this asset. This represents a reduction of the service or the capacity of this asset due to the incident happening. Based to the connections among the asset in the graph, i.e., the dependencies, the state change of one asset might also affect the operational state of all the subsequent assets depending on it and so forth. In this way, the cascading effects of the incident, which triggered the alarm, on the entire infrastructure are described by the TPE. As a result, the TPE delivers two lists: one list containing the most critical assets affected by the alarm and a second list describing the assets that will be affected immediately in the next step.

4   Model Implementation

4.1   Formal Definition

The formal description of the threat propagation model is essentially a network of coupled probabilistic Mealy automata (following [15]): at a high level, consider a set V of assets forming nodes of a graph $G = (V, E)$, where a directed edge $u \rightarrow v \in E$ models a dependency of asset v on asset u (e.g., u may be a supplier for v). Each node $v \in V$ undergoes an evolution over time, switching between different states of operation, ranging from "fully operational" until "outage". The transition from one state to another is triggered by notifications (messages) exchanged between assets, and is in general probabilistic. That is, if asset u experiences troubles and changes its state from "fully operational" to "partly affected", it notifies its dependent asset (in our example node v if there is an edge $u \rightarrow v$) about this change. The dependent asset v, in turn, may not deterministically react upon this, but may change its state probabilistically based on this information. If v undergoes its own state transition (caused by the change of u before), it acts in the same way as u and notifies its descendants (in the asset network G) about its new status, which lets them react likewise.

Probabilistic Mealy automata are a natural description of this intuition, since they process and emit symbols, which are the messages received from other automata. The simulation model thus has two levels (cf. also Fig. 1): (i) the *outer model*, which is a humble directed graph $G = (V, E)$, and (ii) a set of *inner models*, one for each $v \in V$, which are Mealy automata over a common set S describing the states of operation. Each Mealy automaton v describes the transition from state $s_1 \in S$ to state $s_2 \in S$ by the triplet ⟨incoming message m, outgoing notification m', probability p⟩, with the semantics that upon receiving the message m from a parent node/asset of v in G, with probability p, there will be a change into state s_2, upon which another notification m' is published to other assets that depend on this node (in G). With probability $1 - p$, the automaton v will remain in its state (possibly also notifying other assets about this fact, if the transition from s_1 to s_1 is defined accordingly).

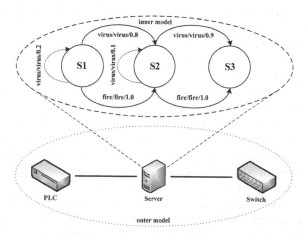

Fig. 1. Schematic illustration of the inner and out model.

Further, an element of time herein can added, if we replace the probability p by some time-dependent value $p(t)$, and let the automata undergo transitions without external forces (this is the behavior of a Markov chain, and as such different to the Mealy automaton model; hence distinguishes the model from a Markov chain in this aspect). We do not explore this possibility further here and leave it for future work.

4.2   Reference Implementation

The model described in Sect. 4.1, has been implemented as a Node.js module using the TypeScript language and is callable through a HTTP-based interface[1]. In addition, a browser-based Single Page Application has been developed to enable users drawing and connecting their own physical or cyber assets. This includes relevant information about each asset such as probabilistic state transitions or which types of alarms affect it. In the current version of the tool, this information needs to be filled in by the user; in particular, the probabilities for all state transitions are chosen based on the experience and knowledge of the infrastructure's experts. It is planned in the future to support the user with these inputs, e.g., by using a small sample set for the probabilities of state transitions, to reduce the effort required for setting up the model. Aside from simulations, all other processing is done in-browser, meaning that it is not reliant on network connectivity.

After a user has modeled his own environment and assets, the underlying implementation allows triggering any of the defined alarms on any asset that responds to it. While the modelling aspects are handled by the web application, any actual calculations related to simulations are offloaded to the HTTP-based application programming interface (API). If the user triggers such an alarm, a configurable amount of simulations are run on the server side, an ordered set of changes will be returned, and the web application aggregates it into distributions. Information valuable to determine appropriate courses of actions can be gleaned from this, including which assets are likely to be affected next or what is the worst possible outcome if no mitigating measures are undertaken.

The web application does not rely on the user drawing their environment within the application. Instead, such environments can be imported from and exported to disk using a human-readable, JSON-based text file. The object schema contained within these network files is strongly based on the visualization library vis.js and requires only a set of nodes composed of unique identifiers and Mealy automaton transition quintuples, and a set of directed edges composed of unique identifiers as well as which two nodes are connected. The operational state of each asset is expressed as an integer of the domain $\{1, 2, 3\}$.

Once a series of simulations for a given scenario has been calculated, the API responds with an ordered set of changes that occurred for each simulation. This also includes a verification, i.e., which transitions have been triggered by which event. As multiple simulations are run, different outcomes are generated and aggregated for further evaluation by human operators. Simulations can either be run until they no longer trigger any transitions within the Mealy automata, or until a predefined logical time has been reached. The minimum number of

---

[1] Online available at https://atlas.ait.ac.at/sauron.

iterations for the simulation required to obtain a statistically significant result can be determined in (at least) two ways: first, conditional on the evolution being only degenerative, i.e., without recovery or repairs, we have all statuses evolve monotonous and bounded, so the status of each CI will necessarily lead to convergence. Consequently, we can stop as soon as the change to the overall status falls below some (small) threshold. The same holds if we treat the simulation outputs as samples from a time series. On these, we may apply a palette of convergence diagnostics known from the field of Markov chains (e.g., [24]). Alternatively, if we want to conduct statistical tests based on simulation results, we can consider each simulation output as one sample from an experiment, and ask for the number of such samples required for statistical significance. Software for statistical power analysis (e.g., G*Power [12]) can do this.

The main output of the application is twofold: the "State Distributions" aggregate each asset's final state distribution across all simulations and the "Worst and Average Outcomes" provides an overview on which assets are at risk after a certain amount of time in a worst case and an average scenario. This information can be directly used for incident handling, i.e., to evaluate the potential consequences when a specific alarm is triggered and show them to the security operator using the tool.

To test the performance of the simulation core functionality, we tracked the processing time for different model configurations (see Table 1) where each test consists of 1000 simulation runs and the initial event was randomly chosen. The smallest model needed half a second to simulate whereas the biggest one needed approximately 3 min and 20 s. This can further be enhanced since the performance is currently limited to Node.js single threaded language JavaScript but can be improved by using worker threads.

Table 1. This table shows the performance of the simulation core for different model sizes.

Test-Nr	Nodes	Edges	Symbols	Transitions	Simulation-time
1	100	200	1	2–3	509 ms
2	500	1200	1	2–3	5254 ms
3	1000	3000	1	2–3	23191 ms
4	1000	3000	5	10–15	32825 ms
5	1000	10000	5	10–15	199592 ms

5   Scenario Description

To showcase the application, we created an example scenario of a simplified port infrastructure with four physical areas: two office buildings with four rooms each, a truck gate that monitors incoming and outgoing traffic and an area where liquid natural gas (LNG) is stored (see Fig. 2). The rooms of the office buildings again contain different ICT assets such as workstations and servers; more important rooms (i.e., B1-4, B2-3 and B2-4) are secured by access control systems. The LNG area and the truck gate have surveillance cameras and access controls installed. All cameras and access controls are connected via the OT network; similarly, all workstations are connected in the ICT network. Further, there are three physical servers located in the infrastructure: one of them is responsible for database management, another one provides the customer relationship management (CRM) services and the access control (ACC) and the third runs the services for surveillance (SUR) and freight management (FRM). The connections between these assets were set according to their physical and/or cyber based dependencies to each other. Hence, the three servers are physically connected to both the ICT and the OT network, since they provide databases and services for the working stations and access to OT devices like cameras and access controls.

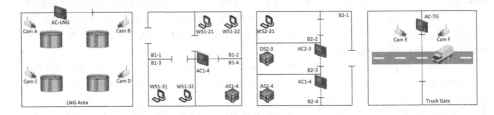

Fig. 2. Schematic set-up of the port infrastructure in our scenario

To model cascading effects, transitions need to be defined for each threat at the corresponding assets. For our scenario, we consider a physical threat, i.e., a fire, and a cyber threat, i.e., a system gets hacked and compromised. In case of a fire, only physical assets have transitions to react to the alert; cyber based assets do not actively react on the input "fire" and thus are not directly affected. However, they can still be affected by the threat because of their dependencies to physical assets. A fire usually reduces the operational state of a physical asset to "outage", i.e., the asset shuts down or is destroyed. To model this effect, the physical assets transform the input fire to the output "offline" or "destroyed" which is then sent to all dependent assets. In a similar way, the cyber threat of hacking a system can also affect physical assets: a room can become "compromised" if the access control system is hacked, it does not provide sufficient protection any more.

6   Results and Discussion

For our first showcase, we simulate two fires happening in different buildings, i.e., in room B1-1 (cf. Figure 3) and B2-1 (cf. Figure 4) and compare the outcome of 1000 simulation runs each. The grey-scale in the figures represent the average state of the CI's assets (white = state "1" to dark grey = state "3"). In Scenario 1, a fire starts in room B1-1. Figure 3 shows the average state of each asset over all simulation runs. The fire caused an outage of all workstations and the server in building B1. Two applications and services run on this server: CRM and ACC. Since the ACC service and application is now offline, all the access controls (triangles) to sensitive areas are affected and don't operate any more. As a result, the LNG area, the truck gate as well as two rooms in building B2 can be accessed without any authorization required.

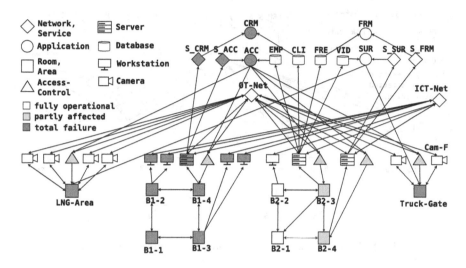

Fig. 3. Average case result of Scenario 1 (fire in room B1-1).

In Fig. 4, the fire starts in room B2-1 but does not affect all adjacent rooms equally. The room B2-3, which contains the database server, is only affected partially because it is more resistant to fire (modelled with a transition probability of only 20%) and is damaged (i.e., changes to state "3") in only 44% of the simulations. As a result, the database server in room B2-3 is less affected than the application server of the adjacent room B2-4. Due to the damage of the application server, the SUR and FRM services are shut down, too. Hence, although the cameras and access controls are still intact, security operators are no longer able to access the video stream. Therefore, the LNG area and the truck gate are partially affected and not considered secure any more.

When comparing both scenarios, we see that due to the fire resistance of room B2-3, fewer assets are in the most severe state "3" and more are only partially affected (i.e., in state "2") in Scenario 2. This indicates that using fire resistant material will lower the overall risk for the CI. However, when computing the average operational state of the entire CI (i.e., the arithmetic mean over the states of all assets), we can see that the difference is not significant (1.77 for Scenario 1 and 1.64 for Scenario 2). Nevertheless, when looking at the worst case (which is not depicted here due to space limitations), the average operational state for the entire CI is much worse compared to Scenario 1, i.e., 2.02 for Scenario 2 versus 1.86 for Scenario 1. That is, the CI is expected to be partly affected but likely remain running ("fully operational" = 1 < 1.86 < 2 = "partly affected") in Scenario 1, as opposed to be probably affected if not endangered to be out of order ("partly affected" = 2 < 2.02 < 3 = "outage").

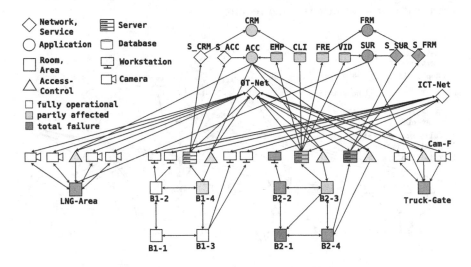

Fig. 4. Average case result of Scenario 2 (fire in room B2-1).

In our second showcase, we assume that the camera "Cam F" at the truck gate is hacked by a malicious party and we again compare two scenarios with 1000 simulation runs: Scenario 3, where there is no special security layer in the OT network, and Scenario 4, where cyber security measures are implemented to protect the OT network. Due to these security measures, we assume that the chance for the OT network to be compromised when one of the devices in the network gets hacked is only 30%, whereas without this security layer, the OT network is always compromised. In Scenario 3, the compromised camera "Cam F" caused many other devices in the OT and ICT network to be compromised (cf. Figure 5), which has a crucial effect on the surveillance of the LNG area and the truck gate (in our showcase, compromised assets are in state "2", since they are still functional but might send or display false information). For this case, the average operational state for the entire CI is 1.47, i.e., more likely fully functional with some (smaller) chance of being partly affected (1.47 is closer to state 1 than to state 2).

When looking at Scenario 4, the devices connected to the OT network are not as easily compromised, leaving them in a much better operational state. Accordingly, also the average operational state for the entire CI is better, i.e., 1.16. The advantage of implementing security measures on the network level are

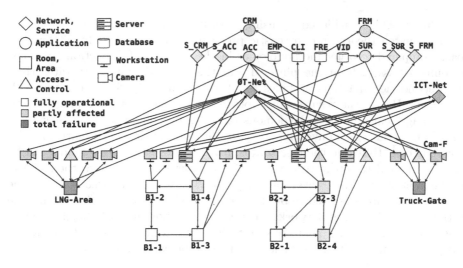

Fig. 5. Average case result of Scenario 3 (insecure OT network).

even more visible, when we observed the likelihood of individual assets to change their operational state directly after "Cam F" has been compromised (i.e., after the initial step of the simulation). Table 2 shows the top five assets, which are most likely to change their operational state within the next three simulation steps. From this table, we can see that the likelihood of the top two assets ("OT Network" and "LNG Area") is reduced drastically. Hence, the results from the simulation can also be used to evaluate the implementation of new security measures or mitigation actions at different assets in the CI.

Table 2. This table shows the top five most likely assets to be affected within the next three simulation steps after "Cam F" has been compromised (with a 85% probability).

Insecure OT network			Secured OT network		
Asset name	State	Likelihood	Asset name	State	Likelihood
OT-Network	2	86.20%	Truck-Gate	2	59.80%
LNG-Area	3	85.50%	OT-Network	2	26.70%
Truck-Gate	3	78.90%	LNG-Area	3	26.30%
IT-Network	2	76.70%	Truck-Gate	3	25.00%
Camera-B	2	74.0%	IT-Network	2	23.80%

7 Conclusion

In this paper, we presented a tool which allows simulating the propagation of a threat though a CI's asset network and estimating the cascading effects of that threat. This is achieved by using a formal model building on graph theory, automaton theory and stochastic processes. The main benefit of the approach compared to other methodologies in the literature (cf. Section 2) is that it combines assets from the physical and the cyber domain, integrates their interdependecies and thus provides a holistic (or hybrid) view on the cascading effects. Hence, the results can improve the CI operator's risk analysis and risk management processes. We demonstrated the functionality in four scenarios, describing the effects of physical and cyber threats on a simplified maritime port infrastructure. Based on these scenarios, it is easy to see that the model can be quickly adapted to integrate new security measures and estimate their effects for different incidents. However, one major drawback of the approach is that the transition probabilities need to be specified for each dependency (i.e., each node in the graph). For large networks, this can be a laborious task which involves expert opinions. Thus, a next steps is to integrate a methodology to formalize this process, making it more efficient and less time-consuming.

Acknowledgement. This work was supported by the European Commission's Project SAURON (Scalable multidimensional situation awareness solution for protecting European ports) under the HORIZON 2020 Framework (Grant No. 740477).

References

1. Bañuls, V.A., Turoff, M.: Scenario construction via delphi and cross-impact analysis. Technol. Forecast. Soc. Change **78**(9), 1579–1602 (2011)
2. BBC News: NHS cyber-attack: GPs and hospitals hit by ransomware (2017). http://www.bbc.com/news/health-39899646
3. Bilis, E.I., Kroger, W., Nan, C.: Performance of electric power systems under physical malicious attacks. IEEE Syst. J. **7**(4), 854–865 (2013)
4. Burnap, P., Cherdantseva, Y., Blyth, A., Eden, P., Jones, K., Soulsby, H., Stoddart, K.: Determining and sharing risk data in distributed interdependent systems. IEEE Comput. **50**(2), 72–79 (2017)
5. Carreras, B.A., Newman, D.E., Gradney, P., Lynch, V.E., Dobson, I.: Interdependent risk in interacting infrastructure systems. In: 40th Annual Hawaii International Conference on System Sciences, 2007, HICSS 2007, pp. 112–112 (2007)
6. Cimpanu, C.: Maersk Reinstalled 45,000 PCs and 4,000 Servers to Recover From NotPetya Attack (2018). https://www.bleepingcomputer.com/news/security/maersk-reinstalled-45-000-pcs-and-4-000-servers-to-recover-from-notpetya-attack/
7. Condliffe, J.: Ukraine's power grid gets hacked again, a worrying sign for infrastructure attacks (2016). https://www.technologyreview.com/s/603262/ukraines-power-grid-gets-hacked-again-a-worrying-sign-for-infrastructure-attacks/
8. E-ISAC: Analysis of the Cyber Attack on the Ukrainian Power Grid. Technical report, E-ISAC, Washington, USA (2016). https://ics.sans.org/media/E-ISAC_SANS_Ukraine_DUC_5.pdf
9. Gordon, T., Hayward, H.: Initial experiments with the cross impact matrix method of forecasting. Futures **1**(2), 100–116 (1968)
10. Guo, H., Zheng, C., Iu, H.H.C., Fernando, T.: A critical review of cascading failure analysis and modeling of power system. Renew. Sustain. Energy Rev. **80**, 9–22 (2017)

11. Hasan, S., Foliente, G.: Modeling infrastructure system interdependencies and socioeconomic impacts of failure in extreme events: emerging R&D challenges. Nat. Hazards: J. Int. Soc. Prev. Mitig. Nat. Hazards **78**(3), 2143–2168 (2015)

12. Heinrich-Heine-Universität Düsseldorf: G*power: Statistical power analyses for windows and mac. http://www.psychologie.hhu.de/arbeitsgruppen/allgemeine-psychologie-und-arbeitspsychologie/gpower.html. Accessed 21 Aug 2019

13. Koc, Y., Warnier, M., Kooij, R.E., Brazier, F.M.T.: A robustness metric for cascading failures by targeted attacks in power networks. In: 2013 10th IEEE International Conference on Networking, Sensing and Control (ICNSC). IEEE (2013)

14. König, S., Rass, S.: Investigating stochastic dependencies between critical infrastructures. Int. J. Adv. Syst. Meas. **11**(3&4), 250–258 (2018)

15. König, S., Rass, S., Rainer, B., Schauer, S.: Hybrid dependencies between cyber and physical systems. In: Arai, K., Bhatia, R., Kapoor, S. (eds.) CompCom 2019. AISC, vol. 998, pp. 550–565. Springer, Cham (2019). https://doi.org/10.1007/978-3-030-22868-2_40

16. König, S., Schauer, S., Rass, S.: A stochastic framework for prediction of malware spreading in heterogeneous networks. In: Brumley, B.B., Röning, J. (eds.) NordSec 2016. LNCS, vol. 10014, pp. 67–81. Springer, Cham (2016). https://doi.org/10.1007/978-3-319-47560-8_5

17. Kotzanikolaou, P., Theoharidou, M., Gritzalis, D.: Cascading effects of common-cause failures in critical infrastructures. In: Butts, J., Shenoi, S. (eds.) Critical Infrastructure Protection VII, pp. 171–182. Springer, Berlin Heidelberg, Berlin, Heidelberg (2013). https://doi.org/10.1007/978-3-642-45330-4_12

18. Laprie, J.-C., Kanoun, K., Kaâniche, M.: Modelling interdependencies between the electricity and information infrastructures. In: Saglietti, F., Oster, N. (eds.) SAFE-COMP 2007. LNCS, vol. 4680, pp. 54–67. Springer, Heidelberg (2007). https://doi.org/10.1007/978-3-540-75101-4_5

19. Little, R.G.: Controlling cascading failure: understanding the vulnerabilities of interconnected infrastructures. J. Urban Technol. **9**(1), 109–123 (2002)

20. Luiijf, E., Nieuwenhuijs, A., Klaver, M., van Eeten, M., Cruz, E.: Empirical findings on critical infrastructure dependencies in Europe. In: Setola, R., Geretshuber, S. (eds.) CRITIS 2008. LNCS, vol. 5508, pp. 302–310. Springer, Heidelberg (2009). https://doi.org/10.1007/978-3-642-03552-4_28

21. McGee, S., Frittman, J., James Ahn, S., Murray, S.: Implications of cascading effects for the hyogo framework. Int. J. Disaster Resilience Built Environ. **7**, 144–157 (2016)

22. Ouyang, M.: Review on modeling and simulation of interdependent critical infrastructure systems. Reliab. Eng. Syst. Saf. **121**, 43–60 (2014)

23. Pagani, G.A., Aiello, M.: The power grid as a complex network: a survey. Phys. A: Stat. Mech. Appl. **392**(11), 2688–2700 (2013)

24. Plummer, M., Best, N., Cowles, K., Vines, K.: Coda: Convergence diagnosis and output analysis for MCMC. R News 6(1), 7–11 (2006). https://journal.r-project.org/archive/

25. PTI: New malware hits JNPT operations as APM Terminals hacked globally — The Indian Express (2017). http://indianexpress.com/article/india/cyber-attack-new-malware-hits-jnpt-ops-as-apm-terminals-hacked-globally-4725102/

26. Qi, J., Dobson, I., Mei, S.: Towards estimating the statistics of simulated cascades of outages with branching processes. IEEE Trans. Power Syst. **28**(3), 3410–3419 (2013)

27. Rahnamay-Naeini, M., Hayat, M.M.: Cascading failures in interdependent infrastructures: an interdependent markov-chain approach. IEEE Trans. Smart Grid **7**(4), 1997–2006 (2016)
28. Rahnamay-Naeini, M., Wang, Z., Ghani, N., Mammoli, A., Hayat, M.M.: Stochastic analysis of cascading-failure dynamics in power grids. IEEE Trans. Power Syst. **29**(4), 1767–1779 (2014)
29. Schauer, S., Rainer, B., Museux, N., Faure, D., Hingant, J., Rodrigo, F.J.C., Beyer, S., Peris, R.C., Lopez, S.Z.: Conceptual Framework for Hybrid Situational Awareness in Critical Port Infrastructures. In: Luiijf, E., Zutautaite, I., Hämmerli, B.M. (eds.) Critical Information Infrastructures Security, pp. 191–203. Springer International Publishing, Lecture Notes in Computer Science (2019). https://doi.org/10. 1007/978-3-030-05849-4_15
30. Seppänen, H., Luokkala, P., Zhang, Z., Torkki, P., Virrantaus, K.: Critical infrastructure vulnerability—a method for identifying the infrastructure service failure interdependencies. IJCIP **22**, 25–38 (2018)
31. Vasilevskaya, M., Nadjm-Tehrani, S.: Quantifying risks to data assets using formal metrics in embedded system design. In: Koornneef, F., van Gulijk, C. (eds.) SAFECOMP 2015. LNCS, vol. 9337, pp. 347–361. Springer, Cham (2015). https://doi. org/10.1007/978-3-319-24255-2_25
32. Wang, Z., Scaglione, A., Thomas, R.J.: A Markov-transition model for cascading failures in power grids. In: 2012 45th Hawaii International Conference on System Sciences, IEEE (2012)
33. Wu, S.J., Chu, M.T.: Markov chains with memory, tensor formulation, and the dynamics of power iteration. Appl. Math. Comput. **303**(C), 226–239 (2017)

Aggregating Centrality Rankings: A Novel Approach to Detect Critical Infrastructure Vulnerabilities

Gabriele Oliva[1]($^{(\boxtimes)}$) (ID), Annunziata Esposito Amideo[4] (ID), Stefano Starita[3] (ID), Roberto Setola[1] (ID), and Maria Paola Scaparra[2] (ID)

[1] University Campus Biomedico of Rome, Rome, Italy
g.oliva@unicampus.it
[2] Centre for Logistics and Heuristic Optimisation (CLHO), Kent Business School, University of Kent, Canterbury, England
[3] Sasin School of Management, Chulalongkorn University, Bangkok, Thailand
[4] University College Dublin, Dublin, Ireland

Abstract. Assessing critical infrastructure vulnerabilities is paramount to arrange efficient plans for their protection. Critical infrastructures are network-based systems hence, they are composed of nodes and edges. The literature shows that node criticality, which is the focus of this paper, can be addressed from different metric-based perspectives (e.g., degree, maximal flow, shortest path). However, each metric provides a specific insight while neglecting others. This paper attempts to overcome this pitfall through a methodology based on ranking aggregation. Specifically, we consider several numerical topological descriptors of the nodes' importance (e.g., degree, betweenness, closeness, etc.) and we convert such descriptors into ratio matrices; then, we extend the Analytic Hierarchy Process problem to the case of multiple ratio matrices and we resort to a Logarithmic Least Squares formulation to identify an aggregated metric that represents a good tradeoff among the different topological descriptors. The procedure is validated considering the Central London Tube network as a case study.

Keywords: Critical infrastructures · Criticality analysis · Ranking aggregation · Analytic Hierarchy Process · Least squares optimization

1 Introduction

Critical infrastructures are prone to disasters, both man-made and natural (e.g., see [1–3] in the case of railway infrastructures). Given the potential consequences of such disasters, it is mandatory to quantify and identify subsystems that are particularly critical, in that their disruption may cause severe consequences on the remaining subsystems. In this view, identifying such vulnerabilities is essential for deciding how to invest resources in order for instance to protect vulnerable subsystems. This is particularly relevant for critical infrastructure *networks* (e.g.,

© Springer Nature Switzerland AG 2020
S. Nadjm-Tehrani (Ed.): CRITIS 2019, LNCS 11777, pp. 57–68, 2020.
https://doi.org/10.1007/978-3-030-37670-3_5

power networks, railway networks, etc.), where the importance/criticality of a subsystem may not depend just on the physical characteristics of such subsystems, but also on the complex web of connections and relations that intertwine such composing elements [4,5]. Assessing critical infrastructure vulnerabilities is paramount to arrange efficient plans for their protection. Critical infrastructures are network-based systems hence, they are composed of nodes and edges. The literature shows that node criticality, which is the focus of this paper, can be addressed from different metric-based perspectives (e.g., degree, maximal flow, shortest path) [6–10]. However, each metric provides a specific insight while neglecting others. This paper attempts to overcome this pitfall through a methodology based on ranking aggregation. Specifically, in this paper we develop a methodology to aggregate topological descriptors based on the Analytic Hierarchy Process (AHP) [11]: first, we convert the numerical topological descriptors into ratio matrices and then we extend the Logarithmic Least Squares (LLS) AHP methodology [12–16] in order to find a least-squares optimal ranking that is a compromise among the considered ones. It should be noted that the problem of aggregating rankings has raised some interest in previous research: in [17] Kendall and Hausdorff distances are used to compare rankings and a median-based approach is used to identify an overall ranking; in [18] interval ordinal rankings are considered; in [19] (and references therein) the *bucket order problem* is considered, i.e., finding an agreement based on several ranking matrices with ordinal information. Notice that, in [6], the authors quantify the correlation of centrality measures with risk levels in *Dependency Risk Graphs* and provide an heuristic algorithm to recursively select a subset of nodes based on the centrality measure with the highest correlation. In this paper we approach such a problem from a different perspective starting from the topological structure of the infrastructure and looking for those nodes that "optimize" a set of metrics which are not limited to the centrality ones. In this way, the aggregated ranking hereby proposed has a number of benefits: (i) being the result of a least-squares minimization problem, it represents the optimal tradeoff among the considered metrics; (ii) it provides a numerical characterization of the criticality of each node; (iii) it is not computationally expensive, as it consists in solving a system of n linear equations with n unknowns, where n is the number of nodes in the network. The remainder of this paper is organized as follows: after some notation, which concludes this section, we present our aggregation methodology in Sect. 2; then, in Sect. 3 we validate the methodology with respect to a case study, namely, the Central London Tube network; finally, we provide some conclusive remarks and future work directions in Sect. 4.

1.1   Notation

We denote vectors via boldface letters, while matrices are shown with uppercase letters. We use A_{ij} to address the (i,j)-th entry of a matrix A and x_i for the i-th entry of a vector $\mathbf{x}$. Moreover, we write $\mathbf{1}_n$ and $\mathbf{0}_n$ to denote a vector with n components, all equal to one and zero, respectively; similarly, we use $1_{n \times m}$ and $0_{n \times m}$ to denote $n \times m$ matrices all equal to one and zero, respectively. We denote by I_n the $n \times n$ identity matrix. We express by $exp(\cdot)$ and $ln(\cdot)$ the component-wise exponentiation or logarithm of a vector or matrix.

2 Aggregating Heterogeneous Rankings

In this section, we describe the methodology adopted to calculate an aggregated ranking that is representative of several rankings over the same set of alternatives.

2.1 The Approach in a Nutshell

Generally, different ranking criteria capture peculiar elements in terms of node criticality. Hence, any one of them provides a useful point of view to better understand the role and the relevance of each node. Consequently, selecting one ranking criterion while discarding another, may lead to misleading prioritizations in the protection strategies. To overcome such a limit we propose to aggregate the different ranking criteria into a single "super-ranking", i.e., an aggregated ranking that potentially collects all the different aspects of traditional metrics. In this view, our main idea is to convert the numerical rankings into square matrices containing the ratios of the importance of pairs of alternatives, and then combine them in a least square sense via the Logarithmic Least Squares Analytic Hierarchy Process (LLS-AHP) methodology [12–16], in order to obtain an aggregated ranking that is a good trade-off among the available ones. This approach has the advantage to allow a fair comparison among the criteria, in that the rankings are compared in terms of ratios of utilities and not in terms of actual utilities, which may have very different scales. Moreover, the least squares approach provides clear information on the degree of conflict among the rankings, in that the smaller the value of the objective function of the least squares problem is, the more data are in accordance, and vice versa.

2.2 Formal Definition of the Method

Let us consider a situation where we are given m cardinal (i.e., numerical) rankings $r^{(1)}, \ldots, r^{(m)}$ over the set of n nodes in a given graph. In particular, each ranking $r^{(i)}$ is an $n \times 1$ vector having positive entries, and $r_j^{(i)}$ represents the numerical value or utility associated to the j-th node according to the i-th ranking. In order to obtain an aggregated ranking that is representative for the given m rankings, our approach is composed of two logical steps: (1) converting the rankings into ratio matrices and (2) calculating the overall ranking. During the first step, we convert each ranking $r^{(i)}$ into an $n \times n$ matrix $W^{(i)}$ such that the (u, v)-th entry $W_{uv}^{(i)}$ is in the form $W_{uv}^{(i)} = r_u^{(i)}/r_v^{(i)}$. In other words, $W_{uv}^{(i)}$ models the relative utility or importance of the u-th alternative over the j-th one according to the i-th ranking. As a second step, we aim at finding the ranking vector w^* that solves the following problem.

Problem 1. Find $\boldsymbol{w}^* \in \mathbb{R}^n$ that solves

$$\underset{\boldsymbol{w} \in \mathbb{R}^n}{\arg\min} f(\boldsymbol{w}) = \sum_{i=1}^{m} \sum_{u=1}^{n} \sum_{v=1}^{n} \left(\ln(W_{uv}^{(i)}) - log(w_u) + log(w_v) \right)^2$$

subject to

$$\left\{ w_u > 0, \quad \forall u \in \{1, \ldots, n\}. \right.$$

(1)

The above problem aims at finding the vector $\boldsymbol{w}^*$ such that the logarithm of the ratio of its components is the least squares compromise among the logarithms of the corresponding ratios $W_{uv}^{(i)}$. In other words, Problem 1 aims at finding the weight w_u, to be assigned to each node, such that the ratios w_u/w_v minimize the deviation from respect to the ratios $W_{uv}^{(i)}$ for the m considered criteria. In order to solve this problem, which is in general non-convex and may have non-unique solution, we aim at finding a vector $\boldsymbol{y}^*$ such that $\boldsymbol{w}^* = exp(\boldsymbol{y}^*)$, where $exp(\cdot)$ is the component-wise exponential; in other words, we aim at solving the following unconstrained problem.

Problem 2. Find $\boldsymbol{y}^* \in \mathbb{R}^n$ that solves

$$\underset{\boldsymbol{y} \in \mathbb{R}^n}{\arg\min} g(\boldsymbol{y}) = \sum_{i=1}^{m} \sum_{u=1}^{n} \sum_{v=1}^{n} \left(\ln(W_{uv}^{(i)}) - y_u + y_v \right)^2.$$

(2)

The above problem is easily solved in a closed form. Specifically, being an unconstrained convex problem, the minimum is attained at $\boldsymbol{y}^*$ such that, for all $u \in \{1, \ldots, n\}$, it holds $\frac{\partial g(\boldsymbol{y})}{\partial y_u}|_{\boldsymbol{y}=\boldsymbol{y}^*} = 0$. By some algebra, it can be shown that the optimal $\boldsymbol{y}^*$ satisfies

$$m(n\,I_n - \mathbf{1}_n\mathbf{1}_n^T)\boldsymbol{y}^* = \sum_{i=1}^{m} log(W^{(i)})\mathbf{1}_n,$$

where $log(W^{(i)})$ is the $n \times n$ matrix collecting the logarithm of the corresponding entries of $W^{(i)}$ (note that we assumed the rankings have positive entries hence the logarithm is always finite). Note further that matrix $n\,I_n - \mathbf{1}_n\mathbf{1}_n^T$ is the Laplacian matrix of a complete graph and is singular [20]; hence, in order to find $\boldsymbol{y}^*$, one may need to resort to a pseudoinverse, i.e., by setting

$$\boldsymbol{y}^* = \frac{1}{m} \left(n\,I_n - \mathbf{1}_n\mathbf{1}_n^T \right)^{\dagger} \sum_{i=1}^{m} log(W^{(i)})\mathbf{1}_n,$$

where $\left(n\,I_n - \mathbf{1}_n\mathbf{1}_n^T \right)^{\dagger}$ denotes the left pseudoinverse of $n\,I_n - \mathbf{1}_n\mathbf{1}_n^T$. An alternative approach is to solve in an approximated way via the differential equation

$$\dot{\boldsymbol{y}}(t) = m(\mathbf{1}_n\mathbf{1}_n^T - n\,I_n)\boldsymbol{y}(t) + \sum_{i=1}^{m} log(W^{(i)})\mathbf{1}_n$$

which is known to asymptotically converges to a vector that satisfies the above singular system of equations [21].

3   Case Study

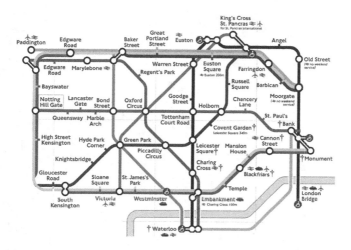

Fig. 1. Central London tube map.

In this section, we consider as an example the Central London Tube network (Fig. 1). Specifically, we represent each station by a node (we consider 50 stations) and we model by directed edges (178 in total) the connections among neighboring stations; in particular, we associate to each edge a weight that corresponds to the average travel time (in seconds) between its endpoints. In other words, we consider a graph that is bidirectional (i.e., there is an edge from i to j whenever there is an edge from j to i) and asymmetric (i.e., the weight associated to the edge from i to j is different from the weight of the edge from j to i.) Fig. 2 reports the resulting asymmetric graph, where edges' color corresponds to the average travel time, according to the provided heatmap; notice that the association between the numerical identifier for each station and the corresponding name can be found in Table 1. With respect to the aforementioned graph, we consider some of the most popular centrality measures in the literature. Specifically, we consider (see [22] and references therein for details):

- **In-degree:** sum of the weights of the edges incoming at each node;
- **Out-degree:** sum of the weights of the edges outgoing at each node;
- **Betweenness:** measures how often a node belongs to the shortest paths between any pair of nodes. If the graph is weighted then path lengths depend on the weights. Specifically the betweenness is defined as $b_u = \sum_{s,t \neq u} N_{st}^{(u)}/N_{st}$, where $N_{st}^{(u)}$ is the amount of minimum paths between nodes s and t passing via node u and N_{st} is the total number of minimum paths between nodes s and t.

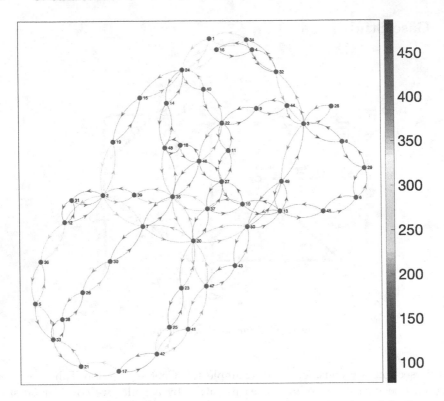

Fig. 2. Central London tube map as a bidirectional asymmetric weighted graph, where weights corresponds to the average travel time (in seconds) between neighboring stations.

- **Pagerank:** it is a measure of importance of the nodes that results from a random walk on the network. Specifically, the random walk is performed with probabilities that depend on the edges' weights. If at some point a node has no outgoing edges, a new random node is chosen. The pagerank measure is the average time spent at each node during the walk.
- **Hubs & Authorities:** such metrics are defined together in a recursive way. The 'hubs-score' of a node is the sum of the 'authorities-score' of its neighbors, and vice-versa. Such values can be regarded as the left (hubs) and right (authorities) singular vectors that correspond to the largest singular value of the adjacency matrix of the graph.
- **Closeness:** this metric is based on the inverse sum of the distances from a node to all other nodes in the graph. Specifically, the closeness is defined as $c_u = A_u/(C_u(n-1))$, where A_u is the number of reachable nodes from node u (not counting u), n is the number of nodes in the graph, and C_u is the sum of the distances from node u to all reachable nodes (if the node is isolated then $c_u = 0$).

- **Eigenvector Centrality:** this metric uses the eigenvector corresponding to the largest eigenvalue of the graph adjacency matrix. The scores are normalized such that the sum of all values is equal to 1.

Overall, we obtain $m = 8$ (numerical) ranking vectors $\boldsymbol{r}^{(i)}$. In Table 1, we report the numerical data for each topological descriptor and for the proposed aggregated metric, while in Table 2 we report the ranking of the stations based, again, on the topological descriptors and on the proposed aggregated metric. In order to provide an immediate understanding of the above data, we show in Fig. 3 the criticality of each node in the network based on the different metrics via a red-blue heat-map, i.e., the more the color of the nodes is red the more the value of the corresponding metric is closer to the maximum value. According to the figure, the different topological indicators identify very different nodes as the most important, and that the proposed aggregated metric represents, indeed, a compromise among the original metrics.

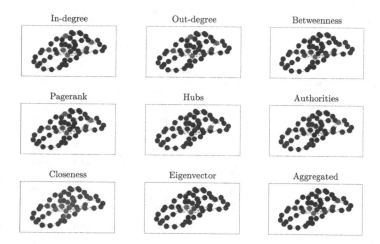

Fig. 3. Visual representation of the nodes' criticality according to the different topological descriptors and to the proposed aggregated measure. (Color figure online)

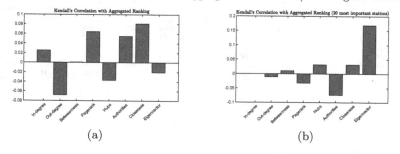

Fig. 4. Kendall's correlation between the ranking obtained based on the proposed aggregated metric and the rankings obtained according to the considered topological descriptors, considering all stations (Fig. 4a) and considering only the 20 most important stations according to the aggregated metric (Fig. 4b).

Table 1. Nodes featured in the case study with the numerical values of the considered topological descriptors and of the proposed aggregated centrality.

Id	Name	In-degree	Out-degree	Betweeness	Pagerank	Hubs	Authorities	Closeness	Eigenvector	Aggregated
1	Angel	461	502	73.33	0.021	0.018	0.004	0.004	0.003	0.013
2	Baker Street	880	872	455.6	0.037	0.023	0.026	0.005	0.037	0.042
3	BankMonument	1089	1003	468.3	0.046	0.035	0.225	0.005	0.010	0.052
4	Barbican	260	252	54	0.013	0.003	0.020	0.004	0.002	0.009
5	Bayswater	342	310	66.16	0.018	0.001	0.001	0.003	0.001	0.006
6	Blackfriars	262	289	39.5	0.016	0.003	0.004	0.004	0.003	0.008
7	Bond Street	595	618	566.21	0.025	0.033	0.040	0.006	0.064	0.044
8	Cannon Street	186	190	79.16	0.012	0.033	0.006	0.004	0.003	0.011
9	Chancery Lane	239	237	87.86	0.013	0.003	0.016	0.005	0.007	0.012
10	Charing Cross	342	357	88.73	0.016	0.017	0.014	0.005	0.042	0.021
11	Covent Garden	230	217	22.73	0.012	0.003	0.003	0.005	0.019	0.009
12	Edgware Road	529	467	196.83	0.025	0.008	0.011	0.005	0.015	0.020
13	Embankment	500	501	236.90	0.022	0.030	0.063	0.005	0.032	0.035
14	Euston	264	267	120.56	0.013	0.006	0.005	0.005	0.011	0.013
15	Euston Square	290	305	140.90	0.014	0.007	0.004	0.005	0.005	0.018
16	Farringdon	418	434	73.33	0.019	0.013	0.003	0.004	0.003	0.012
17	Gloucester Road	317	351	90.66	0.016	0.001	0.001	0.003	0.002	0.007
18	Goodge Street	235	239	7.13	0.012	0.004	0.006	0.005	0.023	0.009
19	Great Portland Street	328	348	162.00	0.015	0.009	0.010	0.005	0.011	0.017
20	Green Park	1024	1037	819.89	0.039	0.071	0.052	0.007	0.090	0.069
21	High Street Kensington	381	348	51.33	0.019	0.000	0.001	0.003	0.001	0.004
22	Holborn	525	533	244.52	0.025	0.006	0.006	0.005	0.023	0.021
23	Hyde Park Corner	283	285	158.83	0.013	0.014	0.023	0.005	0.026	0.021
24	St Pancras	1027	980	322.40	0.042	0.005	0.020	0.005	0.008	0.027
25	Knightsbridge	360	333	89.50	0.016	0.006	0.005	0.004	0.009	0.013
26	Lancaster Gate	297	357	141.16	0.017	0.002	0.002	0.004	0.005	0.010
27	Leicester Square	409	407	101.64	0.019	0.010	0.013	0.005	0.050	0.021
28	London Bridge	155	153	0.00	0.009	0.051	0.010	0.004	0.003	0.000
29	Mansion House	245	220	26.66	0.015	0.002	0.006	0.004	0.002	0.007
30	Marble Arch	294	262	213.16	0.014	0.006	0.007	0.005	0.019	0.016
31	Marylebone	220	225	0.00	0.012	0.006	0.006	0.004	0.014	0.000
32	Moorgate	446	473	178.33	0.022	0.073	0.013	0.004	0.004	0.022
33	Notting Hill Gate	433	452	87.00	0.024	0.001	0.000	0.003	0.001	0.006
34	Old Street	432	380	54.00	0.019	0.004	0.028	0.004	0.002	0.012
35	Oxford Circus	968	899	529.20	0.037	0.039	0.056	0.006	0.093	0.058
36	Paddington	371	398	127.50	0.021	0.004	0.003	0.004	0.004	0.011
37	Piccadilly Circus	572	572	128.55	0.024	0.031	0.034	0.006	0.074	0.035
38	Queensway	282	253	76.16	0.015	0.000	0.001	0.004	0.002	0.005
39	Regents Park	340	350	58.72	0.015	0.022	0.019	0.005	0.035	0.021
40	Russell Square	322	327	80.00	0.015	0.007	0.003	0.005	0.008	0.012
41	Sloane Square	373	380	124.50	0.016	0.011	0.008	0.004	0.010	0.016
42	South Kensington	551	583	158.66	0.024	0.004	0.006	0.004	0.005	0.015
43	St James Park	294	283	51.66	0.013	0.025	0.015	0.005	0.021	0.018
44	St Pauls	315	314	75.00	0.017	0.057	0.011	0.004	0.005	0.017
45	Temple	274	283	104.83	0.015	0.014	0.008	0.004	0.009	0.015
46	Tottenham Court Road	471	491	245.21	0.022	0.013	0.011	0.006	0.052	0.026
47	Victoria	501	512	219.16	0.022	0.020	0.033	0.005	0.032	0.030
48	Warren Street	392	411	186.70	0.018	0.016	0.013	0.005	0.034	0.024
49	Waterloo	695	770	359.63	0.029	0.192	0.043	0.005	0.023	0.049
50	Westminster	620	609	508.06	0.025	0.039	0.086	0.006	0.044	0.047

Table 2. Rankings of the stations according to the considered topological descriptors, and according to the proposed aggregated centrality.

In-degree	Out-degree	Betweenness	Pagerank	Hubs	Authorities	Closeness	Eigenvector	Aggregated
BankMonument	Green Park	Green Park	BankMonument	Waterloo	BankMonument	Green Park	Oxford Circus	Green Park
St Pancras	BankMonument	Bond Street	St Pancras	Moorgate	Westminster	Oxford Circus	Green Park	Oxford Circus
Green Park	St Pancras	Oxford Circus	Green Park	Green Park	Embankment	Bond Street	Piccadilly Circus	BankMonument
Oxford Circus	Oxford Circus	Westminster	Oxford Circus	St Pauls	Oxford Circus	Westminster	Bond Street	Waterloo
Baker Street	Baker Street	BankMonument	Baker Street	London Bridge	Green Park	Piccadilly Circus	Tottenham Court Road	Westminster
Waterloo	Waterloo	Baker Street	Waterloo	Westminster	Waterloo	Tottenham Court Road	Leicester Square	Bond Street
Westminster	Bond Street	Waterloo	Holborn	Oxford Circus	Bond Street	Baker Street	Westminster	Baker Street
Bond Street	Westminster	St Pancras	Edgware Road	BankMonument	Piccadilly Circus	Waterloo	Baker Street	Piccadilly Circus
Piccadilly Circus	Piccadilly Circus	Tottenham Court Road	Bond Street	Cannon Street	Old Street	Victoria	Charing Cross	Embankment
South Kensington	Tottenham Court Road	Holborn	Westminster	Bond Street	Baker Street	Warren Street	Regents Park	Victoria
Edgware Road	Holborn	Embankment	South Kensington	Piccadilly Circus	Victoria	Embankment	Warren Street	St Pancras
Holborn	Victoria	Victoria	Notting Hill Gate	Embankment	Hyde Park Corner	Regents Park	Victoria	Tottenham Court Road
Victoria	Angel	Marble Arch	Piccadilly Circus	St James Park	Barbican	Hyde Park Corner	Embankment	Warren Street
Embankment	Embankment	Edgware Road	Tottenham Court Road	Baker Street	St Pancras	Charing Cross	Hyde Park Corner	Moorgate
Tottenham Court Road	Moorgate	Warren Street	Moorgate	Regents Park	Regents Park	Holborn	Holborn	Leicester Square
Angel	Edgware Road	Great Portland Street	Embankment	Victoria	Chancery Lane	Leicester Square	Waterloo	Charing Cross
Moorgate	Notting Hill Gate	Hyde Park Corner	Angel	Angel	St James Park	BankMonument	Goodge Street	Regents Park
Notting Hill Gate	Farringdon	South Kensington	Victoria	Charing Cross	Charing Cross	Marble Arch	St James Park	Holborn
Old Street	Warren Street	Lancaster Gate	Paddington	Warren Street	Moorgate	St James Park	Covent Garden	Hyde Park Corner
Farringdon	Leicester Square	Euston Square	Farringdon	Hyde Park Corner	Warren Street	St Pancras	Marble Arch	Edgware Road
Leicester Square	Paddington	Paddington	High Street Kensington	Temple	Leicester Square	Euston	Edgware Road	St James Park
Warren Street	Old Street	Sloane Square	Temple	Tottenham Court Road	St Pauls	Great Portland Street	Marylebone	Great Portland Street
High Street Kensington	Sloane Square	Euston	Old Street	Farringdon	Tottenham Court Road	Goodge Street	Great Portland Street	Sloane Square
Sloane Square	Charing Cross	Temple	Leicester Square	Sloane Square	Edgware Road	Russell Square	Euston	Marble Arch
Paddington	Lancaster Gate	Leicester Square	Bayswater	Leicester Square	Great Portland Street	Covent Garden	Sloane Square	South Kensington
Knightsbridge	Gloucester Road	Gloucester Road	Warren Street	Great Portland Street	London Bridge	Chancery Lane	BankMonument	Temple
Bayswater	Regents Park	Knightsbridge	Lancaster Gate	Edgware Road	Temple	Edgware Road	Temple	Angel
Charing Cross	High Street Kensington	Charing Cross	St Pauls	Euston Square	Sloane Square	Euston Square	Knightsbridge	Euston
Regents Park	Great Portland Street	Chancery Lane	Blackfriars	Russell Square	Marble Arch	Sloane Square	Russell Square	Knightsbridge
Great Portland Street	Russell Square	Notting Hill Gate	Knightsbridge	Euston	Holborn	Knightsbridge	St Pancras	Farringdon
Russell Square	St Pauls	Russell Square	Gloucester Road	Marble Arch	South Kensington	Marylebone	Lancaster Gate	Chancery Lane
Gloucester Road	Bayswater	St Pauls	Sloane Square	Knightsbridge	Mansion House	St Pauls	South Kensington	Old Street
Lancaster Gate	Euston Square	Cannon Street	Charing Cross	Holborn	Marylebone	Moorgate	Euston Square	Russell Square
Marble Arch	Blackfriars	Queensway	Mansion House	St Pancras	Goodge Street	Angel	St Pauls	Euston Square
St James Park	South Kensington	Bayswater	Russell Square	South Kensington	Cannon Street	Farringdon	Paddington	Cannon Street
Euston Square	Hyde Park Corner	Angel	Queensway	Goodge Street	Euston	Lancaster Gate	Moorgate	Paddington
Hyde Park Corner	St James Park	Farringdon	Regents Park	Paddington	Knightsbridge	Cannon Street	Cannon Street	Lancaster Gate
Queensway	Temple	Regents Park	Great Portland Street	Old Street	Blackfriars	Old Street	Blackfriars	Blackfriars
Temple	Euston	Old Street	Marble Arch	Chancery Lane	Angel	Barbican	London Bridge	Goodge Street
Euston	Marble Arch	Barbican	Euston Square	Barbican	Euston Square	London Bridge	Angel	Covent Garden
Blackfriars	Queensway	St James Park	Chancery Lane	Blackfriars	Farringdon	South Kensington	Farringdon	Barbican
Barbican	Barbican	High Street Kensington	St James Park	Covent Garden	Russell Square	Paddington	Queensway	Gloucester Road
Mansion House	Goodge Street	Blackfriars	Hyde Park Corner	Lancaster Gate	Covent Garden	Bayswater	Old Street	Mansion House
Chancery Lane	Chancery Lane	Mansion House	Barbican	Mansion House	Lancaster Gate	Blackfriars	Barbican	Bayswater
Goodge Street	Marylebone	Covent Garden	Euston	Gloucester Road	Bayswater	Queensway	Gloucester Road	Notting Hill Gate
Covent Garden	Mansion House	Goodge Street	Cannon Street	Bayswater	Gloucester Road	Mansion House	Mansion House	High Street Kensington
Marylebone	Covent Garden	Marylebone	Covent Garden	Queensway	High Street Kensington	Gloucester Road	Bayswater	Marylebone
Cannon Street	Cannon Street	Piccadilly Circus	Goodge Street	Notting Hill Gate	Queensway	Notting Hill Gate	Notting Hill Gate	Queensway
London Bridge	London Bridge	London Bridge	London Bridge	High Street Kensington	Notting Hill Gate	High Street Kensington	High Street Kensington	London Bridge

In order to validate the above intuition, we calculate the Kendall's correlation coefficient[1] between the ranking obtained based on the proposed aggregated metric and the rankings obtained according to the considered topological descriptors, as shown in Fig. 4; specifically, we show in Fig. 4a the correlation over the entire set of nodes, while Figs. 4b displays the correlations obtained considering the 20 most important nodes according to the aggregated metric. As shown by the figures, it can be noted that the correlations obtained over the whole set of nodes are all less than 0.1 in magnitude, while limiting to a subset of the 20 most important nodes the correlations with most metrics further reduce, except for the eigenvector centrality, which reaches a correlation of 0.2. Overall, the above results suggest that the proposed index, by aggregating different metrics, assigns a criticality to the nodes that can not be exhaustively explained by any of the original metrics. In fact, by looking at Fig. 3, it can be noted that the most influential nodes according to the proposed aggregated metric are indeed represented by the union of the most influent nodes according to all the different topological descriptors (although we observe that the high importance assigned to some peripheral nodes based on the closeness, in-degree and out-degree criteria is reduced in the aggregated metric.

4   Conclusions and Future Work

In this paper we provide a novel methodology to aggregate heterogeneous criticality indices for critical infrastructure networks in order to obtain an overall aggregated ranking that represents a good trade-off among the different metrics. Such an index can be the basis for implementing protection strategies that are not driven by a single factor but consider at the same time multiple facets of node criticality. The main idea is to convert the metrics in ratio matrices and then compute an aggregated metric by means of a generalization of the Logarithmic Least Squares Analytic Hierarchy Process technique to the case of multiple ratio matrices. The experimental results show that the proposed approach assigns

---

[1] Given two pairs of values (a_i, b_i) and (a_j, b_j), we say they are *concordant* if both $a_i > a_j$ and $b_i > b_j$ or if both $a_i < a_j$ and $b_i < b_j$; similarly the pairs are *discordant* if $a_i > a_j$ and $b_i < b_j$ or if $a_i < a_j$ and $b_i > b_j$. If $a_i = a_j$ or $b_i = b_j$ the pairs are neither concordant nor discordant. Given two vectors $\mathbf{a} \in \mathbb{R}^n$ and $\mathbf{b} \in \mathbb{R}^n$, the *Kendall's correlation index* [23] τ is defined as

$$\tau = \frac{\mathcal{C} - \mathcal{P}}{n(n-1)/2},$$

where $\mathcal{C}$ and $\mathcal{P}$ are the set of concordant and discordant pairs (a_i, b_i) and (a_j, b_j), respectively. When $\mathbf{b}$ is a permutation of the components of $\mathbf{a}$, the Kendall's tau can be interpreted as a measure of the degree of shuffling of $\mathbf{b}$ with respect to $\mathbf{a}$, between minus one and one. In this sense $\tau = 1$ implies $\mathbf{a} = \mathbf{b}$, while $\tau = -1$ represents the fact $\mathbf{b}$ is in reverse order with respect to $\mathbf{a}$. The closer is τ to (minus) one, therefore, the more the two rankings are (anti-) correlated, while the closer is τ to zero the more the two rankings are independent.

large relevance to the most influential nodes according to the single indices; yet, the resulting criticality cannot be exhaustively explained by any of the original metrics thus requiring further investigation. Future work will follow three main directions: (i) we will consider different graphs over the same set of nodes (e.g., structural graph, flow graph,. etc.) in order to take into account, at the same time, both structural and dynamical characteristics of the network; (ii) we will extend the framework by implementing a multi-criteria decision procedure to weight differently the different topological descriptors, in order to obtain a synthetic metric that reflects the preferences of stakeholders or decision-makers; (iii) we will inspect the possibility to prioritize ordinal information over cardinal information, extending the framework in [24] to the case of multiple ratio matrices.

Acknowledgements. This work was supported by INAIL via the European Saf€ra project "Integrated Management of Safety and Security Synergies in Seveso Plants" (4STER).

References

1. Anderson, C.W., Santos, J.R., Haimes, Y.Y.: A risk-based input-output methodology for measuring the effects of the August 2003 northeast blackout. Econ. Syst. Res. **19**(2), 183–204 (2007)
2. Popova, O.P., et al.: Chelyabinsk airburst, damage assessment, meteorite recovery, and characterization. Science **342**(6162), 1069–1073 (2013)
3. Setola, R., Sforza, A., Vittorini, V., Pragliola, C. (eds.): Railway Infrastructure Security. TSRRQ, vol. 27. Springer, Cham (2015). https://doi.org/10.1007/978-3-319-04426-2
4. Setola, R.: How to measure the degree of interdependencies among critical infrastructures. Int. J. Syst. Syst. Eng. **2**(1), 38–59 (2010)
5. Faramondi, L., et al.: Network structural vulnerability: a multiobjective attacker perspective. IEEE Trans. Syst. Man Cybern. Syst. (99), 1–14 (2018)
6. Stergiopoulos, G., Kotzanikolaou, P., Theocharidou, M., Gritzalis, D.: Risk mitigation strategies for critical infrastructures based on graph centrality analysis. Int. J. Crit. Infrastruct. Prot. **10**, 34–44 (2015)
7. Chen, X.: Critical nodes identification in complex systems. Complex Intell. Syst. **1**(1–4), 37–56 (2015)
8. Lü, L., Chen, D., Ren, X.-L., Zhang, Q.-M., Zhang, Y.-C., Zhou, T.: Vital nodes identification in complex networks. Phys. Rep. **650**, 1–63 (2016)
9. Rueda, D.F., Calle, F., Marzo, J.L.: Robustness comparison of 15 real telecommunication networks: structural and centrality measurements. J. Netw. Syst. Manag. **25**(2), 269–289 (2017)
10. Starita, S., Esposito Amideo, A., Scaparra, M.P.: Assessing urban rail transit systems vulnerability: metrics vs. interdiction models. In: D'Agostino, G., Scala, A. (eds.) CRITIS 2017. LNCS, vol. 10707, pp. 144–155. Springer, Cham (2018). https://doi.org/10.1007/978-3-319-99843-5_13
11. Saaty, T.L.: A scaling method for priorities in hierarchical structures. J. Math. Psychol. **15**(3), 234–281 (1977)

12. Crawford, G.B.: The geometric mean procedure for estimating the scale of a judgement matrix. Math. Model. **9**(3–5), 327–334 (1987)
13. Barzilai, J., Cook, W.D., Golany, B.: Consistent weights for judgements matrices of the relative importance of alternatives. Oper. Res. Lett. **6**(3), 131–134 (1987)
14. Bozóki, S., Fülöp, J., Rónyai, L.: On optimal completion of incomplete pairwise comparison matrices. Math. Comput. Model. **52**(1–2), 318–333 (2010)
15. Oliva, G., Setola, R., Scala, A.: Sparse and distributed analytic hierarchy process. Automatica **85**, 211–220 (2017)
16. Bozóki, S., Tsyganok, V.: The (logarithmic) least squares optimality of the arithmetic (geometric) mean of weight vectors calculated from all spanning trees for incomplete additive (multiplicative) pairwise comparison matrices. Int. J. Gen. Syst. (2019, to appear)
17. Fagin, R., Kumar, R., Mahdian, M., Sivakumar, D., Vee, E.: Comparing and aggregating rankings with ties. In: Proceedings of the Twenty-Third ACM SIGMOD-SIGACT-SIGART Symposium on Principles of Database Systems, pp. 47–58. ACM (2004)
18. Dopazo, E., Martínez-Céspedes, M.L.: Rank aggregation methods dealing with ordinal uncertain preferences. Expert Syst. Appl. **78**, 103–109 (2017)
19. Aledo, J.A., Gámez, J.A., Rosete, A.: Utopia in the solution of the bucket order problem. Decis. Support Syst. **97**, 69–80 (2017)
20. Godsil, C., Royle, G.: Algebraic Graph Theory. Graduate Text in Mathematics. Springer, New York (2001)
21. Olfati-Saber, R., Alex Fax, J., Murray, R.M.: Consensus and cooperation in networked multi-agent systems. Proc. IEEE **95**(1), 215–233 (2007)
22. Borodin, A., Roberts, G.O., Rosenthal, J.S., Tsaparas, P.: Link analysis ranking: algorithms, theory, and experiments. ACM Trans. Internet Technol. (TOIT) **5**(1), 231–297 (2005)
23. Kendall, M.G.: A new measure of rank correlation. Biometrika **30**(1/2), 81–93 (1938)
24. Oliva, G., Bozóki, S.: Incomplete analytic hierarchy process with minimum ordinal violations. arXiv preprint: arXiv:1904.04701 (2019)

Vulnerability Assessment

Cyber-Physical Systems Security Based on a Cross-Linked and Correlated Vulnerability Database

Yuning Jiang$^{(\boxtimes)}$, Yacine Atif , and Jianguo Ding

School of Informatics, University of Skövde, Skövde, Sweden
{yuning.jiang,yacine.atif,jianguo.ding}@his.se

Abstract. Recent advances in data analytics prompt dynamic data-driven vulnerability assessments whereby data contained from vulnerability-alert repositories as well as from Cyber-physical System (CPS) layer networks and standardised enumerations. Yet, current vulnerability assessment processes are mostly conducted manually. However, the huge volume of scanned data requires substantial information processing and analytical reasoning, which could not be satisfied considering the imprecision of manual vulnerability analysis. In this paper, we propose to employ a cross-linked and correlated database to collect, extract, filter and visualise vulnerability data across multiple existing repositories, whereby CPS vulnerability information is inferred. Based on our locally-updated database, we provide an in-depth case study on gathered CPS vulnerability data, to explore the trends of CPS vulnerability. In doing so, we aim to support a higher level of automation in vulnerability awareness and back risk-analysis exercises in critical infrastructures (CIs) protection.

Keywords: Cyber-physical system security · Vulnerability analysis · Correlated database management · SCADA

1 Introduction

Assessing vulnerabilities supports analytics-based decision-making processes to protect cyber-physical systems (CPSs) such as those prevalent in Critical Infrastructures (CIs), in order to focus on specific risks with varying degrees of impact-severity. The notion of risk remains elusive, as evidenced by the increasing investigations on CI security operations centres (SOCs) where analysts employ various detection, assessment, and defence mechanisms to monitor security events [1]. Normally, SOCs involve multiple automated security tools such as network vulnerability scanners and CVSS[1] calculator, combined with analysis of data

---

[1] https://www.first.org/cvss/specification-document.

This research has been supported in part by the EU ISF Project A431.678/2016 ELVIRA (Threat modeling and resilience of critical infrastructures), coordinated by Polismyndigheten/Sweden.

© Springer Nature Switzerland AG 2020
S. Nadjm-Tehrani (Ed.): CRITIS 2019, LNCS 11777, pp. 71–82, 2020.
https://doi.org/10.1007/978-3-030-37670-3_6

contained and produced by CPS operations as well as alerts retrieved from vulnerability repositories such as Common Vulnerability Exposure (CVE)[2]. The security operators need further to forecast the match between these vulnerabilities and the state of intricate CIs layer networks, while prioritising patching investments using an accurate and a streamlined vulnerability-scoring mechanism [10]. This process is illustrated in Part (a) of Fig. 1, which shows the central role of security operators in SOCs and their need for support to keep pace with dynamically evolving vulnerability-alert repositories.

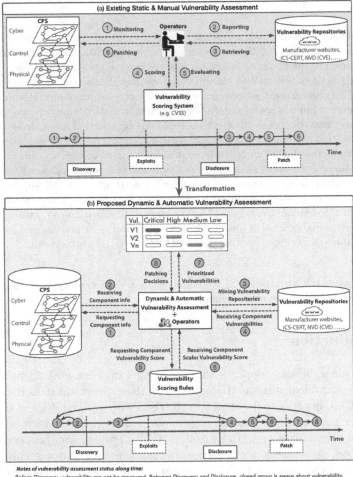

Fig. 1. Vulnerability analysis trends for cyber-physical system.

---

[2] https://cve.mitre.org/.

However, CPS vulnerability analysis faces two challenging issues:

(a) Subjective and Human-Centred Process: Existing vulnerability analysis approaches like CVSS calculator [3] require subjective and manual input, based on qualitative judgments of vulnerability properties such as exploitability, scope and impacts. Relying on individual experts' knowledge could introduce recurrent costs, subjective evaluations and contradicting outcomes. Nevertheless, security operators of CI also need to obey limited budget restrictions, and consider the limited computing resources of CPSs networks.

(b) Static Vulnerability Analysis Lifecycle: Static analysis poses a limitation in security management of safety-critical systems such as CPSs, as malicious attempts may use new exploits that occur between successive analysis milestones [4]. On the contrary, dynamic vulnerability analysis allows mitigations to occur within the time interval that span the discovery and disclosure of vulnerabilities, and giving time for vulnerability patches to be available and deployed before the release time of exploits.

In our research, we propose to support a dynamic vulnerability-analysis approach, as shown in Part (b) of Fig. 1. The proposed streamlined approach employs cross-linked database management techniques to analyse data retrieved from multiple vulnerability-alert repositories with emphasis on CPS network components. This data analysis can be further combined with correlation techniques to produce both component-level and system-level vulnerability instances. Subsequently, retrieved vulnerability instances feed a rule-based scoring system using common industrial scoring standards such as CVSS, to derive a vulnerability-severity score automatically. We suggest to substitute offline, costly, error-prone and subjective vulnerability analysis processes with an automatic, accurate and data-evidenced approach, to improve situation awareness and to support security decision-making mechanisms. Based on this novel method, we did an in-depth case study of CPS vulnerability, to provide insights of the trends in CPS vulnerabilities in the context of CIs protection.

2   Related Works

Security assessment automation in CPS systems is evidenced by the plethora of definitions on Cyber-Threat Intelligence (CTI) in the literature, with an objective to overcome some notorious flaws in manual processes [9]. A recent trend in CPS vulnerability analysis uses computational intelligence approaches, such as graph-based and text-driven mining techniques.

Advances in formal semantics and data visualisation models have been widely used in graph-based applications for CPS security [2,5]. Tree structures, directed graphs and logic diagrams fall into this category. Tree-structured analysis and graph-based methods differ in the semantic of nodes and edges. But many of the previous studies mainly focus on certain vulnerabilities exploited by specific threat types, such as DoS [6]. However, risk analysis of a complex CPS may involve various vulnerabilities across highly-interdependent components of CPS. Current security-related data is mostly text-based, and appear in three types, namely unstructured, semi-structured and structured data. However, graph-based approaches are not suitable to deal with text-based data.

On the other hand, other techniques have been studied and reported to support text-data driven information processing. Tools like cve-search[3] (referring to a Web interface and an API to CVE repository) and Open Vulnerability and Assessment Language (OVAL) are some of the efforts investigated to identify and manage CPS vulnerabilities effectively in a vendor-independent manner, while enabling a certain level of automation. Whereas, it is also desirable to define vulnerability indexes to help with a better categorisation and analysis of vulnerabilities, as well as to automate the analysis process by translating natural language statements found in vulnerability reports into machine-readable formats, as a supplement to automatically generate prevalent topics in vulnerability disclosure [10,12]. A more relevant work employs information-retrieval techniques to facilitate keyword identification, such as malware detection features from researcher papers [7]. However, these models focus on attack-steps and corresponding prerequisites in vulnerabilities instead of the vulnerable nature of the system.

Our method provides near real-time risk-monitoring through an information-fusion approach with multiple input vulnerability-repositories to provide up-to-date information, to extract relevant data for vulnerability analysis. This approach contrasts with traditional rigid management portfolios, which may tolerate security gaps and exploits occurrence beyond disclosure limits.

3   CPS Vulnerability

Typically, a CPS includes a cyber, a control and a physical process layer. The control layer features a network of operational technology (OT) components to coordinate and synchronise operations. The control centre provided by cyber layer incorporates an informational technology (IT) network of workstations and servers, including application and data-store servers. Therefore, each CPS asset confines data from software and physical components, while each component generates data from a list of vulnerability instances.

Considering the power grid as an example, it is a typical CPS empowered by a Supervisory Control and Data Acquisition (SCADA) control and monitoring system to efficiently optimise power generation, transmission and distribution processes [8]. The physical process consists in this case of a power-flow regulated by junction-busbars and power-generation sources. The control layer includes a network of microprocessor-controlled physical objects, such as remote terminal unit devices (RTUs) and programmable logic controllers (PLCs), which interface with physical process sensors. Master Terminal Unit (MTU) is another SCADA control-layer element that concentrates data gathered from RTUs. Thus, the control layer relays measurements from sensors that interact with field devices such as power-transmission lines and transformers, to remote control centres.

---

[3] https://www.circl.lu/services/cve-search/.

Control centre applications process these measurements to support operational power-flow decisions to balance the supplied and demanded power flows.

Systems and softwares that are adopted in the digitalised power industry are interconnected. Meanwhile, more vulnerabilities have emerged due to the interconnections among systems. Considering the nature of CPS, we define a component to be either an application software (e.g. a PLC firmware program), a hardware (e.g. a PLC), a network (e.g. a network based on Modbus protocol), or an operating system (e.g. a Linux-based server). A software is embedded in a hardware, and is physically influenced by the hardware, for instance electricity supply. Different vulnerabilities might contribute to threats that bring different levels of impact, through different levels of losses in confidentiality, integrity and availability (CIA) triad. For example, an outdated software might contain flaws in source code. Such flaws might result in bypass threats materialised by code-injection attack. A hardware is vulnerable by having no physical-access protection, which might be used by an attacker to gain information (e.g. files store in the hardware) through unauthorised USB access, for example. A network protocol without encryption is vulnerable, which might result in threats like information (e.g. data-flows) leakage or man-in-the-middle (MITM). Attackers could trigger a privilege escalation or network reconnaissance attacks by making use of such protocol vulnerability. An operating system (OS) may expose to denial of service (DoS) threats due to resource management errors, which could be exploited by buffer overflow attacks. Most attacks happen in software or network environment. Whereas, a successful attack may also impact the hardware where exploited software is embedded.

4   Cross-linked and Correlated Vulnerability-Database

We propose correlated database management techniques in vulnerability-data processing to discover CPS vulnerabilities and their attributes, to derive a multi-level vulnerability analysis from both component-perspective and asset-perspective, and to visualise the connection between vulnerability, threat and attack. Our research agenda mainly includes three steps, as further analysed below.

4.1   Step1: Vulnerability Database Preparation

We apply information fusion algorithms to extract attributes of vulnerabilities from multiple repositories into one local database, including vulnerability-instance repositories and security-related standard enumerations. According to the Coordinated Vulnerability Disclosure (CVD) guide [11], vulnerability report documents or vulnerability records could be found typically with some formal identifier, e.g. CVE ID. A published vulnerability report has zero or more associated vendor records, preliminary analysis of reported vulnerability severity using CVSS, and some other pertinent metadata. Using CVE ID as index, we build a database of vulnerability reports containing the base reports from CVE, as well as the cross-references from multiple repositories leading to corresponding manufacturer websites and standardised enumerations.

4.2   Step2: Cyber-Physical System Asset Database Preparation

CPS asset information are extracted from multiple repositories using information retrieval algorithms, including manufacturing websites and system configuration-related enumeration like CPE and Common Configuration Enumeration (CCE)[4]. CVE and NVD have been recognised as valuable resources for large-scale security analysis. Some other available security-related data could be gathered from online forums such as ExploitDB[5] and SecurityFocus[6]. To guide cybersecurity analysis process, a number of open standards are advocated to enumerate system configuration, weakness categorisation and attack categorisation. These standards include product dictionary Common Platform Enumeration (CPE)[7]; weakness taxonomy from Common Weakness Enumeration (CWE)[8]; attack patterns from Common Attack Pattern Enumeration and Classification (CAPEC)[9]. Each of these standards have its own syntax and semantics.

4.3   Step3: Correlation Between Asset-Data and Vulnerability-Data

Knowledge-based reasoning approaches are applied to automatically abstract vulnerability attributes for concept-modelling and information-correlation. Features of different vulnerabilities are abstracted and updated with up-to-date vulnerability repositories, and then clustered into vulnerability instances which are stored in a Standardised Vulnerability Database. Meanwhile, component features including component properties, component versions, etc., are also abstracted to be stored in Asset Database. Information from the two databases are queried and correlated, to generate an Asset-based Vulnerability Database.

5   Evaluation and Discussion

In this section, we use our proposed vulnerability-search technique to gain insights about threat landscape in CPS environments via an experimental study conducted using relevant Python APIs.

5.1   Case Study Setup

Following the steps introduced in the previous section, we start by setting-up a vulnerability database that is inherently synchronised with multiple on-line vulnerability-reports repositories. Our database is built on top of cve-search Python API[10], which brings together CVE and enhancing NVD repositories

---

[4] https://cce.mitre.org/.
[5] https://www.exploit-db.com/.
[6] https://www.securityfocus.com/.
[7] https://cpe.mitre.org/.
[8] https://cwe.mitre.org/index.html.
[9] https://capec.mitre.org/.
[10] https://github.com/cve-search/cve-search.

into a local MongoDB system that can handle large unstructured data. When the local MongoDB engine starts running, it is kept synchronised on hourly basis with feeds from repositories data, as shown in Fig. 2.

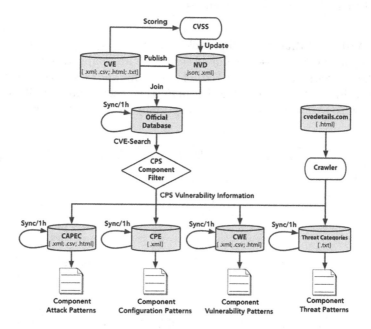

Fig. 2. Security reports from synchronised cross-linked vulnerability-databases

Subsequently, we retrieve CPS-relevant vulnerability instances, that we further cross-reference against a variety of sources including industry-standard CPE used to reveal operating systems, hardware and software information. Other cyber-security sources may also be enclosed in the data fusion process, namely CWE which expand the information-set about the vulnerability regardless the affected product instance, and CAPEC, which provides a dictionary of known attack patterns used by adversaries to exploit the discovered vulnerabilities.

The testing data set we used as a case study are retrieved till the 7th of July, 2019. The CVE database checked on 7th of July 2019 contained 123 687 entries, CPE contained 261 112 entries, CWE entries included 719 elements from CWE, and CAPEC included 463 elements.

We tested our correlated and cross-linked database method with four CPS asset types, namely RTU, MTU, PLC and HMI/SCADA. The four asset types are selected as they are core assets in Critical Infrastructures (CIs) CPS control systems. Next, we report the results obtained from querying our correlated local database to extract CPS assets vulnerability trend, as well as the analysis results about threat types that could exploit these CPS assets.

5.2   Case Study Results

We use our local vulnerability-databases that are kept synchronised on hourly-basis to generate security reports, which reveal CPS vulnerability trends across correlated feeds from third-party sources.

(a) CPS Vulnerabilities: We first look at CPS assets' vulnerability instances. Total vulnerability instances amount of each CPS are mapped to the years from 2000 till 2019, considering that CVE discloses vulnerabilities since 1999 till now, as shown in Fig. 3. Compared to MTU and RTU, more vulnerabilities of PLC and HMI/SCADA have been disclosed, especially in the past 6 years.

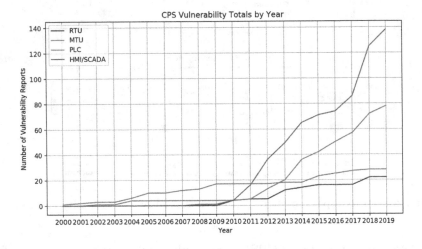

Fig. 3. CPS vulnerability totals trend

Then we look at the severity level of CPS assets' vulnerabilities. Part (a) of Fig. 4 shows vulnerability-instance bar charts and average CVSS-score line, where the reported vulnerability instances related to RTU, MTU, PLC, HMI/SCADA are 22, 28, 78, and 138 instances respectively. Although HMI/SCADA reveal the largest amount of vulnerability reports, their average severity-score is not the highest. This is contrasted against the average CVSS base-scores of reported vulnerability instances in RTU, MTU, PLC, HMI/SCADA, which are 8.15, 6.26, 6.60, and 6.87 respectively. The average vulnerability score for overall CPS is 6.97 (approximately 7.0), which refers to "High" severity[11]. According to the documentation of CVSS v2.0, we mapped each CVSS base-score of vulnerability instances to the qualitative severity rating scale, and concluded that most of these vulnerability instances are evaluated as *Medium* or *High* severity, as illustrated in Part (b) of Fig. 4.

---

[11] https://www.first.org/cvss/v2/guide.

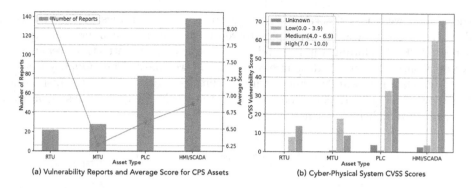

(a) Vulnerability Reports and Average Score for CPS Assets   (b) Cyber-Physical System CVSS Scores

Fig. 4. Vulnerability reports and CVSS score for CPS assets

(b) Threat Types and Vulnerability Categories: We correlated CVE-ID against the threat categorisation provided in www.cvedetails.com to retrieve the threat types that a vulnerability instance may be exposed to. Note that a vulnerability could be exposed to more than one threat types. Three threat types, namely Execute Code, Denial of Service, and Overflow, appear to be the most typical ones that might materialise into attacks targeting CPS assets, as shown in Fig. 5.

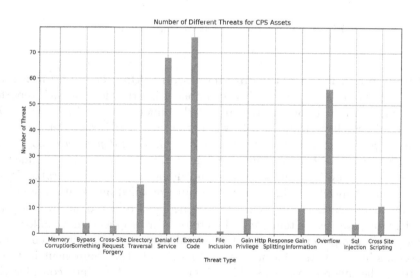

Fig. 5. Threat types targeting CPS assets

Subsequently, we show the results of crosschecking CVE-ID against the weakness categorisation provided in CWE to obtain a list of weakness types. However, there are multiple ways of weakness categorisation in CWE, and different CWE-IDs might refer to the same vulnerability type. Therefore, we gather all the related weakness descriptions, and extract common topics from gathered data. As a result, we get six topics to represent the most common weakness types of CPS, including Input Validation weakness, Authentication weakness, Access Control weakness, Resource Management weakness, Code Quality weakness, and Data Exposure weakness. Vulnerability categories of reported instances are shown in Fig. 6. It could be seen that the weakness type Access Control appears with highest frequency in CPS assets.

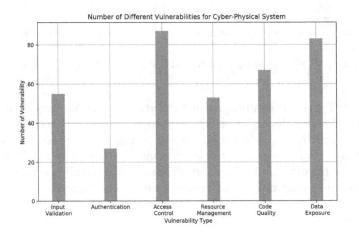

Fig. 6. Vulnerability categories for CPS assets

C) Vulnerable CPS Asset Components and Affected Vendors: From asset configurations, we retrieve their component information for each reported vulnerability. An example is the reported vulnerability *CVE-2013-2810*[12] in RTU-vulnerability, from which we obtain six CPE metadata records, such as *"cpe:2.3:o:emerson:dl-8000-remote-terminal-unit-firmware:2.30"* and *"cpe:2.3:h:emerson:dl-8000-remote-terminal-unit"*. By default, a vulnerable software or operating system makes the embedding asset also vulnerable. Based on CPE naming specification, we further acquire detailed information of vulnerable components, such as component type (where *"h"* refers to hardware device, *"o"* refers to operating system, *"a"* refers to software application), vendor, component name, component version, etc. We calculate the amount of vulnerable components in two ways. One way is to sum-up only the component instances but ignore the different versions. The other way is to take into consideration the different versions and view them as different vulnerabilities. Adopting both ways leads to some interesting results, referring to asset-level vulnerabilities, as shown in Fig. 7. Although application software and operating systems are the main source of vulnerability, there might be larger number of hardware devices embedding those vulnerable components.

---

[12] https://cve.mitre.org/cgi-bin/cvename.cgi?name=CVE-2013-2810.

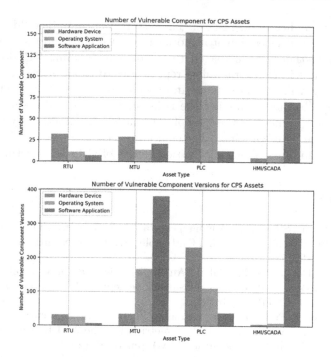

Fig. 7. Number of vulnerability components in CPS Assets

We further retrieve the vendor information for each reported vulnerability, and ranked the vendors based on the total amounts of affected products. The most distinct vendors are listed here. RTU vendors *Schneider Electric SE* and *Yokogawa Electric Corporation* have 14 and 8 affected products separately. MTU vendors *Cisco Systems Inc.* and *F5 Networks Inc.* have 29 and 17 affected products separately. PLC vendors *Schneider Electric SE* and *Siemens AG* have 138 and 32 affected products separately. HMI/SCADA vendors *Schneider Electric SE* and *General Electric Company* have 23 and 14 affected products separately.

6   Conclusion

In this paper, we motivated the need for, and the promises driven by correlated database management approaches to deal with semi-structured vulnerability data and also to address trends in vulnerability-analysis. We introduced a method to cross-check and correlate multiple vulnerability repositories through a step-by-step analysis. We built our local vulnerability database that is inherently synchronised with heterogenous security-related repositories and we employed information fusion techniques to extract relevant information. In doing so, we applied computational intelligence techniques to support classification of vulnerability categories and related threat types. We presented some results of the proposed approach as a case study that investigates vulnerability trends at both

CPS asset-level and component-level. The results we achieved could be obtained through manual processes, but it is more time-consuming and less accurate. By applying our methods, we managed to (a) offer a dynamic CPS-focused vulnerability analysis from several online repositories to assist operators evaluating up-to-date CPS vulnerability trends in order to reduce existing security management gaps, (b) narrow further the risk-window induced by discovered vulnerabilities, and (c) increase the level of automation in vulnerability analysis. In future works, we plan combine other computational intelligence techniques, to improve vulnerability evaluation at various levels of CPS architecture.

References

1. Sundaramurthy, S.C., et al.: A human capital model for mitigating security analyst burnout. In: Eleventh Symposium On Usable Privacy and Security (SOUPS 2015), pp. 347–359 (2015)
2. Lallie, H.S., Debattista, K., Bal, J.: An empirical evaluation of the effectiveness of attack graphs and fault trees in cyber-attack perception. IEEE Trans. Inf. Forensics Secur. **13**(5), 1110–1122 (2018)
3. Joh, H., Malaiya, Y.K.: Defining and assessing quantitative security risk measures using vulnerability lifecycle and CVSS metrics. In: The 2011 International Conference on Security and Management (SAM), pp. 10–16 (2011)
4. Arbaugh, W.A., Fithen, W.L., McHugh, J.: Windows of vulnerability: a case study analysis. Computer **33**(12), 52–59 (2000)
5. Pasqualetti, F., Dorfler, F., Bullo, F.: Control-theoretic methods for cyberphysical security: geometric principles for optimal cross-layer resilient control systems. IEEE Control Syst. Mag. **35**(1), 110–127 (2015)
6. Mavroeidis, V., Bromander, S.: Cyber threat intelligence model: an evaluation of taxonomies, sharing standards, and ontologies within cyber threat intelligence. In: 2017 European Intelligence and Security Informatics Conference (EISIC), pp. 91–98. IEEE (2017)
7. Zhu, Z., Dumitra, T.: FeatureSmith: automatically engineering features for malware detection by mining the security literature. In: Proceedings of the 2016 ACM SIGSAC Conference on Computer and Communications Security, pp. 767–778. ACM (October 2016)
8. Humayed, A., Lin, J., Li, F., Luo, B.: Cyber-physical systems security-a survey. IEEE Internet Things J. **4**(6), 1802–1831 (2017)
9. Kordy, B., Pietre-Cambacedes, L., Schweitzer, P.: DAG-based attack and defense modeling: don't miss the forest for the attack trees. Comput. Sci. Rev. **13**, 1–38 (2014)
10. Hafiz, M., Fang, M.: Game of detections: how are security vulnerabilities discovered in the wild? Empir. Softw. Eng. **21**(5), 1920–1959 (2016)
11. Householder, A.D., Wassermann, G., Manion, A., King, C.: The CERT guide to coordinated vulnerability disclosure (No. CMU/SEI-2017- SR-022). Carnegie-Mellon Univ Pittsburgh Pa Pittsburgh United States (2017)
12. Bogatinov, D.S., Bogdanoski, M., Angelevski, S.: AI-based cyber defense for more secure cyberspace. In: Handbook of Research on Civil Society and National Security in the Era of Cyber Warfare, pp. 220–237. IGI Global (2016)

Climate Change Impact and Vulnerability Analysis in the City of Bratislava: Application and Lessons Learned

Daniel Lückerath[1]([⊠]) [iD], Eva Streberová[2], Manfred Bogen[1], Erich Rome[1], Oliver Ullrich[1], and Eva Pauditsová[3]

[1] Fraunhofer-Institut für Intelligente Analyse- und Informationssysteme, Schloss Birlinghoven, 53757 Sankt Augustin, Germany
daniel.lueckerath@iais.fraunhofer.de
[2] Útvar hlavnej architektky, Hlavné mesto Slovenskej republiky, Bratislava, Slovak Republic
[3] Prírodovedecká fakulta Univerzity Komenského v Bratislave, Ilkovičova 6, 841 04 Bratislava, Slovak Republic

Abstract. Consequences of climate change, like more frequent extreme weather events, are major challenges for urban areas. With diverse approaches for adaptation strategy development available to cities, comparability with respect to risks, vulnerabilities, and adaptation options is limited. The lack of standardized methods and approaches to prioritize and select appropriate adaptation options restricts the exchange of best practices between cities.

This paper presents the application of a vulnerability analysis for the city of Bratislava, Slovakia. It describes how the approach was employed to analyze the effects extreme precipitation has on the road network and reports on how different stakeholders were involved in the process, how relevant data was employed for the assessment, and which results were produced. Based on this process description, typical problems, resulting method adaptations, and lessons learned are described.

Keywords: Risk analysis · Vulnerability assessment · Climate change · Critical infrastructure protection · Climate change adaptation

1 Introduction

Climate models project robust differences in regional climate characteristics between the present-day state and global warming scenarios with average temperature increases of 1.5 °C and 1.5 °C to 2 °C. These differences include significant increases in mean temperature in most land and ocean regions (high confidence), hot extremes in most inhabited regions (high confidence), heavy precipitation in several regions (medium confidence), and the probability of drought and precipitation deficits in some regions (medium confidence). [1] Urban population centers and their critical infrastructure components are increasingly vulnerable to extreme events related to these changing climate characteristics [2], especially fluvial and pluvial flooding, flash floods caused by heavy precipitation, temperature extremes, as well as thunderstorms and other heavy

© Springer Nature Switzerland AG 2020
S. Nadjm-Tehrani (Ed.): CRITIS 2019, LNCS 11777, pp. 83–94, 2020.
https://doi.org/10.1007/978-3-030-37670-3_7

storms [3]. This is also true for the City of Bratislava, capital of Slovakia and home of approx. 430,000 residents, that already suffers from a temperature increase of 2 °C since 1951 and an increase of total annual precipitation amounts. The storms that hit the city today bring as much as 10% more precipitation compared to average records from the previous century. Heatwaves and droughts have been appearing with increased frequency and severity in the last three decades [4].

With an even higher degree of extreme weather events to be expected, Bratislava decided to take part in the EU-H2020 project "RESIN – Climate Resilient Cities and Infrastructures" [5]. RESIN was a research project investigating climate resilience in European cities. Through co-creation and knowledge brokerage between city decision-makers and researchers, the project developed tools to support decision-makers in designing and implementing climate adaptation strategies for their local contexts. Specifically, Bratislava decided to apply "IVAVIA – Impact and Vulnerability Analysis of Vital Infrastructures and Built-up Areas", a standardized process for the assessment of climate change-related risks and vulnerabilities in cities and urban environments that was developed as part of RESIN.

This paper describes the process and key findings of the Bratislava city case. The IVAVIA process was applied over the course of 18 months, contributing key elements to the "Climate Change Impact Atlas of Bratislava" [4].

The paper continues with introducing the background of risk-based vulnerability analysis and a brief description of the IVAVIA process (Sect. 2). It then presents an in-depth description of the application of IVAVIA to assess the risk pluvial flooding, a major threat for the City of Bratislava, poses to its road infrastructure (Sect. 3), and concludes with a short summary of the lessons learned and an outlook on further research steps (Sect. 4).

2   Background

2.1   State of the Art: Impact and Vulnerability Analysis

Several methods and tools for risk analysis exist, with the "Words into Action Guidelines for National Disaster Risk Assessment" from the United Nations Office for Disaster Risk Reduction giving a comprehensive overview for the most frequently employed approaches [6].

On behalf of the German Federal Ministry for Economic Cooperation and Development, Deutsche Gesellschaft für Internationale Zusammenarbeit (GIZ), together with Adelphi and EURAC, developed the Vulnerability Sourcebook [7] in 2014, based on the Fourth Assessment Report of the IPCC. In 2017, the same authors provided a Risk Supplement [8] to the Vulnerability Sourcebook, based on the changes promoted in the Fifth Assessment Report [9] to provide guidance for indicator-based vulnerability and risk assessments. In this method, the usually massive amount of information and data about hazards, exposure, vulnerability, and other risk components is simplified by aggregating it to index scores (i.e. a number out of a full score), which are subsequently combined (e.g. using weighted arithmetic/geometric mean) to present risk levels as a single score.

In contrast, the German Federal Office of Civil Protection and Disaster Assistance (BBK) employs a multi-criteria impact and likelihood analysis based on risk matrices, an instrument also promoted as an ISO standard [10]. In this approach, impacts and probabilities of hazard scenarios are estimated (e.g. based on historical data or simulation models) and classified by defining threshold values for the different impact/probability classes, i.e. in which value range do potential impacts/probabilities have to lie to be classified in a certain way. Typically, risk matrices have four to seven impact classes and a similar number of probability classes. For any combination of impact and probability, a risk level or class (BBK: very high, high, intermediate, low) is determined. Both determining the thresholds and assigning risk levels requires political decisions that have to be taken with extreme care: It requires deciding when a certain number of fatalities is regarded as 'moderate' or 'significant' and which risk level requires which type of reaction, or, more simply put, which risk level is acceptable and which is not.

If no (or not enough) information or means for carrying out an indicator-based multi-criteria analysis is available, expert elicitation approaches might be employed. Here, individuals with a good understanding of the various components of disaster risk components of the area under study conduct a qualitative analysis using their expert judgements. The "Risk Systemicity Questionnaire" developed during the "Smart Mature Resilience project – SMR" [11] and the "UNISDR Disaster Resilience Scorecard for Cities" [12] are recently developed expert elicitation approaches. Both employ spreadsheet- and/or web-based questionnaires to elicit knowledge from experts and combine the gathered information into comprehensive overviews, e.g. by assigning scores to predefined answers and visualizing them using spider charts.

Other research projects investigated climate change-oriented resilience in European cities too: The project "Reconciling Adaptation, Mitigation and Sustainable Development for Cities – RAMSES" [13] developed methods and tools to quantify the impacts of climate change and the costs and benefits of adaptation measures to cities, while the project "Smart Mature Resilience – SMR" [14] aimed at developing a resilience management guideline to support city decision-makers in developing and implementing resilience measures.

The RESIN project developed practical and applicable methods and tools to support decision-makers in designing and implementing adaptation and mitigation strategies for their local contexts and in a participatory way. One of these methods is the risk-based vulnerability assessment methodology IVAVIA, which combines the indicator-based method from the original Vulnerability Sourcebook with the multi-criteria impact and likelihood analysis by the BBK.

2.2 IVAVIA: A Process for Impact and Vulnerability Analysis of Vital Infrastructures and Built-Up Areas

The IVAVIA process consists of seven modules in three stages: the qualitative stage, the quantitative stage, and the presentation of the outcome. Each module consists of three to six individual steps.

The modules and steps are described in detail in the IVAVIA Guideline document [15], with the more technical details of the process and reference information being covered by the IVAVIA Guideline Appendix. A more detailed explanation of the methodology with brief descriptions of example applications in Bilbao, Spain and Greater

Manchester, UK can also be found in [16]. Here, only the key elements of IVAVIA will be introduced briefly.

The central element of the qualitative stage of IVAVIA are impact chains. They are cause-effect models describing the elements that contribute to the consequences a given hazard has on an exposed object (see Fig. 1). Each element of an impact chain is to be described in a qualitative way by specifying attributes[1]. Usually, impact chains are developed during collaborative workshops with domain experts. As a result, impact chains are not exhaustive, but describe the common understanding of these experts.

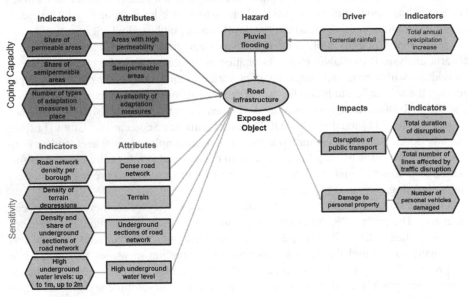

Fig. 1. Impact chain for the hazard-exposure combination "pluvial flooding on road infrastructure" in the city of Bratislava. Hazards and drivers in blue, exposed object in grey, coping capacity in green-blue, sensitivity in green, and impacts in orange. Rectangles: attributes; Hexagons: indicators. (Color figure online)

For each attribute defined in an impact chain, measurable indicators need to be identified and associated data needs to be gathered. To ease the indicator selection process, established directories of standard indicators should be employed, for example, the annex of the Vulnerability Sourcebook ([7], pp. 14–17) or the annex of the Covenant of Mayors for Climate and Energy Reporting Guidelines ([17], pp. 61–67).

Communicating a multitude of complex, multi-dimensional indicators in a comprehensive way can be extremely complicated. Therefore, the calculated indicator values are normalized (e.g. via min-max normalization [18]), weighted, and aggregated (e.g. using weighted arithmetic mean [18]) to composite scores for different risk components.

Subsequently, risks are estimated. If sufficient historical data about impacts and occurrences of hazards for the definition of damage functions is available, these are used

---

[1] Attributes are inherent characteristics of the objects under analysis, such as sensitivity and coping capacity; they are the basis for determining indicators.

to estimate potential consequences, which are then classified using discrete, ordinal classes (e.g. "insignificant", "minor", or "disastrous" for impacts and "very unlikely", "likely", and "very likely" for probabilities). The resulting impacts and probability pairs, i.e. the risk scores, are then assigned to discrete, ordinal risk classes using a risk matrix.

If not sufficient historical data about past consequences and occurrences of hazards to derive damage functions is available, an alternative approach is to employ the available data to define aggregated hazard and exposure indicators as described in the Risk Supplement of the Vulnerability Sourcebook [8]. For example, data about flood depth and velocity can be combined to a single hazard indicator, while data about population density in flood-prone areas and exposed build-up area can be combined to an exposure indicator. These can then be combined with the composite risk components calculated to a single risk score.

3 Analyzing Risks and Vulnerabilities Regarding Climate Change for Bratislava

3.1 Situation in Bratislava

The City of Bratislava, capital of Slovakia, lies in the southern part of the country, which has suffered from a temperature increase of 1 °C since 1988. Higher temperatures in warmer seasons have led to increased evapotranspiration, which results in occasional but heavy rainfall. However, southern Slovakia has suffered an almost 20% decrease in total annual precipitation and serious drought have been occurring almost every year since the 1990s [19]. A more complex analysis on intensity and length of warm and cool weather spells in the period 1951–2017 shows a continuous increase of above-normal temperature warm spells while below-normal cold temperature spells are continually decreasing [20].

Bratislava's sectoral master plan on management of sewage water and rainwater sewage systems dates back to 2008 and is not suited anymore for the amount of urban development that occurred in the past 10 years, which resulted in an increase of impermeable land-cover. As a result, underpasses and whole street segments are often flooded after substantial rainfall, resulting in blockages and traffic jams.

To tackle these and other climate change-related issues, Bratislava committed itself to the Mayors Adapt initiative in 2014 and in the same year completed the EU Cities Adapt program with a climate change adaptation strategy. In 2017 an action plan to implement adaptation measures was developed. However, both the adaptation strategy and the action plan are based on a qualitative vulnerability assessment. Therefore, a new quantitative assessment applicable for spatial planning and permission procedures for development projects needed to be conducted.

3.2 Applying IVAVIA in the City of Bratislava

Following the IVAVIA process as described above, the assessment started with the identification of the most pressing climatic hazards for the city, i.e. heatwaves, droughts, and pluvial flooding, followed by a kick-off meeting with stakeholders from several departments of the municipality as well as external experts including health and environmental authorities, the Slovak Hydrometeorological institute, and other organizations operating in the area of health, sewage water management, and drinking water provision. The goals of this meeting were to introduce the participants to the methodology and design initial impact chains.

The initial workshop yielded three impact chains covering the effects of heatwaves and pluvial flooding on health and quality of life as well as droughts on green infrastructure. These were later on supplemented by two additional impact chains covering the effects of pluvial flooding on buildings and road infrastructure (see Fig. 1). During the initial workshop, the participants were not given explicit guidance on potential attributes, resulting in the identification and definition of more than 90 different potential attributes across all impact chains, mostly based on experience and knowledge of the participating stakeholders.

Therefore, the identified attributes underwent a thorough review to filter out unsuitable and duplicated attributes, re-categorize attributes to correct for misunderstandings (e.g. participants identified "low implementation of building-level adaptation measures for reducing the impacts of rainfall" as a sensitivity attribute), and reducing the number of attributes to a more manageable amount in order to facilitate result validation. Following this process, initial indicators for each attribute where defined and required data identified.

The subsequent months focused on data acquisition: For each indicator the available data, its spatial and temporal resolution, its data format, and the necessary licensing agreements were identified. This included data from the Slovak Statistical Office on borough level, published annually in the statistical yearbook, as well as data by the National Healthcare Information Centre of the Slovak Republic and the Slovak Hydrometeorological institute. In addition, Bratislava City and local research partner Comenius University in Bratislava processed their own data sources as well as open source data (e.g. from OpenStreetMap [21]) to calculate indicator maps. For example, a digital elevation model of Bratislava was used to identify existing and potential drainage basins and their outlets using hydrological and terrain modelling tools. This drainage basin model was then used to identify critical terrain depressions by vectorising the raster output and identifying the lowest sections of the drainage basins with depths up to 1 m. This information was subsequently used to calculate different indicators, e.g. "density of terrain depressions per borough" or "length of infrastructure exposed to terrain depressions". This method has also been used in [22], p. 73f. Figure 2 shows part of the combined drainage basin and terrain depression model with identified critical sections of transport infrastructure and high-density terrain depression zones.

Other calculated indicators include pressure on the sewage system from the amount of surrounding impermeable area and estimated amount of water coming from impermeable areas into the combined sewage system, groundwater level depth, pressure on the sewage system based on population density in every borough and drinking water consumption in households, availability of different types of implemented adaptation measures, and share of (semi-)permeable areas.

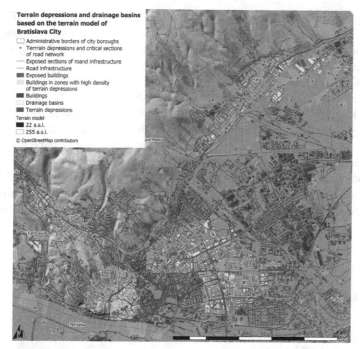

Fig. 2. Elevation model with analysis of drainage basins and terrain depressions, showing also zones of high density of terrain depressions (in yellow) – used for creating exposure indicators. Source: [4]. (Color figure online)

Single indicators were normalized using min-max normalization and combined to composite indicators for sensitivity, coping capacity, exposure, and hazard using weighted arithmetic mean. Initially, an expert judgment approach was to be employed for selecting indicator weights, reflecting the perceived importance of indicators. However, this process was judged as too subjective by the participants and subsequently, weights were chosen based on the results of a correlation analysis, allocating lower weights for indicators that were correlated to correct for statistical effects.

The resulting composite indicators were visualized as choropleth maps (see Figs. 3 and 4) and validated by experts. Afterwards, the composite sensitivity and coping capacity indicators where combined to a vulnerability indicator (see Fig. 5, left), which in turn was combined together with the exposure and hazard indicator (see Fig. 4) to a final risk indicator (see Fig. 5, right). These results were in turn validated by local experts based on historic occurrences of flooding events.

3.3 Results

The assessment approach employed in Bratislava differs from the process description in Sect. 2 in that risk are not estimated based on a multi-criteria impact and likelihood analysis but using an indicator-based approach as described in [8]. This is due to the limited amount of historical records about hazard occurrences and related impacts, which prohibits the definition of robust damage functions and the estimation of likelihoods. However, a non-probabilistic assessment for the present situation can be conducted with the indicator-based approach. In the future these results can easily be expanded to a probabilistic assessment.

The results of the assessment show for all impact chains that the city center located in the "Stare Mesto" (Old town) borough and the adjacent boroughs such as the more urbanized "Ružinov" and "Petržalka" usually yield the highest scores for vulnerability and risk (see Fig. 5). The more peripheral city boroughs have a rather rural character, with the majority of their area covered by permeable land-use or the Danube river running on their territory. These kinds of land use effectively mitigate the negative impacts of pluvial flooding, which is reflected in the assessment. The only exemption in this regard is the peripheral "Čunovo" borough. Although infrastructure density is relatively low here, the infrastructure that is located here is often affected by terrain depressions.

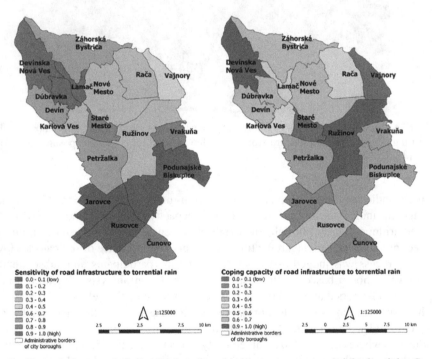

Fig. 3. Choropleth maps, left: Sensitivity of road infrastructure to torrential rain; right: Coping capacity of road infrastructure to torrential rain. Source: [4].

With regard to the morphology of the city area, several boroughs are strongly affected by the vicinity of the Male Karpaty (Small Carpathians) mountain range in the north and northwest. Although the vicinity of the mountains is an asset in mitigation of extreme heat, the terrain also creates natural drainage basins which accumulate precipitation and channel it into the lower and more urbanized sections of the boroughs at the foothills.

The results of the vulnerability assessment were compiled into an Atlas that has been created with the aim to provide useful information for city administration practitioners at all levels, local research institutions, as well as practitioners from private sector (such as architects, landscape architects, and development companies) and be also a supporting tool to decision-makers and policy makers across all scales – borough, city, regional, as well as government level. Besides more than 90 choropleth maps (displaying borough level assessments), there are finer thematic maps showing possible combinations of different indicators, which can be used as stand-alone tools in spatial planning and evaluation of investment projects.

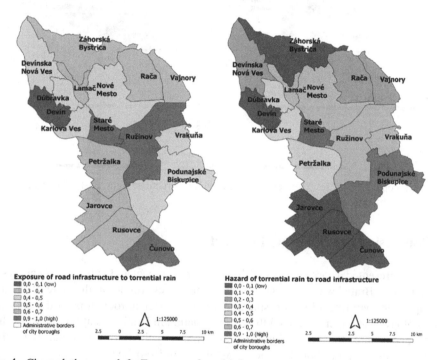

Fig. 4. Choropleth maps, left: Exposure of road infrastructure to torrential rain; right: Hazard indicator for torrential rain. Source: [4].

The city will include the visual outputs into its open map portal after a public consultation process and a formal acceptance of the Atlas by a resolution of the City Parliament.

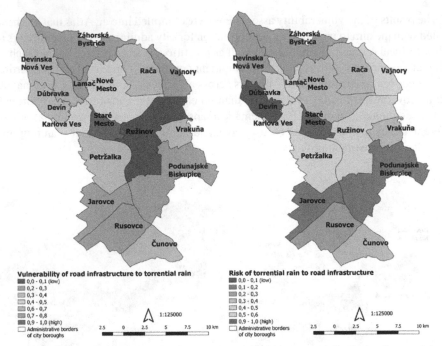

Fig. 5. Choropleth maps, left: Vulnerability of road infrastructure; right: Risk of torrential rain on road infrastructure. Source: [4].

4   Conclusion and Lessons Learned

This paper presented a case study on a climate change impact and vulnerability analysis for the City of Bratislava, Slovakia. It shared some background on the state of the art for impact and vulnerability assessment and gave a brief introduction to the applied methodology. The paper described the initial situation in Bratislava at the outset of the process and detailed the application of the assessment methodology exemplarily for the effects of extreme rainfall on the road infrastructure in Bratislava.

While the initial goal of conducting an indicator-based vulnerability assessment followed by a multi-criteria impact and likelihood analysis could not be met due to lack in historical records, it was possible to conduct a non-probabilistic indicator-based assessment that reflects the present conditions in Bratislava. After further validation of the results by public consultation processes, a probabilistic assessment covering different climate change scenarios is planned, availability of sufficient historical records provided. This assessment should also employ a higher (i.e. sub-borough) resolution to enable detailed planning of adaptation options. This iterative refinement approach is in line with how impact and vulnerability analyses for climate change should be understood: as a continuous process with regular, frequent updates and adjustments accommodating new developments and newly available data.

In addition, applying the methodology in Bratislava showed the need for a European – or even globally – unified reference indicator set for impact and vulnerability analysis in urban areas with standardized temporal/spatial resolution and scope as well as standardized data structures to enable comparability between different urban areas and facilitate development of better supporting tools. The availability of reliable, sufficiently extensive data sources is a serious problem that limits the applicability of probabilistic assessment methodologies (see also BBK [22], p. 94, right box).

Nonetheless, non-probabilistic assessments are highly valuable for a multitude of stakeholders in urban areas. Developing cause-effect models with experts from different municipal departments facilitates joint understanding and better communication of complex climate change-related issues. Discussing these issues across different departments and stakeholder groups can also pave the way for other processes that enable a better assessment in the future. For example, as a result of applying IVAVIA in Bratislava, the Office of the Chief City Architect was invited to join a working group developing a GIS portal for Bratislava that can be employed for further refinement of the assessment results.

The results presented in the Atlas will be an important tool for identifying where to implement adaptation measures listed in the action plan for climate change, e.g. sustainable drainage systems, bio swales, green retention trenches and infiltration basins, rain gardens, or increased permeable paving. On a city-wide level, more initiative needs to be taken in terms of strategic land-use planning by incorporating the results of the assessment into the new master plan. While the city can do this in public spaces, private property owners also need to be incentivized to take action. For example, the city provides municipal grants of up to 1,000 € to encourage the implementation of adaptation measures in households, such as upgrading buildings with sustainable drainage systems or other nature-based approaches for rain water retention.

Acknowledgments. This paper is based in part upon work in the framework of the projects "RESIN – Climate Resilient Cities and Infrastructures" and "ARCH – Advancing Resilience of historic areas against Climate-related and other Hazards". These projects have received funding from the European Union's Horizon 2020 research and innovation program under grant agreement nos. 653522 and 820999. The sole responsibility for the content of this publication lies with the authors. It does not necessarily represent the opinion of the European Union. Neither the EASME nor the European Commission are responsible for any use that may be made of the information contained therein.

References

1. Intergovernmental Panel on Climate Change (IPCC): Summary for policymakers. In: Global Warming of 1.5 °C. World Meteorological Organization, Geneva, Switzerland, 32 pp. (2018)
2. Coletti, A., De Nicola, A., Villani, M.L.: Building climate change into risk assessment. Nat. Hazards **84**(2), 1307–1325 (2016)
3. Rossetti, M.A.: Potential impacts of climate change on railroads. In: Workshop on the Potential Impacts of Climate Change on Transportation, Washington, D.C. (2002)
4. Streberova, E., et al.: Atlas of impacts of climate change in Bratislava City. 66 p. Forthcoming (2019). (in Slovak)

5. RESIN – Climate Resilient Cities and Infrastructures. http://www.resin-cities.eu/. Accessed 11 Nov 2017
6. United Nations Office for Disaster Risk Reduction: National Disaster Risk Assessment. Words into Action Guidelines, UNISDR (2017)
7. German Federal Ministry for Economic Cooperation and Development: The Vulnerability Sourcebook. Concept and guidelines for standardised vulnerability assessments. Deutsche Gesellschaft für Internationale Zusammenarbeit, Bonn and Eschborn, Germany (2014)
8. German Federal Ministry for Economic Cooperation and Development: Risk Supplement to the Vulnerability Sourcebook. Guidance on how to apply the Vulnerability Sourcebook's approach with the new IPCC AR5 concept of climate risk. Deutsche Gesellschaft für Internationale Zusammenarbeit (GIZ), Bonn, Germany (2017)
9. Intergovernmental Panel on Climate Change (IPCC): Summary for policymakers. In: Climate Change 2014. Part A: Global and Sectoral Aspects. Cambridge University Press, Cambridge, pp. 1–32 (2014)
10. German Federal Office of Civil Protection and Disaster Assistance: Method of Risk Analysis for Civil Protection. Wissenschaftsforum 8, BBK, Bonn (2011)
11. Pyrko, I., Howick, S., Eden, C.: Risk systemicity and city resilience. In: EURAM 2017, University of Strathclyde, 21–24 June 2017
12. United Nations Office for Disaster Risk Reduction: Disaster Resilience Scorecard for Cities. UNISDR (2017)
13. RAMSES – Reconciling adaptation, mitigation and sustainable development for cities. http://www.ramses-cities.eu/. Accessed 05 Dec 2017
14. SMR – Smart Mature Resilience. http://smr-project.eu. Accessed 05 Dec 2017
15. Rome, E., et al.: IVAVIA Guideline, Annex to Deliverable D2.3 Realisation and implementation of IVAVIA. EU H2020 Project RESIN, Sankt Augustin, Germany (2017)
16. Rome, E., Ullrich, O., Lückerath, D., Worst, R., Xie, J., Bogen, M.: IVAVIA: impact and vulnerability analysis of vital infrastructures and built-up areas. In: Luiijf, E., Žutautaitė, I., Hämmerli, Bernhard M. (eds.) CRITIS 2018. LNCS, vol. 11260, pp. 84–97. Springer, Cham (2019). https://doi.org/10.1007/978-3-030-05849-4_7
17. Neves, A., et al.: The covenant of mayors for climate and energy reporting guidelines, EUR 28160 EN (2016). https://doi.org/10.2790/586693
18. Organisation for Economic Co-operation and Development (OECD): Handbook on constructing composite indicators: methodology and user guide. Technical report. OECD Publishing, Paris (2008)
19. Faško, P., Lapin, M., Pecho, J.: 20-year extraordinary climatic period in Slovakia. Meteorol. J. **11**(2008), 99–105 (2008). (in Slovak)
20. Výberči, J., Pecho, J., Faško, P., Bochníček, J.: Warm and cool spells in Slovakia (1951–2017) in the context of climate change. Meteorol. J. **21**(2018), 101–108 (2018). (in Slovak)
21. OpenStreetMap Contributors (2018). https://www.openstreetmap.org/
22. German Federal Office of Civil Protection and Disaster Assistance: Abschätzung der Verwundbarkeit von Bevölkerung und Kritischen Infrastrukturen gegenüber Hitzewellen und Starkregen, Praxis im Bevölkerungsschutz; Band 11, BBK, Bonn (2013)

Resilience and Mitigation

Intrusion Resilience for PV Inverters in a Distribution Grid Use-Case Featuring Dynamic Voltage Control

BooJoong Kang[1]($\boxtimes$), David Umsonst[2], Mario Faschang[3], Christian Seitl[3],
Ivo Friedberg[4], Friederich Kupzog[3], Henrik Sandberg[2], and Kieran McLaughlin[1]

[1] Queen's University Belfast, Belfast, UK
b.kang@qub.ac.uk
[2] KTH Royal Institute of Technology, Stockholm, Sweden
[3] AIT Austrian Institute of Technology GmbH, Vienna, Austria
[4] Austrian Power Grid AG, Vienna, Austria

Abstract. ICT-enabled smart grid devices, potentially introduce new cyber vulnerabilities that weaken the resilience of the electric grid. Using real and simulated PV inverters, this work demonstrates how cyber-attacks on IEC 61850 communications to field devices can force an unstable state, causing voltage oscillations or overvoltage situations in a distribution grid. An automated resilience mechanism is therefore presented, combining intrusion detection and decentralised resilient controllers, which is demonstrated to assure stable operation of an energy system by counteracting cyber-attacks targeting embedded PV inverters.

Keywords: Cyber security · Smart grids · Resilient control · Intrusion response

1 Introduction

This work investigates a novel protection scheme against cyber-attacks, based on domain-specific modelling of the physical features of an electrical distribution system where embedded PV inverters are dynamically controlled to manage power and voltage outputs. Many cyber-physical infrastructures use the well-established Supervisory Control and Data Acquisition (SCADA) paradigm, with a central control instance and numerous logical connections to field devices. This work focuses on power grid infrastructure, which is a typical example for that paradigm. With the introduction of participants such as renewable energy generators, new connections to participants are being deployed, and an emerging concern is the rapid increase in field devices that require communications. At the very least, this is required for remote monitoring, but it is also highly desirable to support parameter configuration to enable a range of grid management applications. However, integrating such capabilities increases the cyber-attack surface, presenting a risk that controls may be tampered with, resulting in instabilities.

© Springer Nature Switzerland AG 2020
S. Nadjm-Tehrani (Ed.): CRITIS 2019, LNCS 11777, pp. 97–109, 2020.
https://doi.org/10.1007/978-3-030-37670-3_8

In this work, a use-case is considered where photovoltaic (PV) inverters are remotely controlled via IT network connections to a central distribution system operator (DSO) system. The controller in this case aims to facilitate improved voltage management for distribution lines that have a high proportion of distributed embedded generation. The components of the control loop are thus distributed across subsystems, interlinked via SCADA communications. The specific problem investigated is to enable this control system to detect a cyber-attack, and automatically react to mitigate physical effects in the electrical grid. For this scenario, a resilient controller (RC) is developed that protects the field devices from malicious parameter changes. In parallel, a domain specific SCADA intrusion detection system is developed that uses deep packet inspection to detect manipulated device communications. A realistic physical laboratory demonstration environment is used to show how a novel combination of these two approaches can be integrated to ensure system stability during a set of cyberattack scenarios. The main research contributions of this work are as follows:

- Resilient control theory is deployed in a real environment, supporting decision making for real-time response.
- An active intrusion response mechanism integrates with physical system controls in real-time, going beyond previous passive SCADA IDS approaches.
- Validation in a realistic testbed, comprising hardware linked to a simulated grid environment, interconnected via IT.

2 Related Work and Motivation

Previous work investigating cyber-attacks in cyber-physical systems often models or demonstrates physical effects caused by deliberate interference in the cyber domain. However, research gaps remain regarding: (1) detailed system implementations demonstrating specific cyber-attacks executed to cause direct physical effects; (2) attack mitigation methods to respond to cyber-attacks.

Regarding the first gap, the literature typically addresses the problem from a system modelling perspective [1]. In doing so, it is possible to reveal detail about the impact on electrical parameters across a grid model, such as the IEEE n bus system models [2]. However, such studies primarily reveal effects and constraints pertaining to grid stability, with the issue of cyber security being a motivation, rather than part of the experiments. A few papers take this further by investigating attacks via software/hardware co-simulation. E.g., Hahn [3] introduces a testbed to explore vulnerabilities and physical effects, showing how voltages, flows, and generation could be adversely affected by simple DoS attacks. Such studies remain focused on problem identification.

Regarding the second gap, proposed solutions typically focus solely on cyber or physical aspects. One approach is to reduce the problem of intrusion detection to an "anomaly detection" problem [4]. This often happens in isolation from the cyber domain, and the practicalities of real-time deployment are not generally considered. A weakness is that whereas alerts can be generated, it is difficult to map alerts to consequences in the physical domain. The question arises, how to translate alerts into mitigation actions in the physical domain? To address these issues, this paper investigates a combination of two main components: resilient control and intrusion detection.

Resilient control has gained a lot of interest in recent years. Research on the topic is conducted in different areas, such as control theory, power systems, and security. Resilient control systems can achieve an acceptable level of operational performance and state awareness in the presence of random, malicious, or unexpected disturbances [5]. Urbina et al. [6] define a common taxonomy for the different areas in the field of resilient control. This discussion will focus on power systems. On the substation level, Isozaki et al. [7] show how an adversary can manipulate a centralised tap changer control in the substation to cause voltage violations or to reduce the output power of PVs. Furthermore, they present a detection algorithm, which increases the resilience of the system by improving the operational performance during an attack. At a lower level of the power grid, Teixeira et al. [8] show how a microgrid with a quadratic voltage droop control for PVs can be attacked but no mitigation methods are proposed. The resilient control strategies introduced in this paper are active on the PV level, but in contrast to [8] the commonly used piecewise linear voltage droop control is considered. Furthermore, PVs are protected against attack on the droop law setpoints.

From a cyber-security viewpoint, Genge et al. [9] whitelist allowed traffic and detect prohibited connections based on general information such as IP address, port number and protocol. However, such traditional techniques cannot interpret application layer data to provide information about physical system states. Yang et al. [10] introduce model based detection methods for IEC61850. Caselli et al. [11] adopt discrete-time Markov chains to detect anomalies, and Yoo et al. [12] use one-class support vector machines to learn normal behaviours. However, most research focuses on how to detect attacks, with less attention on how to apply the results to provide mitigation. Recent work has emerged investigating intrusion response systems (IRS) whereby automated actions are applied to mitigate detected attacks. Literature on IRS focuses mainly on traditional IT [13], while IRS in cyber-physical use-cases are broadly unaddressed. He et al. [14] demonstrated that an automated IRS could significantly improve the reliability of cyber-physical systems. Qi et al. [15] investigate distributed energy installations that operate smart inverters and propose mechanisms to automatically respond to cyber-attacks, but the proposal is not supported by an implementation. Li et al. [16] propose algorithms for identifying optimal solutions against cyber-attacks, but mainly focus on how to make a decision (as a response) for cyber-attack(s).

3   Selection of the Smart Grid Scenario

Three broad types of control loop are present in today's digitalised distribution system:

1. Local loops with sensor, controller and actuator in close proximity. E.g., maximum power control of an inverter, or substation voltage control with on-load tap changer. Such loops are common and operate autogenously. Changes must be made on-site.

2. Local control loops with interfaces for remote configuration and monitoring. E.g., communication interfaces to distribution-level generators above a certain power rating. The number of control loops in this category will increase in the coming years.
3. Remote control loops, with dedicated sensor-controller/controller-actuator telecommunications. Due to their time-critical nature these are usually avoided.

The second category is chosen for further study in this work, as it is expected to be the most widely applied concept in future and is widely representative. The scenario that is now developed focuses on residential inverters. To avoid grid congestion, distributed energy resources such as PV and battery systems are required to provide so-called ancillary services to the power system. In a distribution grid scenario, the most relevant ancillary service is voltage control, with the aim to maintain line voltages within the technical specifications EN50160. For example, the use of PV inverters to provide a voltage control service is realised using droop control, with the voltage at the connection point used as input and a droop law changing the unit's reactive power as shown in Fig. 1, based on the voltage at the feeding point (see also EN50438:2013).

The configuration of the droop law is typically done on installation of the unit. However, it is proposed that the four supporting points of the droop law shown in Fig. 1 are updateable remotely using an IP-based communication network. In this scenario a controller is placed in a secondary substation, which supports communication using the IEC 61850 protocol. The controller uses measurements from the low voltage grid to gain the voltage level and variations. It is able to adjust the voltage level using an on-site MV/LV on-load tap changer transformer. However, its relevant functionality in this context is that it also updates the settings for reactive power control for the PV inverters. It does this on a regular basis by transmitting a $Q(U)$ function, via IEC 61850, consisting of four support vectors (see Fig. 1). This function defines the control gain of the proportional reactive power controller implemented in the inverters. Malicious changes in this gain can result in significant voltage limit violations or oscillations.

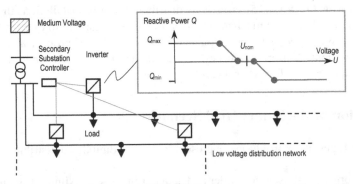

Fig. 1. Low voltage grid scenario and $Q(U)$ of PV inverters to support the local line voltage.

4   Automated Intrusion Resilience

A unified mechanism is now proposed for automated intrusion resilience. The proposed approach assumes that intrusions are possible, thus shifts the emphasis towards resilience of the underlying control loops and system behaviour. Note that the emphasis is on protecting the physical operation of the grid compared to traditional IRS approaches that focus on mitigation in the cyber domain [13]. Therefore, Sect. 4.1 identifies the physical properties and models of the investigated scenario that can be used to verify that a new droop law yields a stable grid operation and to mitigate effects of malicious changes. Section 4.2 describes a custom intrusion detection approach to interact with resilient control components and how each component interoperates.

4.1   Resilience Control

A resilient controller (RC) is proposed to increase the robustness, safety, and security of local controllers with remote action interfaces. Hence, each PV inverter has a local resilient control module, which checks the commands. Although the module increases the inverter's resilience towards attacks and faults, it also limits the remote controllability. Therefore, the module must be designed so the control centre can achieve its control requirement and simultaneously reduce potential damage.

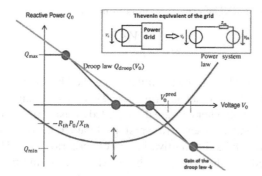

Fig. 2. Intersection between droop and power system law. (Color figure online)

The PV has an anti-islanding system [17] that obtains a Thévenin equivalent of the grid from the PV's local perspective. The Thévenin equivalent consists of a constant voltage source V_{th} and total grid impedance $Z_{th} = R_{th} + jX_{th}$ (see upper right corner of Fig. 2). The model of [18] for the PV inverter is adopted and it is assumed that the voltage at the Point of Common Coupling $V_0 < \theta$ is close to the Thévenin voltage $V_{th} \angle 0$, i.e. $V_0 \approx V_{th}$, $\sin\theta \approx \theta$ and $\cos\theta \approx 1$.

Hence, it is verified that the droop law received from the control centre yields a steady state voltage, which is inside the allowed voltage range. Moreover, it is also verified that the new droop law is stabilising, i.e. it does not induce oscillations of the reactive power. This leads to two resilient control rules:

Rule 1 (Voltage Prediction with the Thévenin Equivalent): With   the   Thévenin equivalent the relationship between the reactive power Q_0 injected in the grid and the PV voltage V_0 of the PV under the active power injection P_0 is expressed as

$$Q_0 \approx \frac{1}{X_{th}}(V_0 - V_{th})V_0 - \frac{R_{th}}{X_{th}}P_0$$

This power system law is used to predict the steady state voltage V_0, called V_0^{pred} by finding the intersection with the new remotely commanded droop law (see Fig. 2). After finding V_0^{pred} a range check is performed to see if the new droop law yields an acceptable steady state voltage: $V_{min} \leq V_0^{pred} \leq V_{max}$. If not, the new droop law is disregarded. Note, for applying this rule it is assumed that the droop law yields stable dynamics, which is checked by the following rule.

Rule 2 (Stability of the Droop Law): If the gain k of the droop law (slope of the orange line in Fig. 2) exceeds a certain critical gain k_{crit} the droop law destabilises the grid. Unstable here means that the reactive power starts to oscillate between the maximum and minimum reactive power possible. This might damage the PV inverter over a longer period of time. To avoid instability the gain of the new droop law is compared with the critical gain and if $k > k_{crit}$ the droop law is rejected.

The crux is to find k_{crit}. Here two methods are presented to obtain estimates of the critical gain. The first method uses the Thévenin equivalent and is a conservative version of the circle criterion [19]. The critical gain is obtained as

$$k_{crit} = \frac{V_{th}X_{th}}{R_{th}^2 + X_{th}^2}$$

and it has the advantage of being locally available, i.e. the Thévenin equivalent is obtained at the PV level without any other information. This critical gain is a heuristic value because the dynamics of all other PVs are disregarded by using the steady-state Thévenin equivalent of the grid and a conservative version of the circle criterion.

The second method uses the multivariate circle criterion [19]. Here, the Thévenin equivalent is not used, but the grid as a whole. After linearizing the grid equations of the reactive power and voltage, the multivariate circle criterion is used to obtain an estimate of the critical gain for all PVs. The advantage is that an estimate with a more solid theoretical foundation is obtained, but it is not possible to obtain the estimate in a completely decentralised fashion, since some knowledge of the whole grid is required. In the experiments in Sect. 5, the first method to estimate the critical gain is used.

4.2   Intrusion Detection and Resilience

The proposed IDS is custom-designed for IEC61850 based SCADA communications, and consists of two layers: local intrusion detection and global intrusion detection. Local units are placed at strategic points to monitor network traffic as shown in Fig. 3. These units apply whitelist, signature detection, and stateful analysis approaches. This is motivated due to the common use of legacy devices, unencrypted communications, and unauthenticated devices typically found in power systems in real-world.

Whitelist defines authorised connections and allowed operations, so any unauthorised connection or operation can be detected. Signature detection is used to detect known cyber-attacks at an individual packet level. Stateful analysis investigates traffic over the time by inspecting flows rather than packet-by-packet analysis. As an IEC 61850 interpreter is implemented in our IDS, the IDS can inspect application data and store the status information. The IDS will alert if a violation has been detected. Local units provide alerts and the status information to the global centre. The global centre provides high-level intrusion detection based on alerts and reports collected across all units. The global centre can identify inconsistencies by applying stateful analysis and anomaly detection on the global view of the network. The global centre can identify:

(1) Man-in-the-middle attacks (MITM): packets are diverted to a wrong destination,
(2) Manipulation: inconsistency or data change in a packet at a point of the network,
(3) Injection: packet identified that is not at the closest local unit of the originator,
(4) Drop: if any packet has failed to arrive at the closest local unit of the destination.

The global centre also provides additional information such as original data that are manipulated, what devices are under attack, status of interested devices, etc. Intrusion resilience is enabled by integrating intrusion detection and resilient control, which interact to share information as shown in Fig. 3. The RCs are placed alongside devices to verify commands and are responsible for device protection. IDS alerts allow RCs to define and enact fine-grained policies against attacks and failures.

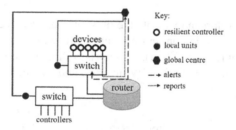

Fig. 3. Intrusion detection and resilience

Table 1 summarises examples of IDS alerts and RC actions. The IDS will alert an attack to relevant RCs. If possible, original data will be provided and RCs can determine whether to adopt the original data or not. By exchanging information between RCs and IDSs, the IDSs can keep track of the RCs' evaluation of the droop laws and alert suspicious setpoints at an early stage. These interactions can be defined as rules depending on systems. The connection between the global centre and RCs enables reaction to attacks in the distribution grid to maintain voltage stability.

Table 1. IDS alerts and RC actions.

Attacks		IDS (Alert to RC)	RC (Action)
Illegal connection	Connection	Timestamp, IP/Port	Reject commands and disconnect the connection (if possible)
	Commands	Timestamp, IP/Port, Commands	Reject commands
	Disconnection	Timestamp, IP/Port	Apply normal rules
Man-in-the Middle (MITM)	Start	Timestamp, IP/Port/MAC	Disconnect the connection (if possible) and apply strict rules
	Manipulation	Timestamp, IP/Port/MAC, Original Commands	Reject manipulated commands and take the original commands
	Injection	Timestamp, IP/Port/MAC, Injected Commands	Reject injected commands
	Drop	Timestamp, IP/Port/MAC, Dropped Commands	Take the dropped commands
	Stop	Timestamp, IP/Port/MAC	Apply normal rules

5   Testbed and Experiments

The testbed used to develop and validate the presented approach consists of a coupled simulation of a power distribution and communication grid infrastructure, linked to laboratory and field equipment [20]. This comprises three systems, shown in Fig. 4: a distribution grid simulation, a physical PV inverter, and a communication network.

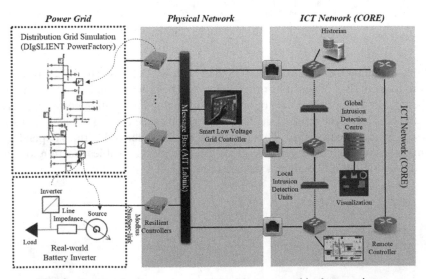

Fig. 4. Communication and power network setup used in the experiment.

DIgSILENT PowerFactory is used to simulate a rural distribution grid consisting of one medium to low voltage transformer, 13 households and 4 PV inverter systems. The PV systems are connected to the Smart Low Voltage Grid Controller (SLVGC) [21], which measures the remote voltage levels and creates reactive power setpoints in the form of $Q(U)$ characteristics for the PV inverters. The distribution grid is simulated with typical household loads and typical PV generation of a sunny spring weekday. To assess the IDS and RC, a real battery inverter is integrated to the coupled simulation. The resulting Power-Hardware-in-the-Loop (PHIL) setup uses a three phase Spitzenberger & Spies power amplifier (G in Fig. 4), representing the grid connection point, controlled by voltage values from one of the simulated nodes. Two impedances (line impedance 240 mΩ, 480 μH and load impedance 70.5 Ω) connect the 2.5 kVA battery inverter to the power amplifier. This PHIL set-up is driven by the real-time PowerFactory simulation and also integrates the inverter into the communication system by its SunSpec communication interface. CORE and AIT Lablink are used to emulate the ICT network and the communication between power grid simulator and the real-world inverter. Under normal operation, the inverters feed (surplus) PV power to the distribution grid. In case the voltage at the feeding point rises over a certain point as specified in the droop law, reactive power is consumed to counteract the voltage rise. This experiment represents a distribution grid use-case with low load and strong PV generation. Like real low voltage distribution grids, the testbed is dimensioned so the default droop law voltages do not rise more than 3% over a nominal value of 230 V.

5.1 Voltage Oscillation Attack

Experiments showed that a voltage oscillation attack can be triggered by an intruder by changing setpoints of the $Q(U)$ characteristic sent from the SLVGC. The $Q(U)$ curve of an inverter (Fig. 5A) describes its voltage support behaviour. It tells the inverter the deviation of the phase angle between voltage and current – in this case proportional to the current node voltage. Depending on the impedance of the PV's connection point, the voltage can be influenced by changing this phase angle and the reactive power.

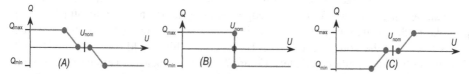

Fig. 5. Typical (A) and attacked $Q(U)$ characteristics (B, C). The high gain in (B) causes oscillations, the inverted curve (C) results in amplification of voltage variations.

An attacker could aim to increase the characteristic gain of the inverter (B in Fig. 5), to cause local oscillation of the inverter around voltage V_0. To achieve this in the testbed, an MITM attack is executed with a custom written code that can intercept and modify IEC 61850 messages to modify the gain settings. The effects of the reactive power oscillation and the grid voltage oscillation are depicted in Fig. 6. By implementing a RC locally at each PV, the oscillation attack can be prevented. Before applying the received $Q(U)$ droop law, it will be checked with Rule 1 and 2 of the RC (see Sect. 4.1). In case of the oscillation attack, the gain of the droop law approaches infinity and therefore it will trigger Rule 2, which checks the stability of the new droop law. When the Rule 2 is triggered the new droop law is rejected and the PV stays with its current droop law. Hence, the attack is automatically mitigated and no oscillations will occur (see dotted lines in Fig. 6). As the stability of a new droop law is judged based on local knowledge, less extreme gain settings which still result in oscillations can also be detected.

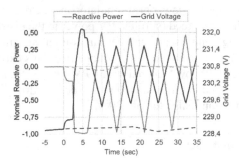

Fig. 6. Laboratory measured effects of the oscillating attack to the PHIL-connected inverter.

5.2 Over-Voltage Attack

The second attack scenario is caused by an MITM attacker who modifies the setpoints of the $Q(U)$ characteristic transmitted by the SLVGC controller. The attacked curve is depicted as (C) in Fig. 5. By inverting the reactive power curve in the inverters, a knowledgeable attacker could force any attacked inverters to revert their reactive power flow. This naturally leads to an omission of the voltage support and a further increase of an already high voltage. With knowledge of this system behaviour, an attacker could provoke such a situation in times of high PV infeed and thus lead the local voltage levels to exceed the voltage limits (e.g. EN 50160). This would cause the inverters to disconnect from the grid immediately. Figure 7 shows the measured effects of this attack in the laboratory PHIL experiment. At time 0 – when the attack happens – the already high grid voltage rises even further because of the inverse reactive power characteristic. The physical inverter as well as the simulated inverters are attacked and contribute to the voltage rise with a time shift of around two seconds due to interface delays. It can also be seen how the observed physical inverter reduces its reactive power support as the voltage rises. After reaching a level of 253 V, the physical inverter disconnects (or rather ramps down) after 1.2 s for safety reasons. This results in a sudden drop in voltage, which afterwards increases again due to the other attacked inverters.

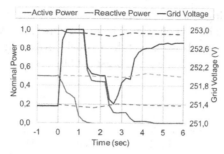

Fig. 7. Laboratory measured effects of the MITM attack to the PHIL-connected inverter. The attack happens at time 0.

The over-voltage attack has two critical consequences: it results in high grid voltages and a sudden loss of PV power. If many units are attacked, this can even have a strong impact on frequency stability. Depending on individual controller implementations of the PV units, it would also be possible to provoke large-scale active power oscillations. Using the interactions described in Table 1 (MITM "Manipulation") the IDS detects the manipulated data in the network and provides alerts to the RC at the real-world inverter (Fig. 4, bottom right). Upon receipt of alert information, the RC will use stricter rules. In this experiment that means it will no longer accept new commands received through the network as long as the MITM attack is active. Here, the combination and interaction of IDS and RC preserves the grid operability and performance even though the attack was successful due to vulnerabilities in the cyber domain. Figure 7 shows two different runs of the scenario. The solid lines show the previously described instabilities that occur when the attack is allowed to succeed. The dotted lines show continued normal operation, whereby the RC determines that it will ignore newly received setpoints based on alert information from the IDS.

6 Conclusion

Many new services are expected to emerge as the digitalization of energy infrastructure continues. It is essential that new services can be integrated without risking the resilient operation of the power system due to cyber vulnerabilities. As a result, there is a significant challenge to understand how cyber vulnerabilities might be used to compromise resilience, and to develop solutions to ensure stable operation when integrated IT systems are attacked. In this work, an intrusion resilience mechanism has been proposed towards enabling an automated response to cyber-attacks against a realistic distribution grid use-case. The use-case focuses on maintaining voltage stability in a distribution system that uses local control loops for remote configuration and monitoring to support local voltage control. The presented approach has been developed in a testbed comprising a distribution grid simulation, a communications network, and physical power system equipment. As shown in Sect. 5, the testbed is highly realistic and combines IP-based real-world communication configurations with a mixed real-world and simulated power distribution setup. Contributions are made beyond studies such as [3] which focus on understanding the potential physical implications of advanced targeted attacks, without investigating mitigation. Contributions are also made compared to IRS solutions such as [13], aimed only at classic IT infrastructure. Finally, a practical solution is realized beyond the comprehensive, yet theoretical, investigations in cyber response and resilience technologies for smart grids presented by [14] and [15].

References

1. Lei, H., Singh, C., Sprintson, A.: Reliability modeling and analysis of IEC 61850 based substation protection systems. IEEE Trans. Smart Grid **5**(5), 2194–2202 (2014)
2. Athay, T., Podmore, R., Virmani, S.: A practical method for the direct analysis of transient stability. IEEE Trans. Power Appar. Syst. **PAS-98**(2), 573–584 (1979)
3. Hahn, A., Ashok, A., Sridhar, S., Govindarasu, M.: Cyber-physical security testbeds: architecture, application, and evaluation for smart grid. IEEE Trans. Smart Grid **4**(2), 847–855 (2013)
4. Ten, C.W., Hong, J., Liu, C.C.: Anomaly detection for cybersecurity of the substations. IEEE Trans. Smart Grid **2**(4), 865–873 (2011)
5. Rieger, C.G., Gertman, D.I., McQueen, M.A.: Resilient control systems: next generation design research. In: Proceedings of 2nd Conference on Human System Interactions, pp. 632–636 (2009)
6. Urbina, D.I., et al.: Limiting the impact of stealthy attacks on industrial control systems. In: Proceedings of ACM SIGSAC Conference on Computer and Communications Security, 2016
7. Isozaki, Y.: Detection of cyber attacks against voltage control in distribution power grids with PVs. IEEE Trans. Smart Grid **7**(4), 1824–1835 (2016)
8. Teixeira, A., Paridari, K., Sandberg, H., Johansson, K.H.: Voltage control for interconnected microgrids under adversarial actions. In: Proceedings of IEEE 20th Conference on Emerging Technologies & Factory Automation (ETFA), Luxembourg, September 2015
9. Genge, B., Rusu, D.A., Haller, P.: A connection pattern-based approach to detect network traffic anomalies in critical infrastructures. In: Proceedings of the 7th European Workshop on System Security, April 2014
10. Yang, Y., Xu, H., Gao, L., Yuan, Y., McLaughlin, K., Sezer, S.: Multidimensional intrusion detection system for IEC 61850-based SCADA networks. IEEE Trans. Power Delivery **32**(2), 1068–1078 (2017)
11. Caselli, M., Zambon, E., Kargl, F.: Sequence-aware intrusion detection in industrial control systems. In: Proceedings of 1st ACM Workshop on Cyber-Physical System Security (2015)
12. Yoo, H., Shon, T.: Novel approach for detecting network anomalies for substation automation based on IEC 61850. Multimed. Tools Appl. **74**(1), 303–318 (2015)
13. Inayat, Z., Gani, A., Anuar, N.B., Khan, M.K., Anwar, S.: Intrusion response systems: foundations, design, and challenges. J. Net. Comput. App. **62**, 53–74 (2016)
14. He, H., Yan, J.: Cyber-physical attacks and defences in the smart grid: a survey. IET Cyber-Phys. Syst. Theory Appl. **1**(1), 13–27 (2016)
15. Qi, J., Hahn, A., Lu, X., Wang, J., Liu, C.: Cybersecurity for distributed energy resources and smart inverters. IET Cyber-Phys. Syst. Theory Appl. **1**(1), 28–39 (2016)
16. Li, X., Zhou, C., Tian, Y., Qin, Y.: A dynamic decision-making approach for intrusion response in industrial control systems. IEEE Trans. Ind. Inform. **15**(5), 2544–2554 (2019)
17. Mango, F.D., Liserre, M., Dell'Aquila, A.: Overview of anti-islanding algorithms for PV systems. Part II: active methods. In: Proceedings of 12th International Power Electronics and Motion Control Conference, pp. 1884–1889 (2006)
18. Andrén, F., Bletterie, B., Kadam, S., Kotsampopoulos, P., Bucher, C.: On the stability of local voltage control in distribution networks with a high penetration of inverter-based generation. IEEE Trans. Ind. Electron. **62**(4), 2519–2529 (2015)

19. Khalil, H.K.: Nonlinear Systems, 3rd edn. Prentice Hall, Upper Saddle River (2002)
20. Lauss, G., et al.: Smart grid research infrastructures in Austria: examples of available laboratories and their possibilities. In: Proceedings of 13th International Conference on Industrial Informatics (INDIN), pp. 1539–1545 (2015)
21. Einfalt, A., Lugmaier, A., Kupzog, F., Brunner, H.: Control strategies for smart low voltage grids - The project DG DemoNet -Smart LV Grid. In: Proceedings of CIRED Workshop (2012)

Mitigating Escalation of Cascading Effects of a Payment Disruption Across Other Critical Infrastructures: Lessons Learned in 15 Simulation-Games

Joeri van Laere[1]([✉]) [iD], Björn J. E. Johansson[2] [iD], Leif Olsson[3], and Peter Määttä[4]

[1] University of Skövde, Skövde, Sweden
joeri.van.laere@his.se
[2] Linköping University, Linköping, Sweden
[3] Mid Sweden University, Sundsvall, Sweden
[4] Combitech, Linköping, Sweden

Abstract. A disruption in one critical infrastructure can quickly lead to cascading effects in several other ones. Much research has been done to analyze dependencies between different critical infrastructures, but little is known about how to mitigate escalation and cascading effects across several critical infrastructures, i.e. how to develop collective critical infrastructure resilience. This research presents the results of 15 simulation-games where groups of 6 to 8 field experts from different sectors were challenged to collaboratively manage a disruption in the payment system that quickly affected food distribution, fuel distribution, transport, health care et cetera. Teams discussed possible strategies, which next were implemented in a computer simulation. Teams could influence the sequence of events on 4 decision points during a 10 day scenario, and play the same scenario several times to test alternative solutions. Each simulation-game session lasted a full day. Data analysis involved the recorded team discussions as well as computer simulation logs of the implemented decisions and their impacts. The results show how escalation and the severity of cascading effects largely depends on the quality of the early crisis response and not so much on the initial disruption. Also, it is shown how cross sectorial collaboration is required. Responses where groups focus too much on cascading effects in one area lead too poor overall performance for society at large. Groups tend to overbalance their mitigating strategies initially, until they arrive at a more balanced strategy that covers challenges in several different critical infrastructures from an integral perspective.

Keywords: Critical infrastructures · Resilience · Gaming-simulation · Cross-sectorial collaboration

1 Introduction

Resilience of interdependent infrastructures increasingly depends on collaborative responses from actors with diverse backgrounds that may not be familiar with cascade effects into areas beyond and outside the own organisation or sector. Our ongoing

S. Nadjm-Tehrani (Ed.): CRITIS 2019, LNCS 11777, pp. 110–121, 2020.
https://doi.org/10.1007/978-3-030-37670-3_9

research project aims to create insight in how critical infrastructure disruptions that create cascading effects in several other critical infrastructures can be collaboratively mitigated. The context of our study is disruptions in the payment system. A severe disruption of the payment system may cause that citizens experience problems to acquire food, fuel or medicine. In addition, transport companies may also be dependent on the payment system to get hold of fuel. When these immediate issues are not addressed or when the measures are not properly communicated, uncertainty may grow in society, which may create further escalation such as hoarding or an increased risk of safety and security problems. As the exact interplay between these cascading events is both uncertain and dynamic, affected actors such as food stores, petrol stations, pharmacies, transport companies, security companies, government and media may have a hard time to develop a well-aligned response.

A simulation-game has been developed to gain a deeper understanding of how cascading effects of a payment solution develop; to explore what mitigating actions can be identified as well as to learn how these mitigating actions interrelate and impact the escalation of the disruptions scenario as a whole. A particular challenge for societal actors is that their response might worsen escalation.

In earlier publications of our study, the focus has been on the development of the scenario (i.e. which cascading effects might occur) [1], what important design choices were identified when developing the simulation-game [2] and how they have been handled [3, 4]. This publication is the first paper where output of the simulation-games is presented regarding what kind of mitigating actions have been identified and how their combined impact influences the escalation scenario.

Innovative collaborative responses have been identified in the playing sessions that might be valuable in a real disruption. Challenges in the cross-sectorial response involve arranging availability of payment options, securing good flows, performing crisis communication and maintaining safety and security.

The outline of the paper is as follows. After presenting related research on cascading effects across different critical infrastructures and studying critical infrastructure resilience with simulation games (Sect. 2), our research design is presented (Sect. 3). The 4th section contains the research results. Finally a discussion (Sect. 5) and conclusion (Sect. 6) complete the paper.

2 Background

2.1 Cascading Effects of Critical Infrastructure Disruptions

Societies rely on well-functioning critical infrastructures such as Energy, Information and Communication Technology, Water Supply, Food and Agriculture, Healthcare, Financial Systems, Transportation Systems, Public Order and Safety, Chemical Industry, Nuclear Industry, Commerce, Critical Manufacturing, and so on [5]. When one or more critical infrastructures break down or provide only limited service, large numbers of citizens, companies or government agencies can be severely affected [6, 7]. Breakdowns can be caused by internal factors (human or technical failure), external factors (nature catastrophes, terror attacks) or by failures of other infrastructures as there are many dependencies between critical infrastructures [7]. Energy and Information Technology or Telecommunications are well-known event-originating infrastructures that generate cascading effects in many other infrastructures, as has been shown in different types of analyses [7, 8]. In times of increasing digitalisation and an ever increasing development towards a digitally interconnected society, security experts argue for more awareness for digital vulnerabilities, more attention for cyber security and a need to educate professionals and citizens on these matters [9].

Resilience of interdependent infrastructures increasingly depends on collaborative responses from actors with diverse backgrounds that may not be familiar with cascade effects into areas beyond and outside their own organisation or sector [10]. In [6] and [7] it is argued that there is limited empirical evidence of cascading effects across many infrastructures, which makes it hard to foresee which interactions may occur across sectors. Risk analysis, business continuity management and crisis management training are often performed within the context of a single organisation or sector and are seldom addressing the holistic analysis of multiple infrastructures [7].

More research is needed to understand collective resilience in the context of critical infrastructure management. In this study, a contribution is made by focusing on one application area, i.e. how payment disruptions impact other critical infrastructures. Despite the long term efforts of public and private actors in the financial sector in Sweden to identify, analyse and understand risks and to develop routines for preventing and mitigating serious disruptions in the payment system in Sweden, there is still a lack of insight into how the proposed action plans exactly need to be executed and how numerous other actors in society (e.g. citizens, food stores, gas stations, voluntary organizations, governmental agencies and so on) will act in case of a temporary or complete breakdown of the payment system [1].

2.2 Exploring Collective Critical Infrastructure Resilience in Simulation-Games

Gaming-simulation is defined as a specific form of simulation. Simulation in general aims at designing a model of a system in a complex problem area in other to be able to experiment with the model. Deeper insight in the behavior of the system is created by evaluating various operating strategies against each other in one ore multiple scenarios. Gaming-simulation differs from other forms of simulation in that it incorporates roles to be played by participants and game administrators, implying that people and their (goal-directed) interactions become part of the simulation [11]. Gaming-simulation is especially relevant when the "*how and why*" of the interaction processes between the participants are of interest and when these interactions cannot easily be incorporated in computer simulation models. In addition, it creates a deeper learning opportunity, as simulation-game participants literally are active participants in the simulation, rather than passive observers of a computer simulation.

In our case, the reason to choose for simulation-gaming is to combine the benefits of role-playing (open system analysis) and computer simulation (closed system analysis). A role-playing game (without the computer simulation) would not be able to address the uncertain, complex and dynamic interaction between mitigating actions and escalations of cascading effects. On the other hand, a computer simulation (without active participation of societal actors) would require a comprehensive insight in all actions, effects and their interrelations, whereas a gaming-simulation can incorporate the creativity and knowledgeability of the playing experts who can come up with innovative out of the box solutions to mitigate the situations occurring in the computer simulation model.

There exist several examples where simulation-gaming has been applied to study dependencies between critical infrastructures or the management of critical infrastructures [12–14] indicating that this is a viable strategy to study critical infrastructure dynamics and resilience. As discussed in [2] our simulation-game design differs considerably from these other approaches and can thus create new insights on how to study the mitigation of cascading effects of critical infrastructure disruptions that escalate across multiple critical infrastructures.

3 Research Design

3.1 Research Method

Our research design is based on an inductive research strategy and a qualitative research method. A clear theory on how the many involved actors collaboratively could manage disruptions that create cascading effects across multiple critical infrastructures is lacking. As such, there is a need for theory building rather than theory testing, which leads us to an inductive research strategy [15]. From an interpretative perspective, we are interested in exploring the many different interpretations of actors involved regarding what challenges disruptions can pose and how they could be handled collaboratively across the affected infrastructures. A simulation-game can be a safe environment where participating actors can experiment with different action alternatives, and demonstrate the core values they hold through their choice and motivation of resilience strategies.

3.2 The Payment Disruption Simulation-Game

The purpose of the game is to learn about consequences and cascading effects a payment disruption and to explore the pros and cons of different sets of mitigating actions. Gameplay involves a group of 6 to 8 representatives from different societal sectors. They play as a team and have universal control over all actors in a fictive society. The objective for the team playing is to mitigate the consequences of a 10-day payment disruption in the best possible way.

The fictive society modeled in the computer simulation represents a typical Swedish region with a large city, some smaller cities and villages on the countryside and is created with Anylogic modeling software. The society contains 77 food stores, 59 petrol stations and 440.000 citizens. The team aims to influence performance on about 35 resilience indicators. Players can come up with any imaginable action that will be implemented instantly (open system design). The first version of the game included 15 different action alternatives. As each playing team has generated new ways to address the scenario, currently about 60 different action alternatives are included. When players suggest an action that is not implemented in the computer simulation, the behavior or impact of that actions is mimicked instantly by influencing computer simulation model variables during runtime.

The scenario starts on Day 1 with the event that card payment disappears as a payment option. The expectation is that the disruption only will take some hours. On Day 2 it is revealed that the disruption cannot be fixed easily and will last several days (not clear how many). The team goes through the scenario and can influence the sequence of events during 4 decision points (day 1, 2, 4 and 6). At each decision point the playing team gets feedback on the situation and the effect of their previous actions. Next they discuss for 20–30 min and implement new actions. The team plays the scenario twice and can as such fine-tune their set of actions or test a completely new approach in the second playing session.

A more detailed discussion of the game design is presented in [3] and [4].

3.3 Data Collection and Data Analysis

The game has been played on15 occasions. Groups playing the game consisted of 4 to 8 professionals representing various sectors of society. Data has been gathered by recording the discussions of the players while playing, by logging their implemented actions (and the effects of their actions in the computers simulation), by 2 observers taking notes, by questionnaires the players filled in, and by recording the oral debriefing.

Data analysis consisted of a qualitative analysis, where themes appeared based on relevance, rather than on frequency. As the scenario in each game sessions is dynamic, i.e. totally depending on the actions that the group who plays chooses, not all challenges have appeared in all game sessions, or they have appeared at different moments. A challenge that only appeared in one game session, but generated very interesting reasoning, can be equally valuable as sequences of events and accompanied reasoning that have been repeated in multiple sessions.

4 Results of the 15 Simulation-Game Sessions

This chapter summarizes the main challenges that the participating groups have been struggling with. Teams pondered about what sets of actions could be effective to arrange for alternative payment alternatives (Sect. 4.1), to perform crisis communication (Sect. 4.2), to secure goods flows (Sect. 4.3) and to warrant safety and security (Sect. 4.4). The final subsection of the results chapter elaborates on tackling the interdependencies between these four areas of attention (Sect. 4.5).

Whereas these four areas of attention were consciously incorporated in the game design, following a thorough scenario validation based on expert opinions from around 37 workshop participants and 6 interviewees combined with 33 analyzed reports [1], this game design consisted primarily of 'effects of the initial disruption' and 'cascading effects when not addressing the initial disruption'. During playing the 15 simulation-game sessions mitigating actions (and their envisioned impact) where generated by the players. They could not choose from a list of available actions, but started suggesting actions given the situation they encountered in the fictive society. As a result, all actions discussed below (and their combined application) are output of the gaming simulation sessions played.

4.1 Challenges with Regard to Arranging Alternative Payment Alternatives

As the scenario starts with the breakdown of card payment transactions, a first point of attention for participants is logically to open up for alternative payment options in different types of shops. When the scenario develops, the participants argue and reason about how to realize this practically and learn (from each other and from the simulation outputs) about limits and drawbacks of different payment options. For instance, too heavily relying on cash payments might create a quick emptying of ATMs, even when withdrawal amounts are limited or when the capacity of collecting and distributing cash is increased. As card payments take about 90% of the payment flow in Sweden today, cash collection and distribution can be increased to a certain extent, but not fully cover the lost capacity of card payments. Moreover, a heavy use of cash in society creates security challenges like potential robberies (see Sect. 4.4) as large amounts of cash are concentrated at stores or at civilians. A heavy use of mobile payment solutions are initially a promising solution, although they are not available for all people in society. Again, capacity is a problem, and too heavy relying in this option results in a technical breakdown due to overload of the services somewhere in the chain of service providers involved. Next, the final major payment option, paying by invoice, raises after a while the question how to handle liquidity problems at stores and the question who will take the credit risk if not all claims are met. Game participants ponder whether the credit risk can be taken by individual shops, by factoring companies or by central government.

A recurring theme in the discussions is that not all payment options are viable for all shops/companies and all citizens. Participants argue that it will be hard for companies that not already have certain payment options installed to install them when crisis hits. First it can be hard to make arrangements with banks or other financial institutions to launch new services when everybody is contacting them, and next it can be hard to create workable routines on the fly. Civilians are faced with similar challenges, not all of them can collect cash before ATMs are empty, not all of them have mobile payment services and not all of them are eligible to buy goods by invoice.

Even those shops, who have alternative payment options 'lying on the shelf' that can be activated rather instantly, are faced with unfamiliar routines that may cause delays at pay desks, irritation amongst customers facing waiting times or denied transactions. This will create a heavier burden on shop employees the longer the disruption lasts.

A final theme that appears in different forms are all kind of juridical issues. While coping with the payment disruption scenario companies, banks and local government representatives give numerous examples of small and more severe legislative issues that will be ignored by themselves of their customers in order to be able to sell as usual. For instance, more capacity is needed to transport and handle cash and staff might be involved that is not really accredited to handle cash. Mobile payments may be accepted on private accounts rather than the company account if the company does not have an existing account. The latter means that the transaction is not registered according to the cash register law. Although these are hypothetical behaviors, professionals playing the game are quite convinced that such behaviors will arise on a small or larger scale. They argue that clarity from governmental institutions is required considering which deviations will be tolerated.

4.2 Challenges with Regard to Performing Crisis Communication

In close connection to arranging alternative payment options, almost all groups argue from the start and throughout the scenario that intensive communication is required. This can involve recommendations to postpone less urgent consumption, information about what payment alternatives are available at different points of sale, or other information about either desired behavior or taken measures. Implementing communicative actions in the game leads to changes in behavior of civilians and consumers in the fictive society that is simulated. Different communicative actions have different impacts on multiple variables (arrivals, hoarding, stealing) & and the communication may be more or less effective. Finally communication might have a certain short time impact and a rather different long term impact. For instance, when informing about the disruption early on this will decrease arrivals of consumers initially, but lead to a rather big increase on the 3rd or 4th day when certain groups start to run out of products they need.

Participants debate rather intensely about the duality of communication. On one hand it can mitigate escalation of the disruption (if people trust public agencies and private companies and follow their instructions). On the other hand the same communication might make things worse: rather than calming down the system, it might evoke panic and/or hoarding if the public interprets that bigger threats are around the corner and that they need to get hold of things before a total breakdown of the consumption system occurs.

A complicating factor is that many points of sale may reason in different ways and might go out with contradicting recommendations. When society at large does not manage to coordinate communications, instructions might be perceived as chaotic, leading to lower trust and more panic. Another way out suggested by participating players is to actually argue for diversity as a resilient strategy, i.e. emphasizing in communication that a rich diversity of solutions is the best strategy (rather than one major alternative which becomes the next Achilles heel).

4.3 Challenges with Regard to Securing Goods Flows

Depending on the type of payment options that will be activated and the type of communication that will be used to promote certain consumer behavior, different points of sale can be confronted with different types of problems. One potential consequence may be a dramatic drop in sales with short term economic consequences and also a risk to have to throw away perishable products that are not sold. On the other hand, shops can also be confronted with a dramatic increase in visits, queuing, stealing and hoarding when the degree of panic and chaos increases in society. Increased visits and hoarding will not result in completely empty shops, but rather empty shelfs for certain types of products, whereas other types of products are not sold at all. Dramatic fluctuations in demand are challenging for today's 'just in time- logistics' that heavily relies on predictable patterns to be able to deliver goods with minimal resources and a slimmed fleet. Irregularities in demand and supply are not only dependent on available payment options and the effects of communication, but also on how the challenges of fuel supply are mastered. Other points of sale can have fantastic solutions in place, but deliveries or consumption might be affected when either customers, or transport companies that supply goods. or both, cannot pay for fuel.

4.4 Challenges with Regard to Safety and Security

When the disruption lasts longer and longer, more and more customers get disappointed, lose faith and get annoyed. As a result, issues like hoarding, threatening behavior towards shop employees and shop lifting may become more and more common. Teams discuss how addressing such issues of safety and security can be managed in different ways. One way is to keep up a positive atmosphere, by offering free coffee or treats. Another way is to increase the presence of employees and guards. Especially when teams start discussing introducing limits to hoarding (i.e. a maximum amount of certain groceries or fuel per customer) they realize that extra personnel is needed to actually be able to enforce such limits. As discussed earlier, a higher circulation of cash requires also measures to limit the chances of robberies.

4.5 Relations Between the Earlier Discussed Sets of Challenges

From the preceding discussions it is evident that there are many interactions between introducing alternative payment options, impact on goods flows, necessity of communication and managing safety/security. When more payment options break down, or when more goods are out of stock (due to hoarding or delivery problems), people get less attentive and less responsive to official communication instructions, and safety and security challenges become larger. The other way around when communication or security measures fail early on, and are interpreted as a sign of government and commerce losing control, consumers might overload one payment option, worsen the logistics of goods distribution by hoarding some products and not buying others, and might create hostile situations in shopping areas. As many actors already are involved in each of the four discussed areas of attention, coordination challenges become immense when even interdependencies across those four areas need to be addressed.

5 Discussion

Whereas the current analysis is based on a qualitative analysis of the performed game sessions thus far, and does not yet incorporate an analysis of the quantitative performance of different teams in the computer simulation model, some interesting observations have been recurrently discussed in the simulation-game evaluations when participating teams and game facilitators reflect on the lessons learned. What is judged as good performance, bad performance, interesting or challenging in the game session experiences is based on common understanding of players and game facilitators.

5.1 The Need for a Cross-Sectorial Coordination at Multiple Levels

Our game sessions confirm the well-known insight that a coordinated cross-sectorial response is needed, because a disruption of one critical infrastructure quickly may affect other critical infrastructures, and because mitigating actions of one actor/sector may influence the sequences of events in other sectors. This sounds self-evident, but from the reasoning in the game sessions, some challenges come forward on a more detailed level.

First, game participants acknowledge that they on a general level know that dependencies exist between their sector and other sectors, but while playing have become more and more aware how tight and critical these dependencies are when disruptions start to reproduce. The trickiest challenge which arises from this first insight is how to accomplish cross-sectorial collaboration in practice. How can many sectors that not necessarily communicate in a big forum on a day to day basis, suddenly gather and tackle strategic and operational assignments on a local, regional, national and international level? Clearly, it is unrealistic to think that all kind of workgroups first need to sit together before any action can be undertaken. That would lead to an all too passive response (see also Sect. 5.2). Instead, actors in any sector and at any level in society need to be able to instantly act independently – and simultaneously start to coordinate bilateral and in larger work groups. When acting instantaneously individually, actors need to be aware of their role in the larger system, and what presumable responses are of other actors and sectors, i.e. collaboratively creating a well-integrated response based on individual holistic understanding. The same holistic understanding is needed to initiate relevant bilateral contacts and cross-sectorial work groups. Note that the kind of actions and the kind of cross sectorial collaboration can differ from disruption to disruption which implies that this cannot be a fixed organization, but needs to be a flexible organism. A final challenge observed frequently is that actors initially may be passive as they have the expectation that *"there must be some national actor that will fix this major disruption"*. Our game design was prepared for this phenomenon. As the players were responsible for all actors in society they had to name which actor needed to do what, or argue for that not any actor should act. Still, it appeared that many actors have large expectations on resources outside their organization and learn (after others have answered that their resources are limited) that they need to act themselves rather than waiting for others coming to solve their problems.

5.2 The Need for a Fast and Determined Response, But Not Too Fast

A typical course of events during a game session is that the playing group in the first game round has a relatively passive response (and are surprised by some unexpected cascading effects they did not addressed), whether they in the next round often move many of their actions to an earlier point in time to timely address issues that will happen later. Some groups overcompensate and end up with a response that is too fierce and too early, which then becomes counterproductive. Instead of being interpreted as a fast and adequate crisis response, the public in the fictive society sees the early forceful actions as a sign that societal actors are panicking and have lost control. Rather than listening to governmental instructions to limit consumption, the 'too early' response evokes a bank run and hoarding of food, fuel and medicine.

In evaluative discussions, players emphasize that communication becomes a challenging balancing act. What actually is too early, too slow, too passive or too forceful is largely situation dependent. Recommendations for practitioners cannot be summarized as *"act as follows on day 2 at 15.15 ..."*, but rather on a more general level like *"be aware that a crisis response can be activated too late and too early and monitor therefore thoroughly signals that would indicate a too early or too slow response"*.

5.3 The Need for a Different Type of Exercises Illuminating System Dynamics

Many participants in the simulation-games were surprised or even initially reluctant to the fact that they would not play "*themselves*" or "*their own organization*". Several of them readdressed this in the evaluative debriefing discussions. It is quite common in the simulation gaming field to let professionals change perspectives. The pedagogical idea of letting them play their adversary is to get a deeper understanding of the larger system, i.e. subordinates and managers could learn how their respective jobs are not as easy as may be assumed by an outsider. In negotiation games, for instance considering rural planning of a limited geographical areas where many stakeholders want to achieve their goals, switching stakeholder roles (i.e. let the industry play the nature protection role and vice versa) can result in either innovative win-win solutions or less extreme standpoints. The common idea is to arrive at a more holistic understanding of the problem at hand and the role and position of yourself in it. The fact that crisis management professionals in our games were insisting so much on playing their own role – rather than adopting a holistic perspective, might indicate that their training culture is rather conservative. Consequently, it would be recommendable to initiate a discussion amongst practitioners whether a larger variety of training forms with different goals are needed. Given the challenges of critical infrastructure resilience – more education forms aiming at understanding overall system dynamics are needed.

In a similar way, participants repeatedly commented that they desired to be put under more time pressure: "*It is a crisis training, but I did not feel that way; we should be put under more pressure and receive more demanding time constraints*". Again, the game design team observed that they consciously have created a game design where participants have plenty of time to discuss. The aim of the game is too collaboratively explore consequences and potential mitigating actions in depth. A risk of putting the participants under time pressure is that they start guessing – rather that carefully arguing for their choices. The learning gains of the game are in the collaborative discussions (why does this happen?), rather than in game figures (if we do action A, variable q goes down and r goes up). For after all, in the next disruption action A might cause variable q to go up and r to go down, and the challenge is to understand why this happens rather than just remembering what happens. The assumption that you need to be put under pressure to be able to learn about crisis management, might indicate a rather narrow learning culture. Apart from learning to act under stress, many other qualities can be developed which are relevant for crisis management professionals. For critical infrastructure resilience, understanding complex system dynamics is such a necessary quality!

6   Conclusion

More research is needed on **how to manage** disruptions that are reproduced across many other infrastructures. Much current (equally relevant) research focuses on understanding dependencies between existing infrastructures, and on how disruptions spread. The important next question is how mitigating actions influence cascading effects of an ongoing disruption, and to what extent these actions evoke new disruptions. Simulation-games are one method that incorporates both quantitative decision modelling as well as qualitative analysis of experts discussing what actions to implement and why.

Results from our 15 game sessions have both generated overall insights considering what needs to be addressed in a crisis response mitigating a disruption in the payment system, and concrete examples on possible strategies. One challenge in such a crisis response is the amount of actors that need to coordinate their actions, and how they quickly can adapt their response strategies to one and another. As that will be hard to realize on the fly, individual actors need to build up holistic system dynamic understanding of all infrastructure systems on beforehand. The latter requires new education and training forms that illuminate holistic system understanding rather than training individual competencies.

Acknowledgments. This research was supported by Grant 2016-3046 of the Swedish Civil Contingencies Agency.

References

1. van Laere, J., et al.: Challenges for critical infrastructure resilience: cascading effects of payment system disruptions. In: Proceedings of the 14th International Conference on Information Systems for Crisis Response and Management, (ISCRAM 2017), Albi, France, 21–24 May 2017, pp. 281–292 (2017)
2. van Laere, J., Ibrahim, O., Larsson, A., Olsson, L., Johansson, B., Gustavsson, P.: Analyzing the implications of design choices in existing simulation-games for critical infrastructure resilience. In: Lukosch, H.K., Bekebrede, G., Kortmann, R. (eds.) ISAGA 2017. LNCS, vol. 10825, pp. 15–23. Springer, Cham (2018). https://doi.org/10.1007/978-3-319-91902-7_2
3. van Laere, J., Berggren, P., Ibrahim, O., Larsson, A., Kallin, S.: A simulation-game to explore collective critical infrastructure resilience. In: Haugen, S., Barros, A., van Gulijk, C., Kongsvik, T., Vinnem, J. (eds.) Safety and Reliability – Safe Societies in a Changing World: Proceedings of ESREL 2018, Trondheim, Norway, 17–21 June 2018, pp. 1305–1312. CRC Press, London (2018)
4. van Laere, J., Ibrahim, O., Larsson, A., Berggren, P., Davis, J.: Iterative game design to develop critical infrastructure resilience. In: Proceedings of the International Simulation and Gaming Association's Conference (ISAGA 2019), Warsaw, Poland, 26–30 August 2019
5. Alcaraz, C., Zeadally, S.: Critical infrastructure protection: requirements and challenges for the 21st century. Int. J. Crit. Infrastruct. Prot. **8**, 53–66 (2016)
6. Boin, A., McConnell, A.: Preparing for critical infrastructure breakdowns: the limits of crisis management and the need of resilience. J. Contingencies Crisis Manag. **15**(1), 50–59 (2007)
7. Van Eeten, M., Nieuwenhuis, A., Luijf, E., Klaver, M., Cruz, E.: The state and the threat of cascading failure across critical infrastructures: the implications of empirical evidence from media incident reports. Public Adm. **89**, 381–400 (2011)
8. Laugé, A., Hernantes, J., Sarriegi, J.M.: The role of critical infrastructures' interdependencies on the impacts caused by natural disasters. In: Luiijf, E., Hartel, P. (eds.) CRITIS 2013. LNCS, vol. 8328, pp. 50–61. Springer, Cham (2013). https://doi.org/10.1007/978-3-319-03964-0_5
9. Hagen, J.M.: Cyber security – the Norwegian way. Int. J. Crit. Infrastruct. Prot. **14**, 41–42 (2016)
10. Ansell, C., Boin, A., Keller, A.: Managing transboundary crises: identifying the building blocks of an effective response system. J. Contingencies Crisis Manag. **18**, 195–207 (2010)
11. van Laere, J., de Vreede, G.J., Sol, H.G.: A social simulation game to explore future coordination in knowledge networks at the Amsterdam Police Force. J. Prod. Plan. Control **17**(6), 558–568 (2006)

12. Grogan, P.T., de Weck, O.L.: Collaborative design in the sustainable infrastructure planning game. In: Proceedings of the Annual Simulation Symposium (ANSS), Spring Simulation Conference (SpringSim16), Pasadena, CA, USA (2016)

13. Rome, E., Doll, T., Rilling, S., Sojeva, B., Voß, N., Xie, J.: The use of what-if analysis to improve the management of crisis situations. In: Setola, R., Rosato, V., Kyriakides, E., Rome, E. (eds.) Managing the Complexity of Critical Infrastructures. SSDC, vol. 90, pp. 233–277. Springer, Cham (2016). https://doi.org/10.1007/978-3-319-51043-9_10

14. Kurapati, S., Lukosch, H., Verbraeck, A., Brazier, F.M.T.: Improving resilience in intermodal transport operations in seaports: a gaming approach. EURO J. Decis. Process. **3**, 375–396 (2015)

15. Eisenhardt, K.M., Graebner, M.E.: Theory building from cases: opportunities and challenges. Acad. Manag. J. **50**(1), 25–32 (2007)

Using Datasets from Industrial Control Systems for Cyber Security Research and Education

Qin Lin[1], Sicco Verwer[1], Robert Kooij[1,2(✉)], and Aditya Mathur[2,3]

[1] Faculty of Electrical Engineering, Mathematics and Computer Science, Delft University of Technology, Delft, The Netherlands
{q.lin,s.e.verwer}@tudelft.nl
[2] iTrust Centre for Research in Cyber Security, Singapore University of Technology and Design, Tampines, Singapore
{robert_kooij,aditya_mathur}@sutd.edu.sg
[3] Computer Science, Purdue University, West Lafayette, USA

Abstract. The availability of high-quality benchmark datasets is an important prerequisite for research and education in the cyber security domain. Datasets from realistic systems offer a platform for researchers to develop and test novel models and algorithms. Such datasets also offer students opportunities for active and project-centric learning. In this paper, we describe six publicly available datasets from the domain of Industrial Control Systems (ICS). Five of these datasets are obtained through experiments conducted in the context of operational ICS while the sixth is obtained from a widely used simulation tool, namely EPANET, for large scale water distribution networks. This paper presents two studies on the use of the datasets. The first study uses the dataset from a live water treatment plant. This study leads to a novel and explainable anomaly detection method based upon Timed Automata and Bayesian Networks. The study conducted in the context of education made use of the water distribution network dataset in a graduate course on cyber data analytics. Through an assignment, students explored the effectiveness of various methods for anomaly detection. Research outcomes and the success of the course indicate an appreciation in the research community and positive learning experience in education.

Keywords: Cyber security · Research and education · Cyber-physical systems · Industrial Control Systems · Cyber Data Analytics · Anomaly detection

1 Introduction

A broad section of cyber security experts from the government, industry and the academia tend to agree that cybercrime has long evolved from an emerging threat to one that is urgent and critical. This is reflected in the estimates of economic losses due to cybercrime. Two estimates of the global annual cost of cybercrime

S. Nadjm-Tehrani (Ed.): CRITIS 2019, LNCS 11777, pp. 122–133, 2020.
https://doi.org/10.1007/978-3-030-37670-3_10

by Symantec [29] and McAfee [16] in 2017 range from $172B to $600B, respectively. In another study [2], set up as a scientific framework for computing the economic cost of cybercrime, the estimated cost was $225B in 2012.

Cyber threats have now infiltrated the domain of cyber-physical systems (CPS) [11,33]. Such systems consist of an Industrial Control System (ICS) that monitors and controls the behavior of the underlying physical process in a CPS through interactions with a network of sensors and actuators. The focus of this work is on distributed ICS found specifically in critical infrastructure such as electrical power grids, water treatment and distribution systems, and transportation systems.

Most countries have responded to the increasing cyber threats by establishing a National Cyber Security Strategy (NCSS). We refer to [18] for a comparison between 19 NCSSs. Typically, such strategies include strengthening the resilience of the Critical Information Infrastructure, the development of a vibrant cyber security ecosystem comprising a skilled workforce, technologically-advanced companies, and strong research collaborations. As cyber threats are borderless, such strategies also include efforts to forge strong international partnerships at a continental or even global level (see for instance [5,7,8]) An important pillar of a cyber security strategy is the ramping up of efforts on research and education. For instance, Singapore's National Research Foundation launched a $130 million, 5-year programme in 2014, with the aim to develop R&D expertise and capabilities in cyber security [25].

In recent years cyber security solutions have started to deploy big data analytics to correlate security events across multiple data sources, providing, amongst others, early detection of suspicious activities. According to a recent survey [3], 90% of those working in cyber security are certain that in a few years Cyber Data Analytics will play a critical role in their field.

Methods employed in the field of Cyber Data Analytics are predominantly based on Machine Learning (ML). Significant amounts of data is needed to train the ML models. While one could generate such data synthetically through simulations, data generated from operational plants is likely to offer more realistic scenarios and challenges to algorithms for training ML models. However, concerned about the safety and privacy of their plants and customers, plant owners are often reluctant to share their data. Though a number of CPS testbeds have been created, e.g., [10,20], the majority of these contain simulated and emulated components. In addition, according to [1], none of the available testbeds openly share data for research and education.

To support research and education in the design of secure CPS, iTrust, a Centre for Research in Cyber Security [13], which belogs to the Singapore University of Technology and Design (SUTD), designed and built three testbeds, that are functional replicas of their larger counterparts. These testbeds are Secure Water Treatment (SWaT), Water Distribution (WADI), and Electric Power Intelligent Control (EPIC). Although the testbeds are scaled down replicas, they contain the essential elements of fully operational critical infrastructure that support cities. The data generated at these testbeds is available [14] for use in research and education.

A recent survey summarized several public datasets from the ICS domain, that can be used for cyber security research [4]. Morris describes datasets with data collected from power systems, gas pipelines, water storage systems and energy management systems [24]. The majority of the Morris datasets [21–23], along with others such as [6,15], contain only network traffic data. The most related data is contained in the Morris-1 dataset [27]; it has been used to apply machine learning to anomaly detection at the power system's process level. We have not found any evidence that the datasets described above, have been downloaded at a large scale, been applied in research competitions or have been used for educational purposes, as is the case for the iTrust datasets.

The aim of this paper is to showcase how the availability of data from live ICS, as well as from realistic simulations, contributes to research and education in the field of cyber security. Towards this end we describe how the dataset from SWaT, a live water treatment plant, has been used to construct an innovative anomaly detection method. In addition we show how simulated data from an international competition around a fictional C-Town water distribution system, has been used effectively in cyber security education.

Contributions: (a) A summary of the impact of six publicly available datasets from operational ICS in both research and education. (b) A case study to understand the impact of using data from ICS for constructing a machine learning model for anomaly detection. (c) A case study to understand the impact of using data from ICS on the learning outcomes in a cyber data analytics class.

Organization: The remainder of this work is organized as follows. Realistic datasets available for education and research are described in Sect. 2. Two datasets, namely the SWaT and the BATADAL datasets, are described in detail in this section. A case study about the use of ICS datasets for research is shown in Sect. 3. Section 4 illuminates our datasets' education value by showcasing the use of the BATADAL dataset in a cyber data analytics course taught at Delft University of Technology. Our conclusions are reported in Sect. 5.

2   Description of Datasets

2.1   Overview

The testbeds hosted at iTrust are used for research, experimentation and training, aimed at the design of secure critical infrastructure. As a contribution to the on-going effort to improve the security of legacy and new critical infrastructure, iTrust generates a large amount of data from the testbeds. The data so generated is made available to researchers across the world[1]. In this section we briefly discuss the six datasets that are currently made available by iTrust, and which can be downloaded upon request. Of these, two datasets, namely SWaT [19] (Secure Water Treatment) and BATADAL (BATtle of Attack Detection Algorithms) [31], were used to showcase the use of real-life data for research and education in cyber security.

---

[1] https://itrust.sutd.edu.sg/research/dataset/.

Secure Water Treatment (SWaT) Dataset. The data collected from the testbed consists of 11 days of continuous operation. Seven days' worth of data was collected under normal operation while 4 days' worth of data was collected while the testbed was under attack. During the data collection, all network traffic, sensor and actuator data were stored in the historian.

S317 Dataset. An event named SUTD Security Showdown (S3) has been organized consecutively for two years since 2016. S3 has enabled researchers and practitioners to assess the effectiveness of methods and products aimed at detecting cyber attacks launched in real-time on SWaT. During S3, independent attack teams design and launch attacks on SWaT while defence teams protect the plant passively and raise alarms upon attack detection, but are refrained from blocking the attacks. Attack teams are scored according to how successful they are in performing attacks based on specific intents while the defence teams are scored based on the effectiveness of their methods to detect the attacks.

WADI Dataset. Similar to the SWaT dataset, the data collected from the Water Distribution testbed consists of 16 days of continuous operation, of which 14 days' worth of data was collected under normal operation and 2 days with attack scenarios. During data collection, all network traffic, sensor and actuator data were collected.

EPIC Dataset. The data collected from the EPIC testbed consists of 8 scenarios under normal operation, where for each scenario, the facility is running for about 30 min. Sensor and actuator data were collected and recorded in an Excel spreadsheet, while network traffic was saved in "pcap" files.

Blaq_0 Dataset. Blaq_0 Hackathon was first organized in January 2018 for SUTD undergraduate students. Independent attack teams design and launch attacks on the EPIC testbed. Attack teams were scored according to how successful they were in performing attacks based on specific intents.

BATADAL Dataset. This dataset is not based on real-life data though is considered realistic as it was constructed using the de facto standard simulation tool for water distribution system modeling, namely the open source software package EPANET [28]. This dataset was constructed for the BATtle of Attack Detection Algorithms (BATADAL), a competition to objectively compare the performance of algorithms for the detection of cyber attacks on water distribution systems [31].

The datasets became available in 2016. As of August 30, 2019, a total of 450 download requests were received and processed. The requests originated from 52 countries, 88% of the requests originated from universities and research institutes. The remaining 12% came from industry. Given the distribution in Table 1,

SWaT dataset is the most requested. Note that some requests were for downloading multiple datasets and hence the sum of entries in the downloads column in Table 1 is more than 450.

Table 1. Downloads of iTrust datasets

Dataset	Number of downloads
SWaT	412
S317	165
WADI	178
EPIC	147
Blaq_0	81
BATADAL	95

2.2 SWaT Testbed and the Dataset

SWaT is a scaled down water treatment plant with a small footprint that produces 5 gallons/minute of doubly filtered water. The SWaT dataset was collected over 11 days of continuous operation. The first 7 days of data was collected under normal operation (without any attacks) while the remaining 4 days of data were collected with 36 designed attack scenarios. All network traffic and physical data (sensor and actuator) were collected. We focus on the detection of attacks through the analysis of physical data, hence the network traffic data is ignored. The physical data was recorded from 22/12/2015 4:00:00 PM to 2/1/2016 2:59:59 PM. The dataset contains a total of 53 columns: 1 for *timestamp*, 1 for *label* ("Attack" and "Normal"), and the remaining 51 are numeric values showing recorded data from 51 sensors and actuators. The sensors and actuators were sampled every second. The description of all 36 attack scenarios can be found on the iTrust website[2].

2.3 BATADAL Event and the Dataset

Recently Taormina et al. [30] have enhanced EPANET with a Matlab® toolbox, which enables the user to design cyber-physical attacks (CPAs) and then assess their impact on the hydraulic behavior of water distribution systems. This toolbox is dubbed epanetCPA. Using data generated with epanetCPA, Taormina et al. [31] organized the BATtle of Attack Detection ALgorithms (BATADAL). BATADAL makes use of the fictional C-Town water distribution network, first introduced for the Battle of the Water Calibration Networks by Ostfeld et al. [26]. C-Town is based on a real-world medium-sized network which contains 388 nodes, 429 pipes, 7 tanks, 11 pumps, and one actionable valve. The BATADAL

---

[2] https://itrust.sutd.edu.sg/dataset/.

dataset consists of three subsets. The first set contains six months of data, whose characteristics (no attacks) can be used to study the normal system operations and is labeled accordingly. The second set consists of three months of data. This dataset contains three attacks, leading to anomalous low levels in one tank, high levels in another tank and overflow in the same tank. In this set, all data are also labeled. The third set consists of only unlabeled data, while the system was running both under normal operations and during attack.

3   Case Study: Using SWaT Data to Construct a Machine Learning Model for Anomaly Detection

One of the drawbacks of general machine learning approaches is that the usage of high-dimensional data leads to opaque models. In this section, we discuss TABOR [17], a novel machine learning model for detecting cyber intrusions of ICS. TABOR is explainable due to its graphical nature, which is based upon the use of Timed Automata (TA) and Bayesian Networks (BNs). The TA is learned as a model of regular behavior of sensor signals, such as fluctuations of water levels in tanks. The BN is learned to discover dependencies between sensors and actuators. As a result, the model is easily readable and verifiable for experts and system operators. Any detection results are tractable and localizable to abnormal nodes in the model. The workflow of TABOR is as follows:

1. Sub-processes of the entire ICS are modeled. Sets of sensors and actuators in the ICS are partitioned into groups according to their locally governing PLCs for the sake of dimension and complexity reduction.
2. Signals from the sensors and actuators are symbolically represented. By doing so, on one hand, the large amount of continuous data is further compressed; on the other hand, meaningful symbols lay the foundation of learning insightful state machine models.
3. The states in the TA are associated with other actuator's states by causality inference using the BN. For example, the status (open or closed) of pumps are associated with the changes of the water level.
4. In the detection phase, irregular patterns and dependencies that do not adhere to the learned model from normal behavior, are considered anomalies.

Figure 1 shows the TA learned from the water level sensor LIT101 in the sub-process P1. In the SWaT system, the function of P1 is just raw water supply and storage - pumping raw water into the tank and pumping the water out to the next sub-process. In Fig. 1 we can observe some repeating regular behaviors such as the state transition path $S0 - S1 - S2 - S4 - S7 - S1$ with the events: 3 (SU, water level Slowly goes Up)-4 (QU, water level Quickly goes Up)-2 (SC, water level Stays Constant)-1 (QD, water level Quickly goes Down)-3 (SU, water level Slowly goes Up) are discovered by the model. This typical loop is essentially a complete description of how the raw water flows into the empty tank until it is full and then flows out of the tank onto the next sub-process. The timed information is used for constructing branches with timed-varied behaviors, but with the same symbolical representation. For instance, due to the different control strategies, the water level may stay for a short or long time at its highest level.

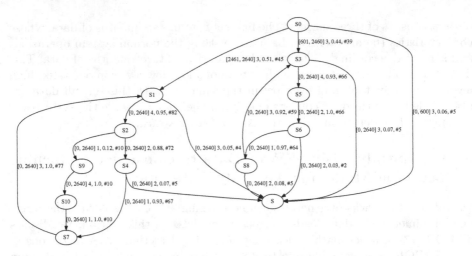

Fig. 1. Timed automaton learned from LIT101. S is the sink state, which is introduced due to fact that some sequences in the training data have very low frequencies of occurrence.

Figure 2 shows the learned BN representing the causalities among the sensors and actuators in P1. In the figure, dependencies are represented by arrows. The conditional probability distribution shows the probability distribution of a node given its parents.

In the testing phase, the new incoming data are represented by discrete events and then they are executed in the TA and BN models. Any abnormal events i.e., invalid transition/state in the TA and zero probability in the BN, are reported as anomalies. The explanation and localization of such detection results are achieved by identifying the nodes, where the anomalies occur. The explanation can be verified by the scenarios description of the SWaT dataset, where the ground-truth (starting/ending time of attacks and names of sensors/actuators under attacks) of every attack scenario is discussed in detail.

Thanks to the public availability of the SWaT dataset, it is possible to directly compare the detection performance and training/testing runtime with two published papers, whose detection methods are based upon deep neural networks [9] and SVM [12], in which exactly the same dataset was used. The results demonstrate that TABOR outperforms the other two methods in terms of effectiveness and efficiency.

4   Case Study: Using BATADAL Data in a Cyber Data Analytic Course

Since 2016 Delft University of Technology is offering a *cyber data analytics* course as part of the Data Science & Technology Track for the master's degree in Computer Science. The course provides a theoretical and practical background

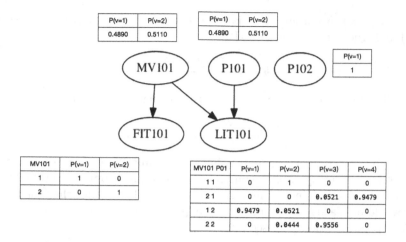

Fig. 2. Bayesian network learned from P1. The first column and the second row of the table about LIT101 indicates that given both MV101 and P101 are closed, the probability that water level quickly decreases (QD) is 0. Note that the actuators' states: open and closed, are denoted as 2 and 1, respectively.

for applying data analytics in the field of cyber security. In 2018, about 150 students registered for the course, which contained an assignment based on the BATADAL dataset. As part of the assignment, the students were asked to apply a machine learning method to detect cyber attacks on the water distribution system.

This section describes the assignments based on the BATADAL dataset and the outcomes based on submissions by the students. A total of 51 student groups took the BATADAL assignment. The results from the groups were scored in the same way as in the BATADAL competition. The score is the average of the time to detect an attack and the detection accuracy [31]. The Time-To-Detection (TTD) is the time needed by the algorithm to recognize a threat and is defined as the difference between the time t_d at which the attack is detected and the time t_0 at which the attack started:

$$TTD = t_d - t_0. \tag{1}$$

Score S_{TTD} is defined as follows to evaluate the performance of the detection algorithm for several attacks,

$$S_{TTD} = 1 - \frac{1}{m} \sum_{i}^{m} \frac{TTD_i}{\Delta t_i}, \tag{2}$$

where TTD_i is the TTD score in i−th attack, Δt_i is the duration of i−th attack scenario and m is the total number of attack scenarios. Note that for the BATADAL competition $m = 7$.

The detection accuracy S_{CM} is defined as the mean of true positive rate (TPR) and true negative rate (TNR):

$$S_{CM} = \frac{TPR + TNR}{2}. \tag{3}$$

Finally, the overall score is computed as the average S_{TTD} and S_{CM}:

$$S = \frac{S_{TTD} + S_{CM}}{2}. \tag{4}$$

Surprisingly, one group of students achieved a competitively high score, namely $S = 0.924$. This group used a combination of results from a discrete Markov model and PCA (Principal Component Analysis). This implies that the student group would be placed fourth among the experienced participants in the original BATADAL competition [31], see Table 2.

Table 2. BATADAL competition ranking

Place	Team	Attacks detected	Score (S)
1	Housh and Ohar	7	0.970
2	Abokifa et al.	7	0.949
3	Giacomoni et al.	7	0.927
4	**Student group**	7	**0.924**
5	Brentan et al.	7	0.894
6	Chandy et al.	7	0.802
7	Pasha et al.	7	0.773
8	Aghashahi et al.	7	0.534

A survey was conducted to assess how the students valued the use of the BATADAL dataset in their assignment. The students were asked to answer five questions related to the use of the real-life data. Because the number of respondents was low (21 students) we have refrained from using a Likert five-point scale. Instead, the respondents simply answered either "yes" or "no" to the questions. They were also allowed to give comments on their answers.

The following five questions were addressed to the students:

Q1: It is important that during the course we use real-life data.
Q2: The use of real-life data increases my understanding of the models we learn in the course.
Q3: I have used real-life data from the cyber domain before.
Q4: I would like to apply the models we learn in the course to more real-life data.
Q5: Machine learning techniques are promising to solve real-life cyber security problems.

A vast majority of the students (86%) agree with the importance of using real-life data (Q1). One student commented: "because in practice we will also use real-life data." Opinions were mixed for Q2 (57%–43%), which polls whether using real-life data increases understanding of the ML models taught in the class. One student feels there is no correlation while another finds real-life data more interesting and hence pushes to study harder. A majority of the students (76%) had not used real-life data from the cyber domain prior to coming to this course (Q3). One student comments that this is a really nice addition to the cyber security track. A majority of the students (76%) would like to apply the taught ML models to more real-life data (Q4). One student deems this important because "techniques are categorized based on their efficiency for certain datasets." Lastly, a majority of the students (95%) find ML techniques promising to solve real-life cyber security problems. The results in this section indicate how the use of real-life data augments education in cyber security.

5 Summary and Conclusions

Data analytics and machine learning classes have sprung up across the research community and many universities. Researchers and instructors in their classes often make earnest attempts to obtain realistic datasets to conduct research and to teach the students. Unfortunately, there are few known ICS datasets available for use. iTrust makes available several such datasets, two of which were used in this work. The objective of the study reported here was to understand how the use of realistic datasets from live and simulated ICS enhance the research and student learning.

An analysis of the results from the two offerings answer some, though not all, questions a researcher or an instructor may pose. First, based on the fruitful research outcome using a live dataset such as SWaT, researchers appreciated a practical platform to develop and test their algorithms. The competition among variate machine learning techniques boosts the flourish of advanced intrusion systems protecting critical CPSs. Second, based on the responses from the survey, we can claim that students appreciated the use of realistic data from an ICS, the simulated BATADAL dataset. However, we do not have any statistical evidence that supports, or does not support, a claim that the use of live data enhances learning of data analytic techniques used in this study. However, we believe that the use of data from an operational plant, SWaT in this study, enhances student motivation and hence learning. Details of SWaT plant are public [14] and thus the students can discuss the pros and cons of using machine learning techniques in detecting process anomalies in a physical context. Such discussions also add to student's knowledge of how ICS operates and the inherent vulnerabilities that could be exploited leading to process anomalies.

Given the above conclusions, we believe that this work is a step towards a more detailed study that would focus on a better understanding of the impact of using live ICS data on research and student learning. Such a study would require both live ICS data as well as synthetic data. A significant amount of synthetic data is already available in the public domain, e.g. the "Electrical Grid Stability Simulated Data" from UC Irvine [32]. Such data can be used, along with live datasets available from iTrust, to conduct a deeper study with research and educational objectives similar to those in the study reported here.

Acknowledgements. This work is partially supported by Technologiestichting STW VENI project 13136 (MANTA), NWO project 62001628 (LEMMA) and the 2+2 PhD program of TUD and SUTD. This work was also supported by the National Research Foundation (NRF), Prime Minister's Office, Singapore, under its National Cybersecurity R&D Programme (Award No. NRF2014NCR-NCR001-040) and administered by the National Cybersecurity R&D Directorate. The testbeds were made possible through funding from Ministry of Defence, Singapore, NRF and the SUTD-MIT International Design Centre (IDC). The authors thank Mark Goh for maintaining the iTrust datasets and processing requests for downloads.

References

1. Almgren, M., et al.: RICS-el: building a national testbed for research and training on SCADA security (short paper). In: Luiijf, E., Žutautaitė, I., Hämmerli, B.M. (eds.) CRITIS 2018. LNCS, vol. 11260, pp. 219–225. Springer, Cham (2019). https://doi.org/10.1007/978-3-030-05849-4_17
2. Anderson, R., et al.: Measuring the cost of cybercrime. In: Proceedings of the 11th Workshop on Economics of Information Security (2012)
3. Balaganski, A., Derwisch, S.: Big data and information security. KuppingerCole and BARC Joint Study, Report No.: 7400 (2016)
4. Choi, S., Yun, J.-H., Kim, S.-K.: A comparison of ICS datasets for security research based on attack paths. In: Luiijf, E., Žutautaitė, I., Hämmerli, B.M. (eds.) CRITIS 2018. LNCS, vol. 11260, pp. 154–166. Springer, Cham (2019). https://doi.org/10.1007/978-3-030-05849-4_12
5. Council of the European Union: European council, council directive 2016/1148 of 6 July 2016 concerning measures for a high common level of security of network and information systems across the union (2016). https://eur-lex.europa.eu/eli/dir/2016/1148/oj
6. Digitalbond: S4x15 ICS village CTF dataset (2015). https://www.digitalbond.com/blog/2015/03/16/s4x15-ctf-ics-village-page/
7. G8: G8 principles for protecting critical information infrastructures (2003). http://www.cybersecuritycooperation.org/documents/G8_CIIP_Principles.pdf
8. GFCE: global forum on cyber expertise (2015). https://www.thegfce.com/about
9. Goh, J., Adepu, S., Tan, M., Lee, Z.S.: Anomaly detection in cyber physical systems using recurrent neural networks. In: 2017 IEEE 18th International Symposium on High Assurance Systems Engineering (HASE), pp. 140–145. IEEE (2017)
10. Holm, H., Karresand, M., Vidström, A., Westring, E.: A survey of industrial control system testbeds. In: Buchegger, S., Dam, M. (eds.) Secure IT Systems, vol. 9417, pp. 11–26. Springer, Cham (2015). https://doi.org/10.1007/978-3-319-26502-5_2
11. ICS-CERT: Cyber-attack against Ukrainian critical infrastructure (2016). https://ics-cert.us-cert.gov/alerts/IR-ALERT-H-16-056-01
12. Inoue, J., Yamagata, Y., Chen, Y., Poskitt, C.M., Sun, J.: Anomaly detection for a water treatment system using unsupervised machine learning. In: 2017 IEEE International Conference on Data Mining Workshops (ICDMW), pp. 1058–1065. IEEE (2017)

13. iTrust: Centre for Research in Cyber Security (2015). https://itrust.sutd.edu.sg/
14. iTrust: Secure Water Treatment (SWaT) Testbed (2015). https://itrust.sutd.edu.sg/research/dataset/
15. Lemay, A., Fernandez, J.M.: Providing {SCADA} network data sets for intrusion detection research. In: 2016 9th Workshop on Cyber Security Experimentation and Test ({CSET}) (2016)
16. Lewis, J.A.: Economic impact of cybercrime-no slowing down (2018). https://www.csis.org/analysis/economic-impact-cybercrime
17. Lin, Q., Adepu, S., Verwer, S., Mathur, A.: TABOR: a graphical model-based approach for anomaly detection in Industrial Control Systems. In: Proceedings of the 2018 on Asia Conference on Computer and Communications Security, pp. 525–536. ACM (2018)
18. Luiijf, E., Besseling, K., De Graaf, P.: Nineteen national cyber security strategies. Int. J. Crit. Infrastruct. (IJCIS) **9**(1/2), 3–31 (2013)
19. Mathur, A.P., Tippenhauer, N.: SWaT: a water treatment testbed for research and training on ICS security. In: International Workshop on Cyber-physical Systems for Smart Water Networks (CySWater), pp. 31–36. IEEE, USA, April 2016
20. McLaughlin, S., et al.: The cybersecurity landscape in industrial control systems. Proc. IEEE **104**(5), 1039–1057 (2016)
21. Morris, T., Gao, W.: Industrial control system traffic data sets for intrusion detection research. In: Butts, J., Shenoi, S. (eds.) ICCIP 2014. IAICT, vol. 441, pp. 65–78. Springer, Heidelberg (2014). https://doi.org/10.1007/978-3-662-45355-1_5
22. Morris, T., Srivastava, A., Reaves, B., Gao, W., Pavurapu, K., Reddi, R.: A control system testbed to validate critical infrastructure protection concepts. Int. J. Crit. Infrastruct. Prot. **4**(2), 88–103 (2011)
23. Morris, T.H., Thornton, Z., Turnipseed, I.: Industrial control system simulation and data logging for intrusion detection system research. In: 7th Annual Southeastern Cyber Security Summit, pp. 3–4 (2015)
24. Morris, T.: Industrial control system (ICS) cyber attack datasets (2015). https://sites.google.com/a/uah.edu/tommy-morris-uah/ics-data-sets
25. NRF: Singapore, national cybersecurity R&D programme (2013). https://www.nrf.gov.sg/programmes/national-cybersecurity-r-d-programme
26. Ostfeld, A., et al.: Battle of the water calibration networks. J. Water Resour. Plan. Manag. **138**(5), 523–532 (2012)
27. Pan, S., Morris, T., Adhikari, U.: Developing a hybrid intrusion detection system using data mining for power systems. IEEE Trans. Smart Grid **6**(6), 3104–3113 (2015)
28. Rossman, L.A.: EPANET 2: User Manual (2000)
29. Symantec: Norton cyber security insights report, global results (2017). https://www.symantec.com/content/dam/symantec/docs/about/2017-ncsir-global-results-en.pdf
30. Taormina, R., Galelli, S., Tippenhauer, N.O., Salomons, E., Ostfeld, A.: Characterizing cyber-physical attacks on water distribution systems. J. Water Resour. Plan. Manag. **143**(5), 04017009 (2017)
31. Taormina, R., et al.: The battle of the attack detection algorithms: disclosing cyber attacks on water distribution networks. J. Water Resour. Plan. Manag. **144**(8), 1–11 (2018)
32. UC Irvine: Machine learning repository (2007). https://archive.ics.uci.edu/ml/index.php
33. Weinberger, S.: Computer security: is this the start of cyberwarfare? Nature **174**, 142–145 (2011)

Transport and Finance

Securing Software Updates for Trains

Tatiana Galibus[✉]

Crypto Group, UCLouvain, Louvain-la-Neuve, Belgium
tatiana.galibus@uclouvain.be

Abstract. We propose the secure procedure for the automated railway update and maintenance. The proposed procedure is derived from the Uptane update framework. Testing and validation phase, additional manual approval procedure and update progress control are integrated into the Uptane framework in order to conform to the railway safety requirements and norms. The possible metadata and repository customization is proposed and specific railway update attacks are discussed.

Keywords: The Update Framework · Railway transportation system · Resilient security · Uptane framework · Secure repository · Secure update

1 Introduction

Railway transportation security relies on correct, safe and secure maintenance. That's why configuration management is the critical aspect of railway security. Configuration management and update are important processes in railway transportation as they assure the correct and uninterrupted functioning of the signaling devices. This process is part of any standard railway system [1,2] but as the role of complex digital components grows, the manual maintenance of thousands of trackside digital devices becomes more and more difficult and costly. The automobile industry has already developed robust and secure procedures for such automatic update and maintenance [5,6], validated in the industrial environment. Railway industry has not yet undergone such transformation but with all the complexity of infrastructure and number of devices to maintain, an automatic solution is inevitably in demand. The paper is focused on the security of the automation of trackside device update, which can deliver significant benefits for the railway industry. Additionally, the railway applications should conform to safety requirements [3,4], i.e. SIL3 safety constraints are highly recommended for the server part and communication board on a device [3] and SIL4 constraints for the signalling board on a device [4].

In order to conform to these safety requirements, we adapt the update model from the automobile transport industry where the automated over-the-air (OTA) updates are a commonly accepted standard. The security of ground vehicle updates lies on the efficient implementation of TUF (The Update Framework) [7]. TUF is a framework that supports the compromise-resilient security of software

© Springer Nature Switzerland AG 2020
S. Nadjm-Tehrani (Ed.): CRITIS 2019, LNCS 11777, pp. 137–148, 2020.
https://doi.org/10.1007/978-3-030-37670-3_11

updates. An adaptation of TUF, Uptane is a de facto standard for automobile updates: in July 2018 the IEEE/ISTO Federation began formally standardizing Uptane under a non-profit consortium called the Uptane Alliance [8]. Uptane is currently is part of Airbiquity [6], the leading automatic update and orchestration platform for more than 40 million ground vehicles. Airbiquity deploys updates for such companies as Ford, Renault, Bosch, Toyota among others. In this paper, we customize the Uptane procedures i.e. the update workflow and metadata verification process to the specifics of the railway industry. We demonstrate how these adaptations protect from the specific attacks on the trackside device updates.

Our main contribution is adaptation of TUF/Uptane key principles for the railway updates. The specifics of the railway system require several enhancements such as:

1. Unique *target.json* files for each trackside device in order to avoid the installation of the wrong software.
2. Keeping track of successful updates in order to manage the uni-cast update process.
3. Full verification on each device i.e. verifying target metadata on each device against the target metadata approved by the installation manager.

2 The Railway Update Workflow

We shall consider the generic railway update workflow in order to demonstrate the specifics and complexity of the train and trackside update process[1]. The railway company should support the development of its products at the 3 life-cycle stages: generic, specific and installation. Unlike Uptane model, frequently, the chain of component suppliers is completely within the control of the company. In other words, OEM has greater responsibility on the software and firmware code as well as configuration files which demands stricter security requirements. The railway company should assure the integrity and authenticity of all components developed by all subcontractors on all levels and all sites whereas in the automobile industry the components might originate from the chain of independent suppliers and a single signature of a manufacturer is enough to verify the authenticity. The update framework should support the security and safety of each component, baseline and the whole update package.

2.1 Level 1: Generic Product/Subsystem Design

A generic trackside subsystem is composed of several components, each of them being composed of several LRU (line-replaceable unit). Each LRU component binary may include software, a configuration or data preparation file and

---

[1] The industrial partner of our research is an important stakeholder in railway transportation. We can not specify the details of update process due to project specifics. We outline the generic norms and procedures, based on railway specification documents such as [3,4] and discussion with our partners.

firmware and can be used in multiple projects. The generic design tests can be delivered along with the product in order to support its testing and validation [3]. All generic products/tools are maintained by independent developer teams located on multiple sites and coordinated by the design team. The design team is in charge of the integration and validation of generic products. It delivers a baseline of all components to the customer. The generic baselines can be stored in the generic repository of railway environment. Further, they can be used by the project design.

2.2   Level 2: Project Design

The project design team is responsible for a dedicated location on the rail (i.e.: a station or a city) specified by the corresponding configuration. In order to initiate a project, one generic baseline can be chosen in order to maintain the compatibility of the component versions. It can be upgraded later. The generic repository can keep track of the baselines in use or permit the customers to manage it. Additionally, it is sometimes necessary to design specific products or features. In this case, the specific developer group is in charge of design, tests and validation of project specific products. A specific product can be tested and stored in a dedicated repository or together with the generic ones depending on the complexity of the project. The project binaries can be stored on the project repository of railway environments in order to be downloaded by the independent installation teams.

2.3   Level 3: Project Installation and Maintenance

Once the update is ready for the installation, railway safety protocols [3,4] require CB (Control Board) to be organized including the customer authorities in order to initiate the download of the new version on the target devices. The new version once approved needs to be securely transferred to all devices and be validated by all of them. As railway safety protocols [4] require additional installation tests and validations for the new version, it should first be tested during the limited time slots. Once the tests and safety activities are finished successfully, a second CB has to be organized in order to definitively switch to a new version. The project installation teams coordinated by an installation team manager are in charge of installation, validation and delivery of the installation on the device.

2.4   Security Procedures in Railway Update

The architecture of the railway update framework is based on a hierarchy of community repositories and requires security guarantees at each level. The community repositories have suffered the series of devastating attacks in the last 2 decades [9] and developed robust and transparent security mechanisms based on secure package managers and metadata support [10]. On the contrary, to our knowledge, no railway company provides robust secure channels between its distributed repositories. The security on the update is based on TLS/SSL, which was shown to be unreliable for community repositories with multiple developer teams in [10,11]. Strictly speaking, currently, there is no security guarantee on the contents of update in the railway infrastructure. An adversary with knowledge of processes and protocols can easily execute a damaging attack i.e. install malicious software or provide outdated or incorrectly formulated update package. This can put the railway at the risk of critical incidents. The secure update framework should be adapted to the specific security requirements of each level. In this paper, we focus on the security of update delivery at the installation level. Currently, the thousands of devices are updated manually which requires a lot of time, effort, money and does not provide enough security guarantees, being dependent on the human factor.

3   TUF and Uptane Background

The Update Framework (TUF) [7] is a security framework designed to protect the software repositories, such as Microsoft Windows Update, Ubuntu, the Python Package Index (PyPI), RubyGems, or Docker Hub, from attacks on update functions. The core of TUF security is based on signed metadata related to files or images kept on the repository. Attacks can be detected and prevented when the metadata is verified before the software installation. TUF does not prevent a compromise but limits its impact when it happens. TUF is designed around 4 key principles:

1. Separation of duties, i.e. different metadata files are signed by the repository administrators using 4 basic roles: the root, timestamp, snapshot, and targets.
2. Threshold number of signatures. The metadata file must be signed using a minimum threshold t out of n keys.
3. Key revocation by signing new metadata or by setting up an expiration date.
4. Using offline keys physically disconnected from the Internet.

Uptane is the first software update framework for automobiles that addresses a comprehensive threat model [5]. It enhanced the security principles of TUF [7] by adding several principles in order to increase the resilience to automobile attacks:

1. using additional storage to recover from attacks;
2. broadcasting metadata to prevent incorrect version distribution;
3. using a vehicle version manifest, or data file signed by every ECU about what it has installed, to detect compatibility attacks;
4. using a time server to limit the denial of the latest updates.

4   Attacks on a Railway Update System

We consider the intruder or insider with capabilities to intercept/modify network messages, compromise device or update server components and pretend to be a device and ask for update. On the high-level the attacker in the railway update context has same generic goals as described in [5].

1. Read update: steal the contents of an update;
2. Deny update: Prevent the updates to reach the trackside equipment;
3. Misuse update: Make a device install an outdated or badly packaged update;
4. Malicious update: Modify the update in a malicious way so that the valid device functionality is affected causing it to fail or behave incorrectly;

4.1 Generic Security Attacks

The railway update is vulnerable to almost all the generic update attacks. We reproduce the list of generic attacks mentioned in [5]:

1. **Read updates:** the man-in-the middle attack permits the adversary to get access to update contents, even if it is protected with a signature.
2. **Deny updates:** adversary can block the update in one of the following scenarios
   (a) **Drop-request attack:** the network traffic can be blocked for some track-side devices so that they cannot receive the update. The human factor excludes the drop-request attack on the generic and project design level i.e. this attack is possible between installation team and device.
   (b) **Slow-retrieval attack:** causes the update to be received so slowly that a vulnerability can be exploited meantime. This attack can happen on all levels.
   (c) **Freeze attack:** does not permit to receive actual update. This attack is possible between the on-site installation team server and device.
   (d) **Partial bundle installation attack**: the latest update is not installed by all device components.
3. **Misuse updates:** an adversary can make an update harmful for a device in one of the following scenarios
   (a) **Rollback attack:** Device installs outdated update. The known vulnerabilities are still present on the device.
   (b) **Endless data attack:** Sending an indefinite amount of data to a device.
   (c) **Mixed-bundles attack:** Causes device to install incompatible component versions.
   (d) **Mix-and-match attack**: Attacker is able to release a random mix of software versions by compromising repository keys.
4. **Malicious updates**: adversary substitutes the contents of update forcing the device install a malware.

Apart from these we discovered specific attacks on trackside equipment that do not exist in the automobile update.

4.2 Specific Attacks

We derive the classes of specific attacks analyzing the implementation of the safety requirements [4] to the railway update process. We didn't apply formal vulnerability analysis which can be the subject of another paper. We suppose that the attacker can target any of 3 specific railway procedures:

1. **Distribution of update to multiple devices.** The update is not distributed for each single device independently but in a synchronized manner for the entire network segment (or one trackside line of the project) which may contain hundreds or thousands of control devices to be upgraded. All of them have to receive the validated update within a short time slot. In other words, an attacker can perform a malicious action to a single device in the update network which should be prevented with minimal consequences.
2. **Testing phase.** The new version undergoes a series of tests before being approved for a commercial use, so there is a time delay between the update installation and actual switch to the new version.
3. **CB approval confirmation.** If the installation team was compromised and has got access to a non-approved version from the project repository, it can make devices install the non-legitimate version bypassing the installation team manager.

We may formulate the specific railway attacks:

1. **Device mismatch**: The update is correct, but is distributed to a wrong device in the network. This can lead to an installation of the incompatible software on a device, incorrect functioning of the signal device and errors in train positioning and interlocking. This attack is not covered by Uptane functionality, as Uptane is focused on the mismatch attacks on the device components or on the version mismatch of the update for the whole system or network. This attack is easier to execute if the metadata file is not composed specifically for each device i.e. the components to be installed on a trackside device are selected from the complete metadata file received by the device for the whole network in the project. In order to protect from a mismatch attack, the verification procedure on a device has to correspond to the specifics of this metadata format.
2. **Test phase attacks**: the tests start before all devices confirm the update installation or the new version is compromised during the testing phase. If the tests start before the devices confirm the installation of the fresh version, this could lead to incompatibility errors and failure of the testing phase which would make the whole update inefficient i.e. the attacker is able to deny the update. If the version is compromised during the testing phase it could lead to the successful end of the testing phase and installation of erroneous version. Uptane does not consider this phase at all as it does not exist in the automobile context.
3. **CB approval absence**: The device switches to the updated version before the CB approval due to a compromised installation team server. If the version

is not approved by CB it can't be used by the devices as in this case the major responsibility on the failure is on the manufacturer of the update. This phase does not exist for automobiles, so Uptane framework does not protect against it.

To conclude, we have identified that all major attacks on the automobile update are also possible in the trackside update process. However, there are some specific aspects of train updates that cannot be protected without adaptation of the generic update TUF/Uptane framework. The first security requirement is a strong compromise-resilience i.e. it would be infeasible for an attacker to achieve the attack goal even for a single device as the failure of a single device can be critical for the train interlocking resolution. The second requirement is secure recovery: the system should to be able to recover from attacks in the most secure way possible. Physical attacks, remote exploits and random failures are out of the scope of the system.

5   Uptane Application for Train Updates

The update framework can be applied on all 3 levels of the railway update process: generic, project design and installation. In this paper, we focus on the application of TUF/Uptane at the on-site installation level, including metadata verification and specifics. It is considered, that the update package has already arrived at the installation server verified and signed by the project director. This section is our contribution to the railway update process. We propose the procedures and metadata verification based on the attack and context analysis. Other Uptane adaptations can be proposed later.

5.1   Customizing Uptane Design at the Installation Level

In this section, we present a straightforward application of Uptane to the installation process. We propose the scenario, when the devices pull an update from the installation or team manager (TM) repository which corresponds to the image repository in Uptane framework, where the team manager signs the canonical image metadata [5]. Team manager on his/her behalf should verify and sign the binaries from the project repository, get CB approval and upload the images and freshly generated metadata (with his/her signature as a root) to the repository. Sometimes, in order to simplify the task, TM could directly sign the root metadata for the approved update or just add his/her signature on top of *root.json* file from project repository. Specifying the secure link between the project repository and TM repository is a subject of another paper. Ultimately, the devices trust the signature of the TM root, not the project director's one as CB is the final decision instance represented by TM root of trust. It is important that there is no link between the project repository of the design phase and installation phase other than CB-approved repository. This process is not specified in the Uptane framework so additional security procedures are necessary to protect it.

After that, installation team (IT) servers pull the specific approved images from this secure repository, sign and encrypt them and forward to the trackside. The installation team coordinates and orchestrates the updates of all devices on a specific line. The devices pull the update as directed by the IT server. The IT repository corresponds to the director repository in the Uptane framework, which is responsible for selecting and encrypting the customized set of images for the specific device. Obviously, the IT repository should maintain the inventory database in order to make a decision on the version and baseline to be installed and a set of device keys in its network zone. The IT repository might contain encrypted images of an update if additional security is required. In the railway framework, the multiple independent director (IT) repositories correspond to a single image (TM) repository.

When a device would contact the IT repository, it would identify itself with the ID, serial number and signature. Given the device ID the IT director should consult the inventory database, perform dependency resolution for the required images and sign the unique metadata or instructions on the names, sizes and hashes of the images to be downloaded and installed by the device. This guarantees immunity to man-in-the-middle device mismatch attacks.

In the full verification scenario of Uptane [5], each device is required to download one set of metadata from the IT server and another, generic one, from the TM repository. The first set should be specifically customized for this device and the latter is required in order to verify the specific set against the metadata approved by CB and signed by the team manager. This Uptane procedure requires customization as TM metadata contains the signed instructions for all images to be installed in the network. Each device should verify only specific information on hashes, names and sizes for several files from this generic metadata. In the Uptane framework such verification is optional, but we propose to make it obligatory for the railway update in order to achieve greater compromise resilience and avoid non-approved version installation. The following Fig. 1 illustrates the proposed application of the Uptane process in the railway context. All components and procedures of Uptane are applicable in this scenario. Additional safety requirements to SIL4 boards on the trackside will require additional safety checks to be performed after Uptane metadata verification. The update

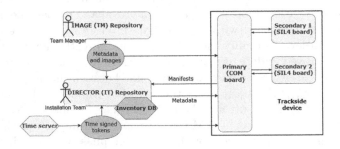

Fig. 1. Update high-level diagram.

of a single device in such scenario will not be an independent procedure but a part of network update. In order to control the network update, it is suggested to maintain an update progress database as a temporary file or a part of the inventory database. This database would contain the confirmation of successfully validated and installed updates for each trackside device. Once all devices will confirm the successful installation of a fresh version the testing phase may start. The procedure is not specified in Uptane, so this customization is obligatory in order to comply with railway security requirements. The Uptane repositories and roles in the railway framework can function as proposed on the following Fig. 2. We may conclude that the principal adaptations of the Uptane framework at this level are:

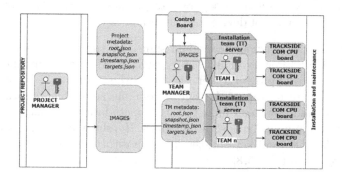

Fig. 2. On-site repositories and roles.

1. Separate *target.json* files for each trackside device in IT (director) repository in order to protect from the device mismatch and device freeze attacks.
2. Target metadata in the TM and IT repository are not identical and its verification includes only comparison of device component file names, sizes and hashes. This allows to manage multiple director repositories corresponding to common shared image repository (TM).
3. In order to proceed to testing phase, the IT repository needs to keep track of successful updates of all devices. The update progress database allows to control the start time of the testing phase and manage the update failures.
4. Full verification on each device is required as this it assures the identity of the installed version and CB approved one. This allows to support the strong compromise-resilience and minimize the risk to install a non-approved update version.

5.2   Roles and Keys

The proposed IT repository roles and keys are presented in the Fig. 3. Each IT server would be an Uptane director repository with 4 basic TUF roles so that each single device can verify the authenticity and timeliness of update:

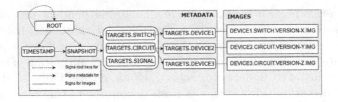

Fig. 3. Installation team repository roles.

- *root*: recommended minimum 8 keys with 5 keys valid signature threshold [8].
- *timestamp* and *snapshot*: one single key per role.
- *targets*: if possible, set up a separate target key for each type of device to reduce the possibility of device mismatch attack.

When the TM receives project metadata signed by the project director, he/she should verify it and download the binary images. After that, he/she must call the CB and ask to approve the version. Once the approval is received he/she will put a signature on top of the signed root metadata file or formulate new root metadata, add download links to target metadata and re-sign it, and generate fresh timestamp and snapshot metadata. He/she will forward it to each IT repository. The roles and keys on the TM repository are identical to those on Uptane image repository [5,8].

6   Security Considerations

Essentially, the TM and IT repositories function similarly to Uptane image/director repositories. Similarly, the informal security considerations [5] hold for the railway update as the same distribution of roles and responsibilities and key validity threshold support compromise resilience. The security analysis

Table 1. Specific attacks and measures.

Attack type	Measures and adaptations
Device mismatch:	Uniquely tailored targets metadata
	Temporary inventory database
	Targets key corresponding to the specific device type
CB approval absence:	Full verification for each device
	Image repository metadata signed by TM
	Direct upload URL in the targets metadata
Test phase attack:	Temporary inventory database
	TM as a link between OT and CB
	Final version verification after the testing phase

of the railway framework in generic part is identical to the Uptane framework security analysis [5].

The proposed adaptations allow to address specific trackside attacks (see Sect. 4.2), as TUF and Uptane do not have tools for such scenarios (Table 1).

It can be concluded, that the proposed enhancements: testing phase protection, full verification of CB-approved version, device-specific metadata and update progress control database provide the stronger compromise-resilience and a solution to balancing between safety and security requirements for the trackside update as none of these specific attacks is considered in TUF and Uptane.

Regarding the formal approach evaluation, to our knowledge, the protocol security proof, similar to [13] does not exist for this framework, though it is a state-of-the-art standard in the automobile industry and community repository updates. The intuitive security analysis [5,7,11] has clear foundation on compromise-resilience, based on the number of keys and targets a well defined class of attacks. In future work, it should be feasible to design a formal model of secure update similar to [13] and prove its consistency for a railway framework.

7   Conclusion

The paper proposes an adaptation of TUF and Uptane for securing railway updates. We studied the generic update process in the railway environment in collaboration with an industry partner and identified generic and specific attacks on the trackside infrastructure in order to address the security and safety requirements. We studied the Uptane/TUF secure update system as the industrially validated solution in order to design the customization.

We propose the design of repositories, roles and metadata management adapted to the railway update process. As the railway update is more demanding compared to that of automobiles the additional security measures are taken into consideration such as testing phase, full verification and update progress control. Uptane is currently being validated in the testbed of the Digitrans demonstrator. Uptane update framework is expected to be implemented on a simulated section of trackside. Some devices will be virtual, and some will be implemented on Raspberry PI computers. The interface of Uptane should be adapted for the needs of signaling devices according to the recommendations given above. Each signaling object should be represented by COM board and one or two SIL4 boards.

Currently, TUF and Uptane are state-of-art mechanisms used by multiple automobile companies and the corresponding standard is in the approval process by IEEE to be adopted as secure update for ground vehicles [8]. It is used by IoT update frameworks as well, such as ASSURED [12]. Though it introduces new risks such as the key theft or compromise, the framework security guarantees allow to recover with minimal damage after such incidents. In our future work, we plan to adapt it to all levels of the railway update process i.e. for securing generic and project repositories as well as developer groups contributing binaries to the trackside components.

Acknowledgements. I would like to thank Dr. Florentin Rochet and François Koeune (UCL, Crypto group) for the valuable comments on the paper and Eric Denayer and Michel Rousseau (Alstom research) for the valuable discussions on the railway update process. This work has been funded in part by the Walloon Region (competitiveness pole Logistics in Wallonia) through the project Digitrans (convention number 7618).

References

1. Standard: CENELEC - EN 50159. Railway applications - safety-related communication in transmission systems (2010)
2. Standard: ISA/IEC 62443: Industrial Network and System Security
3. Standard: EN 50128: railway applications - software for railway control and protection
4. Standard: EN 50129; railway applications - safety related electronic systems for signalling
5. Uptane: securing software updates for automobiles (2019). https://uptane.github.io/. Accessed 5 Apr 2019
6. Airbiquity: OTAmatic update and management (2019). https://www.airbiquity.com/product-offerings/software-and-data-management. Accessed 5 Apr 2019
7. TUF: The Update Framework (2019). https://theupdateframework.github.io/. Accessed 25 Apr 2019
8. Uptane IEEE-ISTO Standard for Design and Implementation (2019). https://uptane.github.io/uptane-standard/uptane-standard.html. Accessed 5 Apr 2019
9. Bellissimo, A., Burgess, J., Fu, K.: Secure software updates: disappointments and new challenges. In: Proceedings of the 10th Conference on USENIX Security Symposium-Volume 10, p. 22. USENIX Association (2001)
10. Cappos, J., Samuel, J., Baker, S., Hartman, J.: A look in the mirror: attacks on package managers. In: Proceedings of the 15th ACM Conference on Computer and Communication Security, pp. 565–574. ACM Press, New York (2008)
11. Samuel, J., Mathewson, N., Cappos, J., Dingledine, R.: Survivable key compromise in software update systems. In: Proceedings of the 17th ACM Conference on Computer and Communications Security, pp. 61–72. ACM Press, New York (2010)
12. Asokan, N., Nyman, T., Rattanavipanon, N., Sagedhi, A.-R., Tsudik, G.: ASSURED: architecture for secure software update of realistic embedded devices. In: Proceedings of EMSOFT 2018, Turin, Italy, article No. 16. IEEE Press, Piscataway (2018)
13. Lewi, K., Kim, W., Maykov, I., Weis, S., Facebook: Securing update propagation with homomorphic hashing (2019). https://eprint.iacr.org/2019/227.pdf. Accessed 24 June 2019

A Comparison Between SWIFT and Blockchain from a Cyber Resiliency Perspective

Luisa Franchina and Guido Carlomagno(⊠) (iD)

Hermes Bay S.r.l., 00143 Rome, RM, Italy
guido.carlomagno137@gmail.com

Abstract. Payments critical infrastructure is subject to rapid technological change. Increasingly sophisticated threats must be addressed to ensure the banking and financial system security and integrity. Several high-profile cyber-incidents have recently shaken the global financial community and stimulated renewed efforts to reinforce and bolster its security framework. Two different cross border payments management approaches have emerged over the years: the SWIFT financial messaging standard and the innovative peer-to-peer transaction model based on the blockchain technology. Debates about which one will prevail as the best practice are currently a very popular topic. Security, and more specifically resiliency to evolving cyber threats, will likely be the main point of concern. Both the SWIFT and the blockchain models present potential exposure to such vulnerabilities. Ultimately, the discussion boils down to an assessment of whether a decentralized, distributed system like the blockchain better meets the integrity requirements of a modern payments infrastructure and is more suitable to mitigate the root cause of cyber incidents, which is human error.

Keywords: Swift · Blockchain · Distributed ledger · Payments · Banking · Cybersecurity · Cyberattacks · Financial services · Networks · ICT · Digital transactions · Peer-to-peer systems

1 Introduction

The payments landscape is changing rapidly. Customer demands are up, in terms of 24/7 availability, real time settling and enhanced cost efficiency. A constant stream of technology innovations is bringing interesting new tools to the payments sector and driving change in market dynamics, regulation and industry initiatives. Banks, financial institutions, fintech companies are required to do more and faster for less, while maintaining compliance, operational excellence and, most of all, security.

Such an evolving scenario is characterized both by opportunity and threat: the biggest challenge is improving the payments infrastructure resiliency to evolving cyber threats, thus ensuring transaction safety and integrity and financial data security. Evidence shows

---

The original version of this chapter was revised: One of the references in the original paper referred to a paper that has since been retracted due to plagiarism. The correction to this chapter is available at https://doi.org/10.1007/978-3-030-37670-3_19

© Springer Nature Switzerland AG 2020, corrected publication 2020
S. Nadjm-Tehrani (Ed.): CRITIS 2019, LNCS 11777, pp. 149–160, 2020.
https://doi.org/10.1007/978-3-030-37670-3_12

that in the last few years attackers are increasingly building advanced capabilities to target core banking systems, particularly around payment messaging and transaction authorization. Cybersecurity is therefore becoming the primary concern in the financial sphere for the years to come.

In this paper, we will draw a brief rundown of the digital cross-border payments historical evolution, then we will analyze the current situation in terms of leading technologies and recent cyber incidents that have affected the payment system. Finally, we will compare the two preeminent models (the SWIFT and the blockchain) from a cyber resiliency perspective.

2 Evolution of Cross Border Digital Payments

2.1 SWIFT History and Functioning

In 1973, 239 banks from 15 countries got together to solve a common problem: how to communicate about cross-border payments. The banks formed a cooperative utility, the Society for Worldwide Interbank Financial Telecommunication (SWIFT), headquartered in Belgium [1]. Before SWIFT came into existence, international interbank telecommunication was handled through Telex-Messages. They were not very secure and not automated. Telex Networks were developed from the 1930 s onwards and they have been on the decline since the 1980s [2]. SWIFT was founded with the vision of creating a global financial messaging service, and a common language for international financial messaging. Today SWIFT connects more than 11,000 banking and securities organizations, market infrastructures and corporate customers in more than 200 countries. The system provides about 1.8 billion messages per year [1, 3].

All payments involving a seller and a buyer who do not have their respective accounts in the same bank, trigger secondary "street side" transactions, such as clearing and settlement. SWIFT plays the intermediary for transactions in which banks are involved (business-to-bank and bank-to-bank). While national payment systems often rely on a clearing system where banks clear their account after a certain time period at one central location – i.e. the clearing-house - cross border payments are largely managed through correspondent banks, a method facilitated by SWIFT. SWIFT messages are programmed in a language know as FIN. It is heavily influenced by the Telex messages it replaced. A very simple SWIFT message could look like this:

```
            :20:MT101 - Test
         :28D:00001/00001
              :30:040403
          :21:Start B - Seq
             :32B:EUR1
             :23E:CMTO
      :50G:/Account Number
          BANKDEM0XXX
      :59A:/Account Number
          BANKDEM0XXX
             :71A:SHA
```

The SWIFT translation system combines several components: its own information transmission network, software that makes it possible to connect to the network and an algorithm for assigning each participant a unique SWIFT code. It is the SWIFT bank code that makes it possible to accurately determine the sender/payee and make the transfer within the shortest possible time. The risk of error in this case is minimal, because the SWIFT code is unique for each participant in the system and contains complete information about it. The SWIFT system aims to help organizations and individuals transferring money to each other in any required currency, regardless of borders between countries and other obstacles [4].

2.2 Blockchain History and Its Applications in the Payment Infrastructure

In 2009, an anonymous author who called himself Satoshi Nakamoto published the article "Bitcoin: A Peer-to-Peer Electronic Cash System", thus giving birth to the distributed ledger technology (also known as "Blockchain") [5].

Blockchain technology is an integrated multi-field infrastructure construction, containing elements of cryptography, computer science and game theory. A peer-to-peer network that uses a distributed consensus algorithm to solve traditional distributed database synchronizing problem. Blockchain key elements are decentralization, transparency and immutability [5]. One of its main applications is funds transferring achieved by using an encrypted technique without relying on a central bank or other trusted third parties. In other words, blockchain is a cryptographically secure system of messaging and recording in a shared database that makes it possible to transact value from point A to point B without the intervention of a third party (see Fig. 1). What's more, having a single blockchain database to which all users have access not only eliminates the need for a central authority, but also eliminates the need for maintaining multiple individual databases [6].

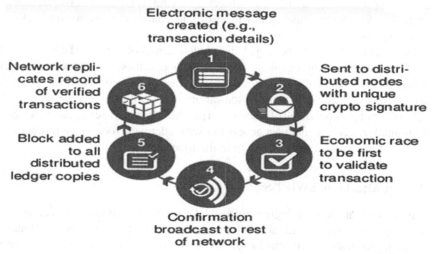

Fig. 1. Graphic elaboration of a digital transaction run on a blockchain network (McKinsey & Company - Blockchain Technology in the Insurance Sector, 2017)

It is important to stress that blockchain comes in many different types: the main distinction is between a public and a private blockchain. A public blockchain is a permission-less peer-to-peer network. Anyone can join the network, meaning that they can read, write, code, or operate within. On the other hand, a private blockchain is a permissioned network. Permissioned networks place restrictions on who is allowed to participate in the network and in what transactions. Private blockchains partially reintroduce the intermediary that the very concept of a distributed ledger had eliminated [7] This distinction will come in handy later in the paper when we specifically discuss about security challenges related to the blockchain implementation.

Many banks and financial institution have been studying distributed ledger technology attributes and launching blockchain-related projects. Ripple, a California company created in 2012 promising to make payments faster, cheaper and more secure, teamed up with Banco Santander in April 2018 to launch a service based on its blockchain messaging technology that allows the Spanish bank's customers in the UK, Spain, Poland and Brazil to send money in many currencies around the world. Santander is only one of more than 100 financial institutions that have registered with Ripple to use its blockchain-based messaging system, known as XCurrent [8]. Other noteworthy blockchain-related projects are the ones involving The Enterprise Ethereum Alliance [9], whose members include the likes of Credit Suisse Group AG and JPMorgan Chase & Co., who also said to be planning to include the mathematical operation known as "Zero Knowledge Proof" [10] in Quorum, its own private distributed ledger [11].

3   Vulnerabilities of the Existing Financial Infrastructure

Banks and financial institutions have always been prime targets for attackers, who are increasingly taking advantage of technological enablers (connectivity, complexity) and are developing new tools and techniques to conduct their malicious activity. In the past decade, the capability and motivation of threats to the financial sector have transformed from small-scale opportunistic crimes to efforts to compromise entire networks and payment systems.

In 2011 and 2012, hackers staged distributed denial-of-service (DDOS) attacks against U.S. banks to disrupt banking services. Although these attacks were basic and caused minimal long-term damage, they were a preview of the cyber-incidents wave that was about to come [12]. Since then, a wide variety of sophisticated cyber-attacks, often characterized by the deployment of malware on payment systems to create a smokescreen for the fraudulent activity and gain access to user credentials, took place repeatedly in many parts of the world, causing concern in the financial sector [13].

3.1   Recent Attacks on SWIFT Systems

There have been at least six high-profile attacks on SWIFT systems in recent years (among many other lower-profile attacks), some of which resulting in significant financial loss. The number of successful attacks against these systems shows how SWIFT security architecture needs improvements and customers must do more to protect their local infrastructures.

Sonali Bank (2013). Attackers were able to infect the bank's internal systems with key-logger software that was used to harvest user credentials. These credentials were then used to laterally move through the bank's network in order to gain access to the bank's internal SWIFT systems, where $250,000 worth of transactions were made [14].

Banco del Austroz (January 2015). Attackers stole the credentials of a bank employee and used these credentials to access the employee's Outlook email account. Using this access, the attackers located, cancelled and rejected SWIFT transfer requests, altered their details, and reissued them, resulting in $12,000,000 worth of legitimate transfer requests being sent [15].

Tien Phong Bank (December 2015). Attackers used malware that specifically targeted the Foxit PDF reader, which was known to be used by the bank employees when viewing SWIFT statements. Attackers were able to install a malicious version of the Foxit PDF reader on employee workstations, which altered statements (when opened) in order to hide evidence of any malicious activity. This malware was found to be installed on infrastructure provided by a third-party vendor. Employees at the Tien Phong Bank identified suspicious SWIFT messages and rapidly contacted all parties involved. This prevented the transfer requests from being completed and the attempt to steal $1,130,000 was halted [16].

The Bank of Bangladesh (February 2016). Investigations found that the attack had been patiently executed over the period of almost a full year. Attackers gained access to the bank's internal systems in order to monitor employee activity. Using this initial foothold, attackers were able to move laterally across the bank's internal network in search of SWIFT-connected systems. Once access to SWIFT systems was obtained, the attackers monitored employee behavior, stole user credentials, and deployed specifically-designed malware named evtdiag.exe, an executable file designed to hide the attackers' activity by changing the logs on a SWIFT database. The malware targeted the SWIFT Alliance Access application, bypassed its security controls, and removed evidence in order to cover the tracks of their fraudulent transfers [17]. A total of 35 SWIFT transactions worth $951,000,000 were made. However, only $81,000,000 of this was successfully exfiltrated from the Bangladesh Bank's account at the Fed Reserve in New York. The transfers were made towards Philippine casinos bank accounts between February 4 and February 5, 2016 [18].

The Far Eastern International Bank (October 2017). Attackers used malware to gain access to and move through the bank's internal network in order to infiltrate SWIFT systems. Attackers then compromised employee credentials and used this information to authenticate to the SWIFT Alliance Messaging Hub and issue a total of $60,100,000 worth of fraudulent transactions. Although it was initially understood that $500,000 was lost, the Financial Supervisory Commission (FSC) reported that the final amount lost by Far Eastern Bank was $160,000. Following an investigation, it was found that the bank's security posture was not in line with the requirements outlined by Taiwan's banking law [19].

The NIC Asia Bank (October 2017). Attackers specifically targeted the bank during the Hindu festival Tihar, one of Nepal's largest holidays. According to reports, $4,400,000 of fraudulent SWIFT transactions were issued during the heist. However, NIC identified the suspicious activity and informed Nepal Rastra Bank (which is Nepal's central bank), resulting in the recovery of all but $580,000 of the $4,400,000 [20].

The main common factor amidst these incidents is the deployment of some type of malware onto a bank's internal systems. We can also see that attackers frequently pair this with the compromise of user credentials. Overall, it can be concluded that none of the attacks directly compromised the SWIFT network itself, and that they were frequently the result of flaws in the security controls within the local targeted bank's IT environments. Another common element is the presence of some type of user error. This should come as no surprise, as showed by the 2014 IBM's Cyber Security Intelligence Index, which reported that 95% of all cyber incidents recognize "human error" as a contributing factor [21]. In fact, regardless of how resilient and strong a system is, human error can nullify any security framework and architecture.

3.2 SWIFT New Security Architecture and Blockchain Experimentation

Previously mentioned cases of data breaches and hacks involving banks linked to the SWIFT network have renewed the debate around SWIFT security and cyber resiliency.

As a countermeasure to the current cyber-threat landscape, SWIFT recently introduced the Customer Security Program (CSP) to support SWIFT customers in securing their local SWIFT infrastructure. This program requires that all customers implement a set of mandatory and advisory security controls outlined within SWIFT's Customer Security Controls Framework (CSCF) [22]. The main focus of CSP is to isolate all SWIFT systems into a secure zone. Without this type of security, attackers would have the opportunity to access SWIFT systems from a variety of entry points across the general enterprise network. With the implementation of all controls within CSCF, the attack surface of the SWIFT infrastructure is considerably reduced, removing a wide range of attack paths that could previously be exploited. However, CSP remains a compliance challenge, and as such it cannot be relied upon alone to mitigate and prevent the compromise of these complex payment systems. Within the CSP document itself, it is stated that CSP should not be considered an exhaustive approach to security and it does not replace a well-structured security and risk framework.

In April 2016, SWIFT and global consulting services company Accenture released a joint report that looked at the use of distributed ledger technologies (DLT) in financial services. Specifically, the paper acknowledged some strengths of the blockchain like efficient information propagation, traceability, simplified reconciliation and high resiliency [23]. In March 2017, SWIFT revealed that they had finished the Proof of Concept phase of its own distributed ledger prototype. According to SWIFT's R&D head Damien Vanderveken, blockchain's implementation would require a significant infrastructure overhaul for banks that had already invested in centralized solutions. "A substantial number of banks would have to drastically modernize their systems before they could turn to a blockchain-based system for their cross-border payments" he said. Reportedly, the testing involved the creation of 528 sub-ledgers for 28 participating banks to avoid confidential information being revealed to rivals. All of the SWIFT members, thousands of banks, would require 100,000 sub-ledgers to be established, which is technically and economically burdensome, inefficient and presents maintenance issues [24].

4   Blockchain and Cybersecurity

It is common sense that blockchain can help fortify the cyber security landscape. The potential of a strong, decentralized security proposition which represents an alternative to fully or partially-centralized systems that contain single access points of vulnerability is worth to be assessed and explored.

4.1   Security Benefits of Decentralization

With respect to the specific field of finance and payments, there are reasons to believe that blockchain features and applications can help deal with the type of malicious tactics implemented in the aforementioned attacks.

DDoS Risk Mitigation and Operational Resilience. We live in an age where DDoS attacks will only grow over time. Considering a rising number of unsecured IoT devices are connected to one another, the potential for DDoS attacks to creep in and overpower an organization is very real. With the number of IoT devices in operation expected to climb from around 8.4 billion in 2017 to 20.4 billion by 2020, according to Gartner research [25], the ease of launching massive DDoS attacks will increase and no existing system can address this problem unless it is truly distributed. That's where the blockchain solidly comes in handy. When it comes to a DDoS attack, the blockchain has protections to ensure transactions can continue even if several nodes go offline. Multiple blockchain nodes across many different institutions must be attacked to overwhelm the full infrastructure. If several nodes are offline, nodes under attack can be made redundant while the others continue working as usual, protecting the operational continuity of the whole system. The protocol recovers as nodes are brought back online and are re-synched to ensure that consistency and integrity is preserved [26]. Several blockchain startups have even claimed that they are able to protect against DDoS attacks by allowing users in a network to rent out their extra bandwidth to support networks who are being overloaded with traffic as a result of an attack [27].

Improved Data Validation and Hacks Prevention. Million new forms of malware are created every year [28]. They are often difficult to spot and come as a software download or a phony application update. Settings such as automatic updates can inadvertently include malware. The blockchain has the capacity to assign unique hashes to downloads and updates. This allows users to compare the hash on their would-be download with the developer's hash to significantly reduce the chances of infecting their systems with fraudulent, well-disguised malwares [29]. Furthermore, experts are relying upon blockchain technology to recognize invalid or potentially corrupt commands and inputs. Data that is filtered through a decentralized network tends to be more trustworthy, as the multi-node security lends itself to greater verification and tamper prevention. The use of advanced cryptographic techniques makes it more probable that data is coming from correct sources and that nothing is intercepted in the interim [30].

Evolved Identity Authentication. The username-password login framework is rapidly growing obsolete, as clearly shown by the ever-increasing numbers of compromised user credentials [31]. As it currently stands, usernames and passwords for a given site or application are stored in central databases that are vulnerable to the typical single-point-of-failure hacking hazard. A superior method of digital access management is definitely needed. One of the main features of the blockchain is that it doesn't require passwords because it relies on either biometric data or private keys and multi-step authentication to verify the identity of a user. This kind of identity and access management process makes it more difficult for hackers to enter the network and leave undetected, preventing them the possibility to hide their tracks or erase records of their unwarranted access. Combining the decentralized architecture of the blockchain and the biometrics on the mobile device, this multi-signature/multi-factor authentication model is a more secure mean of granting access to a network, assigning digital identities not only to users but also to each device registered on the network. Only a combination of the authenticated user and device can provide an entry to the data [32].

4.2 Security Issues of Decentralized Systems

In spite of all the points made above, someone could argue that Bitcoin and cryptocurrencies have been the ultimate hacker honey pot for many years now, with many renowned cases of cyber-theft connected to them [33]. It is very important to highlight that this argument is inconsistent with this paper's topic of discussion, as it only relates to the operational usability of cryptocurrencies exchanges, private wallets security and secure storage of cryptographic keys. It has nothing to do with the blockchain technology core network integrity and security. Actually, "Bitcoin Core" – the Bitcoin's open-source blockchain software underpinning - to date has successfully withstood cyber-attacks for many years [34]. Having cleared that up, there is no doubt that decentralized systems like blockchain are not per se immune to any issue regarding cyber security.

Consensus Mechanisms Alteration. The blockchain is updated via the consensus protocol that ensures a common, unambiguous ordering of transactions and blocks and guarantees the integrity and consistency of the blockchain across geographically distributed nodes. Since the consensus model maintains the sanctity of data recorded on the blockchain, it is important to ensure that it functions correctly in normal as well as adversarial conditions. In other words, a blockchain based system is as secure and robust as its consensus model [35]. Especially in a permission-less setup, the number of nodes is expected to be large, and these nodes are anonymous and untrusted since any node is allowed to join the network. Consensus mechanisms for such a setup need to account for maliciousness: particularly Sybil attacks, which can allow a single user to generate several online identities to influence and manipulate the consensus process. Dominance can also be achieved by other means, as consensus round outcomes can be manipulated by a single or group of entities that is able to control the majority of the hash rate. In such a scenario, the attacker would have enough mining power to intentionally exclude, reverse or modify the ordering of transactions [36]. However, the key problem a hacker would need to solve to create a 51% attack is acquiring the majority of the power that supports that specific blockchain. This process becomes increasingly unlikely as the dimension on the blockchain network grows. The bigger the network, the stronger the protection against attacks and data corruption. With the rising price of Bitcoin as a currency, numerous new miners entered the system aiming to compete for the block rewards (currently set as 12.5 BTC per block) [37]. Such a competitive scenario is one of the reasons why Bitcoin is perceived as being highly secure. At least this is what conventional wisdom currently asserts: the mining protocol is incentive-compatible and secure against colluding minority groups, as it incentivizes miners to follow the protocol as prescribed (they have no incentive to invest large amounts of resources if it is not for acting honestly and striving to receive the block reward). Nonetheless, recent scientific paper shows that even a 25% share can incentivize selfish miners to join the set of colluding nodes, presenting an attack with which colluding miners' revenue is larger than their fair share and thus challenging the widespread 51% notion [38].

4.3 Operational Challenges for Blockchain in Payment Infrastructures

It needs to be understood that the undeniably great cyber resiliency potential of the distributed ledger technology is not automatically applicable to the very complex and articulated modern payment infrastructures.

As previously discussed, not all blockchain networks are equal, and a particular network's robustness largely depends upon its diversity and number of nodes and its hash rate. We have seen that the maximum degree of security is provided by public, sizable and globally distributed blockchains like the Bitcoin's one, whose number of full nodes validating its transactions is close to 60,000 - according to prominent Bitcoin Core developer Luke Dashjr [39]. However, implementation of such distributed public networks must be evaluated on a large scale. If blockchain technology could be deployed on a large scale for payments, it would improve the level of security significantly, but it is evident that a fully open and public blockchain infrastructure is, at the current state of the art, not entirely applicable to the field of interbank cross border payments. Main reasons for this are issues related with redundancy, scalability and data sharing, which ultimately lead to inevitable inefficiencies that could make blockchain overall inferior to alternatives, including existing systems. Current claims that public ledger platforms can conduct financial transactions more efficiently ignore the inefficiencies associated with the huge computational power that is needed to maintain a widely distributed ledger (one study found that the electricity wasted in Bitcoin mining is comparable to the average electricity consumption of Ireland [40]). In addition, the feasibility of using a public blockchain employing a Proof-of-Work consensus for a high volume of payment transactions still remains a big question mark, as demonstrated by the low amount of transactions per second supported by Bitcoin if compared to the VISA or MasterCard numbers [41]. Finally, blockchain experimentation conducted by the SWIFT organization showed how incompatible is confidential data privacy protection with a public ledger implementation: real-banking and financial institutions praxis would require the establishment of thousands of private small sub-ledgers [24], which is technically and economically burdensome because of operational and maintenance issues and, most of all, partially nullify the security benefits of large distributed ledgers.

5   Conclusion

In the present-day cyber-threat landscape, attacks on SWIFT systems have been the focus of advanced persistent threats. Specifically-designed malwares and advanced tactics are used to achieve the goal of performing fraudulent financial transactions. As with most compromises, the root cause of vulnerability will frequently remain human error, whether this error be made by administrators in a configuration file, developers in their application code, or employees being deceived into opening a malicious email attachment. In this respect, blockchain solutions have the potential to help mitigating this fundamental flaw in security (i.e. human error), due to their inherent trustless, automated operational structure. Blockchain is decentralized by nature, which means there is no single point of penetration for hackers to invade, no centralized weak points to exploit as the information never passes through a single server. It also offers improved capacity to recognize invalid or potentially corrupt commands and inputs, and enhanced data validation and identity authentication. In other words, with blockchain systems in place of legacy ones the window of opportunity and the attack surface for hackers are significantly reduced, whereas room for human error impact is kept as minimal as possible.

However, one thing is assessing and recognizing security benefits of this new technology, another thing is implementing its features in the extremely complex modern payment infrastructure. SWIFT has been so successful and widely adopted over the years because it offered a standardized solution completely tailored to the technical and operational demands of existing financial institutions. It should not be taken for granted that this will be the case with blockchain. Recent SWIFT's own distributed ledger experimentation demonstrates that there is interest around this new emerging technology's potential, yet its implementation presents quite a few areas of criticality. This includes, firstly, the trade off between the level of resiliency, integrity that a fully open, public, sizable chain like Bitcoin (which should be assumed as a central point of reference security-wise) ensures and the actual impossibility to adapt anything remotely resembling it to the existing cross-border digital payment management system. One of the reasons why being the fact that banks can't allow confidential information being revealed to rivals. This creates the need to implement a number of private ledgers, whose network size and inherent consensus mechanism does not necessarily grant the type of security and operational resiliency that characterizes a public chain.

It is for all these reasons that a step in the direction of a necessary reconciliation between blockchain systems and banks systems interoperability needs to be made before being able to exploit the great cybersecurity potential of the new decentralized paradigm. Furthermore, technology improvements on the scalability and energy consumption sides must occur before blockchain can be considered ready to be efficiently used. It is highly likely that, rather than completely replacing all major financial processes, the blockchain model will instead take its place beside and integrate with existing systems.

References

1. SWIFT Website. https://www.swift.com/about-us/history. Accessed 09 Sept 2019
2. Huurdeman, A.A.: The Worldwide History of Telecommunications. Wiley-Interscience Publications, Hoboken (2003)
3. Köppel, J.: The SWIFT Affair: Swiss Banking Secrecy and the Fight Against Terrorist Financing, 1st edn. Graduate Institute Publications (2011)
4. Scott, S.V., Zachariadis, M.: Origins and development of SWIFT, 1973–2009. Bus. Hist. J. **54**, 462–482 (2012)
5. Nakamoto, S.: Bitcoin: A Peer-to-Peer Electronic Cash System, 24 February 2013. http://bitcoin.org/bitcoin.pdf
6. Crosby, M., Pattanyak, P., Verma, S., Kalyanaraman, V.: Blockchain technology: beyond bitcoin. Appl. Innov. Rev. **2** (2016)
7. Yaga, D., Meel, P., Roby, N., Scarfone, K.: Blockchain Technology Overview. National Institute of Standards and Technology Internal Report 8202 (2018)
8. Ripple Website. https://ripple.com/ripplenet/process-payments/. Accessed 09 Sept 2019
9. EEA. https://entethalliance.org/. Accessed 09 Sept 2019
10. Pandit, V., Dayama, P.: Privacy in blockchain collaboration with zero knowledge proofs. IBM Blockchain Blog (2019)
11. J.P. Morgan Website. https://www.goquorum.com/. Accessed 09 Sept 2019
12. Bank Info Security Website. https://www.bankinfosecurity.com/7-iranians-indicted-for-ddos-attacks-against-us-banks-a-8989. Accessed 09 Sept 2019
13. Nish, A., Naumaan, S.: The Cyber Threat Landscape: Confronting Challenges to the Financial System. In: Cyber Policy Initiative Working Paper Series, pp. 8–9. Carnegie Endowment for International Peace (2019)
14. Reuters Website. http://uk.reuters.com/article/us-cyber-heist-bangladesh/exclusive-bangladesh-probes-2013-hack-for-links-to-central-bank-heist-idUKKCN0YG2UT. Accessed 09 Sept 2019
15. Nettitude Website. https://www.nettitude.com/wp-content/uploads/2016/12/Nettitude-SWIFT-Threat-Advisory-Report-client.pdf. Accessed 09 Sept 2019
16. TrendLabs Security Intelligence Blog. https://blog.trendmicro.com/trendlabs-security-intelligence/high-profiled-cyber-theft-against-banks-targeted-swift-systems/. Accessed 09 Sept 2019
17. LIFARS Website. https://lifars.com/2016/04/bangladesh-bank-hackers-used-malware-swift-software/. Accessed 09 Sept 2019
18. Reuters Website. https://www.reuters.com/article/us-bangladesh-bank-idUSKCN0WF0IL. Accessed 09 Sept 2019
19. Bae Systems Threat Research Blog. https://baesystemsai.blogspot.com/2017/10/taiwan-heist-lazarus-tools.html. Accessed 09 Sept 2019
20. The Himalayan Times Website. https://thehimalayantimes.com/business/kpmg-team-seek-time-draw-conclusion-nic-asia-bank-case/. Accessed 09 Sept 2019
21. IBM Website, Research Report: IBM Security Services 2014 Cyber Security Intelligence Index, p. 3. https://www.ibm.com/developerworks/library/se-cyberindex2014/index.html. Accessed 09 Sept 2019
22. SWIFT Website. https://www.swift.com/myswift/customer-security-programme-csp/security-controls. Accessed 09 Sept 2019
23. SWIFT Website. https://www.swift.com/insights/press-releases/swift-and-accenture-outline-path-to-distributed-ledger-technology-adoption-within-financial-services. Accessed 09 Sept 2019

24. Financial Times Website. https://www.ft.com/content/966f5694-22c6-11e8-ae48-60d3531b7d11. Accessed 09 Sept 2019
25. Gartner Website. https://www.gartner.com/en/newsroom/press-releases/2017-02-07-gartner-says-8-billion-connected-things-will-be-in-use-in-2017-up-31-percent-from-2016. Accessed 09 Sept 2019
26. Rodrigues, B., Bocek, T., Lareida, A., Hausheer, D., Rafati, S., Stiller, B.: A blockchain-based architecture for collaborative DDoS mitigation with smart contracts. In: Tuncer, D., Koch, R., Badonnel, R., Stiller, B. (eds.) AIMS 2017. LNCS, vol. 10356, pp. 16–29. Springer, Cham (2017). https://doi.org/10.1007/978-3-319-60774-0_2
27. Liu, Z., Cheng, X.: Application of block chain technology in the field of network security. Int. Core J. Eng. 5(7) (2019)
28. G-Data Blog. https://www.gdatasoftware.com/blog/2017/04/29666-malware-trends-2017. Accessed 09 Sept 2019
29. Nasonov, D., Visheratin, A.A., Boukhanovsky, A.: Blockchain-based transaction integrity in distributed big data marketplace. In: Shi, Y., et al. (eds.) Computational Science – ICCS 2018. ICCS 2018. LNCS, vol. 10860. Springer, Cham (2018). https://doi.org/10.1007/978-3-319-93698-7_43
30. Sigwart, M., Borkowski, M., Peise, M., Shulte, S., Tai, S.: Blockchain-based data provenance for the internet of things. arXiv:1905.06852v2 (2019)
31. Ismail, R.: Enhancement of Online Identity Authentication Though Blockchain Technology (2018). https://doi.org/10.18517/ijaseit.8.4-2.6838
32. Delgado-Mohatar, O., Tolosana, J.F.R., Vera-Rodriguez, R.: Blockchain and biometrics: a first look into opportunities and challenges. arXiv:1903.05496v1 (2019)
33. ZDNet Website. https://www.zdnet.com/article/bitcoin-blues-this-is-how-much-cyptocurrency-was-stolen-last-year/. Accessed 09 Sept 2019
34. Deloitte Website, Research Report: Blockchain & Cyber Security. Let's Discuss, p. 10. https://www2.deloitte.com/content/dam/Deloitte/us/Documents/financial-services/us-blockchain-and-cyber-security-lets-discuss.pdf. Accessed 09 Sept 2019
35. Baliga, A.: Understanding Blockchain Consensus Models. Persistent Systems Ltd White Paper, pp. 3–8 (2017)
36. Lin, I.C., Liao, T.C.: A survey of blockchain security issues and challenges. Int. J. Netw. Secur. 19, 53–659 (2017)
37. Bitcoin Visuals website. https://bitcoinvisuals.com/chain-block-reward. Accessed 09 Sept 2019
38. Eyal, I., Gun Sirer, E.: Majority is not enough: bitcoin mining is vulnerable. Commun. ACM 61(7), 95–102 (2018)
39. Luke Dashjr Website. https://luke.dashjr.org/programs/bitcoin/files/charts/software.html. Accessed 09 Sept 2019
40. O'Dwyer, K.J., Malone, D.: Bitcoin mining and its energy footprint. In: ISSC 2014/CIICT 2014 (2014)
41. DataLight Website. https://datalight.me/blog/researches/longread/bitcoin-becomes-the-main-method-of-international-payment/. Accessed 09 Sept 2019

Short Papers

On the Importance of Agility, Transparency, and Positive Reinforcement in Cyber Incident Crisis Communication

Tomomi Aoyama$^{(\boxtimes)}$, Atsushi Sato, Giuseppe Lisi, and Kenji Watanabe

Nagoya Institute of Technology, Gokiso-cho, Aichi 4668555, Japan
aoyama.tomomi@nitech.ac.jp

Abstract. Cyber incident crisis management protocols often overlook the importance of crisis communication. This paper reviews the crisis communication literature to define explicit communication strategies for each stage of a cyber incident. We applied the proposed model to analyze the Norsk Hydro case: a Norwegian aluminum and renewable energy company halted operations due to a ransomware attack. By combining traditional communication outlets and social media, the company kept high transparency of their recovery operation, with frequent (i.e., agile) updates about the cyber incident. The positive presence of Norsk Hydro on social media allowed them to manage reputation throughout the process. Employees' creativity and loyalty were crucial in the recovery process, and it was promptly publicized globally. This empowered other employees at other branches to act creatively and inspired the community. We conclude the study by suggesting the agility, transparency, and positive reinforcement were the success factor of this crisis communication operation.

Keywords: Cyber incident response · Crisis communication · Information sharing · Communication agility · Transparency · Positive reinforcement

1 Introduction

Cyber-attacks continue to pose risks to critical infrastructure. Due to the increasing connectivity, digital and non-digital assets are both vulnerable to threats via Information Communication Technologies [16]. Unlike natural hazards, a cyber incident is caused by the malicious intent of an attacker. Attackers can take advantage of the responding organization's visibility and counteract to the defense.

An example is the Protonmail DDoS (Distributed denial-of-service) attack in 2018 [11]. The initial DDoS attack for the End-to-end encrypted email service provider ProtonMail caused service outage of several minutes. The small hacker group Apophis Squad targeted ProtonMail at random while testing a beta version of a DDoS booter service. Although it was not their intention to persistently attack ProtonMail, but decided to conduct a more massive attack after ProtonMail's CTO, Bart Butler, responded to one of their tweets addressing the group

© Springer Nature Switzerland AG 2020
S. Nadjm-Tehrani (Ed.): CRITIS 2019, LNCS 11777, pp. 163–168, 2020.
https://doi.org/10.1007/978-3-030-37670-3_13

provocatively [3]. Especially during the cyber incident, the communicator should be aware of the risk of provocation, which leads them to be cautious and be hesitant to communicate to the public.

This study aims at understanding the advantage of active crisis communication operation to the public during a cyber incident. Although the theoretical work on modern crisis communication is extensive, it lacks in reflecting the challenges and benefit from the empirical case studies, particularly in the field of cyber crisis management. We addressed this problem by developing the cyber crisis communication strategy model from the literature review highlighting the shortcomings. Then, we conducted an empirical study of a Norwegian aluminum company's case to analyze the benefit of employing a coordinated communication operation.

2   Cyber Incident Crisis Communication Strategy Model

Crisis communication during the cyber incident should be concurrent with incident response activities. Figure 1 shows the crisis communication strategy model based on the literature review. In the field of crisis management study, Coombs grouped the crisis communication stages to pre-crisis, crisis-event, and post-crisis [4] as the macro-level framework. Kulikova et al. studied the challenges organization face in cyber incident information disclosure [10]. Steelman [12], Coombs [4], Weiner [17] worked on the best practices of crisis communication.

The research work of Veil [15] is dedicated to determining the advantage and disadvantage of social media use during the crisis. Their findings are incorporated into the Fig. 1, as the cyber incident crisis management activities.

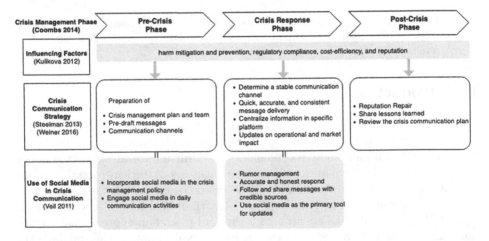

Fig. 1. Cyber incident crisis communication strategy and best practices of social media use in three phases.

From the literature review, we found that previous literature is missing case studies specifically to understand the benefit of utilizing social media in the cyber incident crisis communication. Here, we review a recent cyber incident case and the victim organization's use of social media from the crisis communication perspective.

3   Case Study: Norsk Hydro

The company underwent the production stoppage due to a ransomware attack on the 19th of March 2019. In the following paragraphs, we reconstruct the incident timeline as described on media outlets and the official update by Norsk Hydro (top panel of Fig. 2). As of April 30th 2019, the overall impact on the first quarter of 2019 is NOK 400–450 million (Euro: 45 million; US Dollars: 51 million) [2].

In this section, we describe the crisis communication timeline reconstructed from the social media channels of Norsk Hydro (bottom panel of Fig. 2). On March 19th, the official website of the Norsk Hydro becomes inaccessible. Immediately, the company reports the incident through Twitter and Facebook and establishes the latter as the main channel of communication (i.e., 'Updates regarding the situation will be posted on Facebook'). In the following 24 h, the Twitter and Facebook accounts of Norsk Hydro posted 7 and 6 updates about the incident, respectively. On March 20th, the company organizes the first press release and Q&A, open to the public via the webcast service webtv.hegnar.no, to provide updates about the cyber incident, and publicizes the event via Twitter and Facebook. On March 21st, the official website is recovered, and a new webpage is explicitly created to report about the cyber-incident, and provide the contacts of the public relations personnel.

In the first two weeks after the incident, the company kept a transparent behavior, providing updates on the website and social media (post count on Twitter: 13, Facebook: 8) regarding the operation status. At this stage, the company used the re-tweet function of Twitter to acknowledge the good behavior and creativity of the employees. In early April, the count of social media posts totaled 11 for Twitter and 3 for Facebook. The first Youtube video [8] highlighting the operational personnel's effort was released on April 2nd. On April 9th, the company releases on the official website an article titled 'Employees find creative solutions in response to cyber-attack' [1], and publicizes it on social media. In late April, the count of social media posts decreased to 7 for Twitter and 3 for Facebook, and a second Youtube video [9] was released on April 16th. Finally, on April 30th a preliminary report [2] is published on the official website, while the official report for Q1 2019 is delayed to June 5th, due to the cyber attack impacting the availability of several systems and data. Consistently with the transparent behavior of the company, the report contains the estimated financial and operational loss.

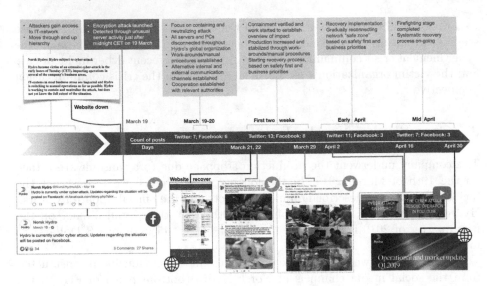

Fig. 2. Timeline of the Norsk Hydro incident [2] (top panel, modified by the author) and the reconstructed highlights of the organizations crisis communication (bottom panel).

4   Lessons Learned

The Norsk hydro case highlighted the benefit of incorporating social media as the medium of crisis communication. During the incident response, the organization continued to show its agility, transparency, and acts of positive reinforcement.

Agility. When the website became unreachable, the organization was quick to determine the alternative platform for communication (facebook and twitter). During the event, multiple platforms were used, including social media and web services. The organization seemed to have a good understanding of each platform; the audience, type of interactions, and its shortcomings. The responding organization has to incorporate the agile process management during the demanding cyber incident response. Agile organizations allow the sharing of information on different levels and between different disciplines, which increases situational awareness and effectiveness [14].

Transparency. Periodic updates on operational status and short documentary videos featuring operators showed honesty and openness. Cornelissen defined transparency as "the state where the image or reputation of an organization held by stakeholder groups is similar to the actual and projected identity of an organization [5]". Transparency creates, maintains, or repairing trust between the organization and stakeholders.

Positive Reinforcement. In the area of psychology and organizational behavior, numerous research has addressed ways to enhance motivation by creating success-focused environments. Interestingly, Norsk Hydro used social media to communicate with the employees. The organization acknowledged the contributions of the employees by retweeting them and created articles and videos highlighting the operators and responders as heroes. Sveen et al. have studied this mechanism in the security incident reporting system in an organization. The result indicates that the increased number of reporting indicates high information security awareness among the system users, and the increase in user motivation causes an increase in the reporting rate, and vice versa [13].

5   Conclusion

In this paper, we studied the Norsk Hydro case from the perspective of crisis communication. From our analysis, we find that risk communication is not only about apologizing or meeting a reporting duty. Instead, it is crucial to promote good behavior of employees by acknowledging their effort. Moreover, by keeping a transparent communication, lessons learned during the recovery operations can be shared with the community.

In the past, information regarding cyber security incidents was shared internally or with close allies. It is because protecting private information is commonly considered as a critical aspect of cyber incident management. Here, we advocate that companies should be more open about sharing information. Haas et al. [7] suggest that Information Sharing and Analysis Organization (ISAO)s create an atmosphere of transparency and inclusion while emphasizing that information sharing, similar to social networking activity, is a group activity and requires active and frequent involvement. In the Norsk Hydro case, in the two weeks following the incident, the company provided updates about the cyber incident with a frequency of at least one post per day, either on Twitter or Facebook.

Undoubtedly, it is still a challenge to ensure the right balance of disclosing and protecting information to defeat an immediate attack and to prepare for long-term security [6]. For this reason, companies should design protocols about what can be shared and what cannot.

The Norsk Hydro demonstrated that agility, transparency, and positive reinforcement are essential principles to promote the good behavior of employees, facilitate cooperation with the relevant authorities and managing reputation.

References

1. Employees find creative solutions in response to cyber-attack, April 2019. https://www.hydro.com/en-NO/about-hydro/stories-by-hydro/employees-find-creative-solutions-in-response-to-cyber-attack/
2. Operational and market update q12019, April 2019. https://www.hydro.com/Document/Index?name=Hydro%20Q1-2019%20Update&id=42133

3. Cimpanu, C.: Protonmail ddos attacks are a case study of what happens when you mock attackers, June 2018. https://www.bleepingcomputer.com/news/security/protonmail-ddos-attacks-are-a-case-study-of-what-happens-when-you-mock-attackers/
4. Coombs, W.T.: Ongoing Crisis Communication: Planning, Managing, and Responding. Sage Publications, California (2014)
5. Cornelissen, J.P.: Corporate communication. The International Encyclopedia of Communication (2008)
6. Goodwin, C., et al.: A framework for cybersecurity information sharing and risk reduction. Microsoft (2015)
7. Haass, J.C., Ahn, G.J., Grimmelmann, F.: Actra: a case study for threat information sharing. In: Proceedings of the 2nd ACM Workshop on Information Sharing and Collaborative Security, pp. 23–26. ACM (2015)
8. Hydro, N.: Cyber attack on hydro magnor, April 2019. https://www.youtube.com/watch?v=S-ZlVuM0we0
9. Hydro, N.: The cyber attack rescue operation in hydro toulouse, April 2019. https://www.youtube.com/watch?v=o6eEN0mUakM
10. Kulikova, O., Heil, R., van den Berg, J., Pieters, W.: Cyber crisis management: a decision-support framework for disclosing security incident information. In: 2012 International Conference on Cyber Security, pp. 103–112. IEEE (2012)
11. ProtonMail: a brief update regarding ongoing ddos incidents, July 2018. https://protonmail.com/blog/a-brief-update-regarding-ongoing-ddos-incidents/
12. Steelman, T.A., McCaffrey, S.: Best practices in risk and crisis communication: implications for natural hazards management. Nat. Hazards 65(1), 683–705 (2013)
13. Sveen, F.O., Sarriegi, J.M., Gonzalez, J.J.: The role of incident reporting in reducing information security risk. In: Twenty Seventh International Conference of the System Dynamics Society. The System Dynamics Society (2009)
14. Van Veelen, B., Storms, P., van Aart, C.: Effective and efficient coordination strategies for agile crisis response organizations. In: Proceedings of ISCRAM 2006 (2006)
15. Veil, S.R., Buehner, T., Palenchar, M.J.: A work-in-process literature review: incorporating social media in risk and crisis communication. J. Contingencies Crisis Manage. 19(2), 110–122 (2011)
16. Von Solms, R., Van Niekerk, J.: From information security to cyber security. Comput. Secur. 38, 97–102 (2013)
17. Weiner, D.: Crisis communications: managing corporate reputation in the court of public opinion. Ivey Bus. J. 70(4), 1–6 (2006)

SealedGRID: A Secure Interconnection of Technologies for Smart Grid Applications

Aristeidis Farao[1](✉), Juan Enrique Rubio[2], Cristina Alcaraz[2],
Christoforos Ntantogian[3], Christos Xenakis[3], and Javier Lopez[2]

[1] Neurosoft S.A., Athens, Greece
a.farao@neurosoft.gr
[2] Computer Science Department, University of Malaga, Campus de Teatinos s/n,
29071 Malaga, Spain
{rubio,alcaraz,jlm}@lcc.uma.es
[3] Department of Digital Systems, University of Piraeus, Piraeus, Greece
{dadoyan,xenakis}@unipi.gr

Abstract. In recent years, the Smart Grid has increasingly integrated cutting-edge technologies that generate several benefits for all the stakeholders involved, such as a more accurate billing system and enhanced Demand Response procedures. However, this modernization also brings with it diverse cyber security and privacy issues, which sets the necessity for developing a security platform specifically tailored to this scenario. In this paper, we present SealedGRID, which proposes a flexible architecture that provides security services at all levels by implementing Trusted Execution Environments on their devices, together with advanced authentication and authorization mechanisms, as well as privacy preserving techniques. These technologies are presented in depth and a final security analysis is conducted, which highlights the contributions of this project.

Keywords: Smart grid · Interoperability · Trust · Scalability

1 Introduction

The rapid evolution of Information and Communications Technologies (ICT) has fostered the evolution of traditional power grids to the Smart Grid (SG). It supports a two-way information exchange between customers and the Utility companies that enables a sustainable energy management and flexible tariffs that result in lower bills. EU regulations require member nations to ensure that 80% of residential households will be fitted with Smart Meters (SM) by 2020. However, the power grid will be also exposed to security threats inherited from the ICT sector, while privacy issues and new vulnerabilities related to the specific characteristics of the SG infrastructure will emerge. In this context, this paper highlights the main contributions of the SealedGRID project for the protection of the SG against these and other sophisticated attacks, providing a scalable,

S. Nadjm-Tehrani (Ed.): CRITIS 2019, LNCS 11777, pp. 169–175, 2020.
https://doi.org/10.1007/978-3-030-37670-3_14

highly trusted, and interoperable SG security platform. It is applicable to modern industrial networks as well as traditional control infrastructures like SCADA and telemetering systems, abiding the existing standardization work.

The architecture of this solution complies with the following requirements:

- **Scalability**: concerning the protection of utilities, which are vulnerable target due to the centralization of the grid
- **Trust**: SG nodes will be accessible by customers creating a fertile field for malicious users that may intercept personal information or alter energy measurements and costs;
- **Interoperability**: multiple heterogeneous technologies with multiple network operators and other stakeholders are involved.

In the next paragraphs, we present an overview of state-of-the-art technologies used in SealedGRID. Beginning with **key management**, some schemes in the SG are based on shared secret keys, which in turn hinder scalability. Other schemes utilize ID-based cryptography [1], whose main issue is that Private Key Generator should always be online and available, being a single point of failure.

There have also been efforts to integrate **trusted computing** on the SG, mainly with the use of the Trusted Platform Modules (TPM) [2] and the Trusted Execution Environments (TEE) [3]. In this project, we prioritize the use of TEEs, since TPMs usually imply higher costs, they do not offer protection against runtime attacks, they are not suitable for embedded devices and do not provide runtime attestation of executable programs; which can be met on the TEE and are required by the SealedGRID concept.

Regarding **privacy**, a lot of research has been done to prevent data disclosure by means of cryptography, using homomorphic encryption, traditional encryption, and masking. Based on standardization organizations in [4], the efficiency and privacy requirements of a privacy preserving mechanism for the SG can be met using masking. Solutions like [5] lack protection against non-repudiation and adaptability to node joining or leaving.

Authentication is also an important issue by the industry, leading to standards like DNP3 Authentication [6] and IEC 62351-5 [7]. In [8], a device-to-device authentication framework based on a two-layer approach is presented, where SMs are authenticated globally by a PKI and locally by channel signatures. In [9], an authenticated aggregation protocol is presented based on asymmetric keys, which preserves the authenticity of exchanged messages.

The design of secure **authorization** and interoperability mechanisms is also complex task [10], since the inter-connection between systems that are not originally envisioned to interoperate may present unanticipated problems. In [11], authors propose a dynamic authorization-based architecture based on Role Based Access Control, Policy Enforcement Points (PEPs) and Policy Decision Points (PDPs) to collect data streams from multiple sources connected to the Advanced Metering Infrastructure. Lastly, [12] presents a solution based on the use of PEPs and PDPs to interconnect large distributions with different vendor technologies.

The rest of the paper is organized as follows: Sect. 2 presents the different technologies used in SealedGRID, whereas Sect. 3 describes how they are integrated by the different components of its architecture. Section 4 analyzes how SealedGRID solutions address certain operational and security requirements, concludes the paper and adds the future work.

2   SealedGRID Technologies

In this section we briefly present the applied technologies in the proposed Sealed-GRID architecture which are the following: (a) Federated Login [13]; (b) SOMA [14]; (c) MASKER [15]; (d) TEE [16] and (e) Context Awareness Manager [17].

The SealedGRID deploys **Federated Login** achieving interoperability and ensuring communication among its components. Then, it utilizes OpenID Connect and OAuth2.0. However, we will not analyze these technologies, since they preexist the SealedGRID and are borrowed from the field of online services, [13].

SOMA [14] is a certificate-based authentication infrastructure that creates a secure authentication system for mesh networks without a TTP. It creates an efficient, self-organized and scalable authentication infrastructure based on a PGP-like architecture. The nodes independently decide with whom to interact, since the SOMA is built on a Peer-to-Peer (P2P) and Web-of-Trust (Wot) infrastructure. This way, SOMA does not use a Credential Authority (CA) and avoids delegation of trust to a TTP. Moreover, SOMA demands the existence of TEE for its secure execution and storage of the generated certificates.

MASKER [15] provides a privacy-preserving aggregation solution that responds to the following issues: (a) it assists the privacy and security of energy consumer and (b) facilitates DR. The SMs share cryptographically generated pseudo-random values with the Utility. These act as masks and obfuscate the real SMs consumption readings; an intermediate Aggregator provides the Utility with an aggregated consumption by several SMs. The Utility subtracts the used masks from the received sum, resulting the real combined consumption. Only, the SM has access to its real energy consumption value. All sensitive computations are protected by a TEE, which stores data and executes crucial operations.

As mentioned above, SealedGRID uses a **TEE** to protect its components from being manipulated and achieve these goals: (a) to protect device private keys and its sensitive data through secure storage; (b) to endorse remote attestation, and (c) to secure critical procedures like key management. Particularly, SOMA is executed within the TEE, where its certificates are stored. Furthermore, MASKER utilizes the TEE to provide confidentiality and authenticity to the executed code and stored data, and to prove the trustworthiness of Sealed-GRID nodes, components and modules. Finally, the Federated Login demands trustworthiness among the participating devices/nodes, which is ensured by the remote attestation mechanism.

It is necessary to implement an Access Control Management Service to control the information within the grid. However, it is also crucial to pair this control with the continuous assessment of the network in terms of security, as to permit or deny the use of certain services in case of risk. This is enabled by **context-awareness mechanisms**, which retrieve data about the production chain in real time (e.g., network events, alarms, raw traffic). Here we leverage Opinion Dynamics [17], a multi-agent collaborative algorithm capable of detecting attacks during their entire lifecycle, from a holistic perspective. It is designed as a framework to analyze information from external sources (e.g., IDS) together with Machine Learning techniques in a distributed way.

3   SealedGRID Components

In this section, we analyze the SealedGRID architecture focusing the SG different components: SMs, Aggregators, Utility, as well as the different technologies that each component encompasses (see Fig. 1). Moreover, the fundamental SG operations are briefly elaborated, depicting how the set of requirements discussed in the previous sections are met.

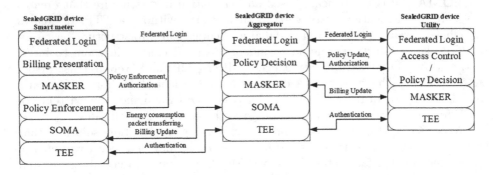

Fig. 1. Architectural components and integrated modules for SealedGRID

The **SealedGRID SM** communicates with other components without extra authentication using the Federated Login module. Also, it deploys the SOMA module, which includes: (a) the SOMA client to request to join in a domain and become part of the SOMA network, and (b) the SOMA authenticator used by an already authenticated SM in a SOMA network to handle a new join request; its certificate is issued by the domain's CA and stored within the TEE. Moreover, it generates the energy consumption readings and constructs the related packet within the MASKER where the TEE is involved. After its construction, it is forwarded to a SealedGRID Aggregator. Also, it receives periodical reports with billing updates through the MASKER. Finally, it plays the role of a PIP and PEP. The PIP determines the severity degree of the area, which can be requested by the PDP placed in the intermediate nodes of that domain. The PEP's role is utilized to access data or request the control of another SealedGRID SM from the same or different domains.

The **SealedGRID Aggregator** authenticates and authorizes new devices in a domain (using SOMA) and aggregates individual readings without being able to infer private information from these messages (using MASKER). As explained before, the security of these operations is ensured by the TEE. As for the authorization, it plays the role of the PEP, since it is responsible for policy enforcement in its domain, according to the policy defined by the Utility. Therefore, it is also considered as an intermediate level PDP, taking access control decisions in a local level.

The SealedGRID Utility is responsible to maintain DR and to calculate the billing by computing the total consumption of customers at the end of the billing period (for which MASKER is leveraged). Moreover, it is liable for issuing the system's policy, integrating the Federated Login module to provide seamless communication between SealedGRID components from different domains. Finally, a Utility plays the role of the PDP role to issue the system access control policy. However, it is also considered as an individual PEP, since it should ensure the enforcement of the security policy in its domain.

4   Discussion and Future Work

This section briefly outlines the fundamental operational and security requirements (i.e., service, infrastructure, and customers) that SealedGRID satisfies.

Service Requirements: Energy distribution services, require availability and accuracy in DR. SealedGRID utilizes the SOMA module to ensure availability, which creates a mesh network for providing authentication and trust management, avoiding single points of failure. Moreover, it employs the MASKER module to inform the Utility about the aggregated energy consumption in real-time, limiting the imposed overheads to the Utility.

Infrastructure Requirements: The SG infrastructure requires a scalable network as the number of customers' varies, while its components should interoperate and communicate to each other for seamless energy distribution. To ensure it, system's monitoring is required for detection of abnormal operation. Moreover, the issuance and enforcement of a system policy guarantees the appropriate system operation. The SOMA module provides scalability regardless of the number of involved components and the frequency of components join and leave. The Federated Login module grants unstoppable communication to the participated components without repetitive identification/auhtentication. In addition, Context Awareness Manager module monitors the system behavior based on information from real time events. Finally, SealedGRID sets the role of PDP in the Utilities to issue the system policy and the PEP's role in Aggregators for enforcing it in their domain, to ensure that system operations run smoothly and the participated components follow the policy.

Customer's Requirements: The SG customers require an authentication procedure to access multiple energy distribution systems with a single instance of identification. Moreover, they demand confidentiality to their personally identifiable information and stable energy supply without energy cutoffs. SealedGRID uses the SOMA module to authenticate new SMs and the Federated Login module to provide single-sign-on to access energy distribution systems by employing only one identification/authentication step within the whole SealedGRID domain. Finally, it implements the MASKER module which not only protects customers' personal data utilizing a TEE, but also enables the DR functionality for persistent and steady power supply.

Altogether, we achieve a federated, dynamic and secure SG architecture where the access control to critical resources, trust and privacy are considered. As future work, we intent to implement the proposed architecture in order to show the feasibility of the security components for practical use cases based on federated, complex and heterogeneous Smart Grid environments.

Acknowledgement. This work was supported by the European Commission under the SealedGRID project (H2020-MSCA-RISE-2017) with GA no. 777996.

References

1. Mohammadali, A.: A novel identity-based key establishment method for advanced metering infrastructure in smart grid. IEEE Trans. Smart Grid **9**(4), 2834–2842 (2018)
2. Trusted Computing Group, TPM Mobile with Trusted Execution Environment for Comprehensive Mobile Device Security, Whitepaper, June 2012
3. GlobalPlatform: Trusted Execution Environment System Architecture (2011)
4. CEN/CENELEC/ETSI, Smart Grid Information Security, December 2014
5. Knirsch, F., et al.: Error-resilient masking approaches for privacy preserving data aggregation. IEEE Trans. Smart Grid **9**(4), 3351–3361 (2018)
6. DNP3 Users Group Technical Committee. DNP3 Secure Authentication Specification Version 2.0, DNP Users Group Documentation as a supplement to Volume 2 of DNP3. Technical report, DNP Users Group, 2008
7. IEC TS 62351 series, Power systems management and associated information exchange - Data and communications security, Technical specification (2007)
8. Chin, W., et al.: A framework of machine-to-machine authentication in smart grid: a two-layer approach. IEEE Commun. Mag. **54**(12), 102–107 (2016)
9. Lu, R., et al.: Eath: an efficient aggregate authentication protocol for smart grid communications. In: 2013 IEEE Wireless Communications and Networking Conference (WCNC), pp. 1819–1824, April 2013
10. Alcaraz, C., Lopez, J.: Secure interoperability in cyber-physical systems. In: Security Solutions and Applied Cryptography in Smart Grid Communications, pp. 137–158. IGI global (2017). https://doi.org/10.4018/978-1-5225-1829-7.ch008. Accessed 19 Apr 2019
11. Veichtlbauer, A., et al. Advanced metering and data access infrastructures in smart grid environments. In: The Seventh International Conference on Sensor Technologies and Applications (SENSORCOMM), p. 638 (2013)
12. Alcaraz, C., et al.: Policy enforcement system for secure interoperable control in distributed smart grid systems. J. Network Comput. Appl. **59**, 301–314 (2016)
13. Killing the Password and Preserving Privacy with Device-Centric and Attribute-based Authentication. Zenodo, February 2019. https://arxiv.org/abs/1811.08360

14. Demertzis, F.F., Karopoulos, G., Xenakis, C., Colarieti, A.: Self-organised key management for the smart grid. In: Papavassiliou, S., Ruehrup, S. (eds.) ADHOC-NOW 2015. LNCS, vol. 9143, pp. 303–316. Springer, Cham (2015). https://doi.org/10.1007/978-3-319-19662-6_21

15. Karopoulos, G., et al.: Masker: masking for privacy-preserving aggregation in the smart grid ecosystem. Comput. Secur. **73**, 307–325 (2018)

16. Karopoulos, G., et al.: Towards trusted metering in the smart grid. In: 2017 IEEE 22nd International Workshop on Computer Aided Modeling and Design of Communication Links and Networks (CAMAD), pp. 1–5, June 2017

17. Rubio, J.E., Roman, R., Alcaraz, C., Zhang, Y.: Tracking advanced persistent threats in critical infrastructures through opinion dynamics. In: Lopez, J., Zhou, J., Soriano, M. (eds.) ESORICS 2018. LNCS, vol. 11098, pp. 555–574. Springer, Cham (2018). https://doi.org/10.1007/978-3-319-99073-6_27

A Dynamic Risk Assessment (DRA) Methodology for High Impact Low Probability (HILP) Security Risks
Short Paper

Carlo Dambra[1]([✉]), Chanan Graf[2], Jordi Arias[3], and Alex Gralewski[4]

[1] ZenaByte s.r.l., Genoa, Italy
carlo.dambra@zenabyte.com
[2] Railsec Ltd., Magshimim, Israel
chanan@railsec.com
[3] ETRA Investigacion y Desarrollo SA, Valencia, Spain
jarias.etraid@grupoetra.com
[4] PROPRS Ltd., Oxford, UK
alex.gralewski@proprs.com

Abstract. This paper proposes a Dynamic Risk Assessment (DRA) methodology applicable to the so-called High Impact Low Probability (HILP) security risks which, by their very nature, are difficult to identify or occur only infrequently. DRA is based on the processing of Weak Signals (WSs) to protect critical infrastructures and soft targets against HILP security risks before they materialise. DRA allows to rank WSs according to the reliability and credibility of the sources and to correlate them to obtain threat precursors. Experimental results have shown that DRA is effective and helps suppressing irrelevant alerts.

Keywords: Dynamic Risk Assessment · Low probability high impact risks

1 Introduction

This paper proposes a methodology to dynamically assess High Impact Low Probability (HILP) security risks which, by their very nature, are either difficult to identify or occur only infrequently [1]: in this category fall, for example, terrorism, extremism, and lone wolf actions. The dynamic assessment of risks is an essential element of any decision support tool aimed at improving the situational awareness while protecting critical infrastructures and/or soft targets against HILP security risks. Related probabilistic approaches (e.g. [2–4]) have two major drawbacks: typically present a high number of false positives and, to characterise the problem, require substantial statistical evidence that is not available for HILP security risks that manifest themselves as "black swans". The proposed Dynamic Risk Assessment (DRA) approach tries to overcome these drawbacks, by processing Weak Signals[1] (WSs) [5] collected from heterogeneous sources

---

[1] A WS can be defined as "*A seemingly random or disconnected piece of information that at first appears to be background noise but can be recognized as part of a significant pattern by viewing it through a different frame or connecting it with other pieces of information*" [14].

S. Nadjm-Tehrani (Ed.): CRITIS 2019, LNCS 11777, pp. 176–181, 2020.
https://doi.org/10.1007/978-3-030-37670-3_15

taking inspiration from Intrusion Detection Systems [6]. WSs, once detected and correlated with other WSs, can generate precursor alerts of threats related to HILP security risks to be deeper and further investigated. The paper is organised as follows: Sect. 2 discusses the DRA approach, Sect. 3 proposes an application of DRA to a mass gathering event, and finally Sect. 4 presents conclusions and future work.

2 The Proposed DRA Approach

The proposed DRA approach bases its reasoning on the processing of WSs, the minimum managed quantum of information. Starting from a static risk assessment, the DRA logic can be summarised in the following steps:

1. Continuously **collect** the WSs potentially representing precursors of threats;
2. **Analyse** each collected WSs and verify if, alone or correlated/grouped with other existing WSs, can represent a more **significant precursor** of a threat;
3. **Present** the potential detected precursor to a security operator for evaluation;
4. **Re-assess the risks** for the considered target accordingly.

Each WS, detected by a given source, contains the following minimal information:

- A unique **ID** that has embedded the reference to the source of the WS;
- The absolute time **t** in which it has been collected;
- The **geolocation** (x, y) - if available;
- A **snapshot** of what has been detected using a pre-defined semantic to help the operator to confirm, discard (false or nuisance alarms) or amend the detection.

Each detected WS is characterised by a **Significance (S)** value that is a combination of:

- The **Reliability (R)** of the source that characterises the ability of a source to give a true information in a particular context of use;
- The **Credibility (C)** of the information generated by the source, that introduces a measure of the degree of confirmation: the more an item of information is confirmed, the higher its credibility and, conversely, the more an item of information is contradicted by others, the less credible it becomes [7].

The Significance of the considered WS detected by the source m ranges in the [0, 1] interval and is computed as follows:

$$S(WS_{ID}) = (\alpha \cdot R_m + \beta \cdot C_m)/NF \qquad (1)$$

where:

- C_m and R_m are integer in [0, 5] (where 1 is very low and 5 is very high);
- The Normalising Factor NF keeps $S(WS_{ID})$ in [0, 1];
- α and β are correcting factors to tune the role of each factor in the product.

If the proposed methodology is applied to an event (e.g. a concert in a stadium) it is possible to add a further element that consider the Time Distance (TD_t) of the WS from the event date: the closer the detection of the WS to the event date the bigger the TD_t. $S(WS_{ID})$ then becomes:

$$S(WS_{ID}) = (\alpha \cdot R_m + \beta \cdot C_m + \gamma \cdot TD_t)/NF \qquad (2)$$

Once received, it is necessary to process WSs to evaluate if they can become, alone or together with other WSs, a **significant precursor** of a threat related to a specific HILP security risk. To this end three structures of **Precursors** are introduced:

- **Suspicious Sign (SS)**, represents a single WS that has either sufficient significance to become a SS or is related to a high-risk threat. In both cases, $S(SS) = S(WS)$;
- WSs coming from the intelligence services, i.e. **Intelligence Alerts (IA)**, can be considered a special Suspicious Event with maximum Significance $S(IA) = 1$;
- **Suspicious Pattern (SP)**, two or more WSs can create a SP if they have sufficient significance and are linked together according to one of the criteria described below.

The Precursors can be generated combining already collected WSs, SSs, IAs or SPs using either the experts' knowledge to define the rules for grouping WSs or data analytics applied to WSs [8–10] as follows:

- **Group**: a set of precursors without time and geographic constraints independently of the time sequence in which they are detected;
- **Sequence**: a set of precursors that need to be received in the correct sequence;
- **Area**: a set of precursors within the same area and in a given time interval;
- **Distance from Hot Spots**: a set of precursors in a given time interval all at a distance from Hot Spots (e.g. embassies, police offices, etc.) shorter than a given threshold;
- **Simultaneous Group**: the grouping is generated using the strategy of "**simultaneous events**", i.e. three or more WSs detected within a short period of time;
- **Data Analytics**: the grouping of precursors is generated using **data analytics** approaches for example through the generation of new rules on the basis of data collected in the past. A possible approach is described in [11], where Suspicious Activity Reports (SAR) collected by 911 emergency operators are analysed to identify and prioritise cases of interest from the large volume of SARs;
- **Operators Group**: generated by the operator according to his/her experience.

Precursors' Significance value is computed using the Significance values of all the WSs connected to it. The approach to combine Significance values for an SP with two WSs contributing to it, with significance S_1 and S_2 respectively, is derived from Certainty Factors [12] theory using the following formula

$$S_{1\,and\,2} = S_1 + (1 - S_1) \cdot S_2 \qquad (3)$$

Having more than two WSs contributing to the same SP, it is possible to iteratively apply the same formula.

Precursors, when triggered by WSs, can be then classified as either **Non-Critical** or **Critical**, i.e. elements that constitute an immediate threat for a given risk. **Critical Precursors** shall be triggered and brought immediately to the attention of a security operator that should take the necessary mitigation actions.

Using the above methodology, the **Risk Level** can be re-assessed using escalation approaches [13]. An example, when dealing with a mass gathering event, based on an IF-THEN-ELSE approach is given in the following:

- IF (Time Distance is Big) AND (no Critical precursors are triggered) THEN (the Risk Level is Very Low);
- IF (Time Distance is Big) AND (some Non-Critical Precursors are triggered) THEN (the Risk Level is Low);
- IF (Time Distance is Big) AND (at least one Critical Precursor is triggered) AND (Crowd Density is Low) THEN (the Risk Level is Medium);
- IF (Time Distance is Small) AND (at least one Critical Precursor is triggered) AND (Crowd Density is Low) THEN the Risk Level is High;
- IF (Time Distance is Small) AND (at least one Critical Precursor is triggered) AND (Crowd Density is High) THEN the Risk Level is Very High.

Clearly, exact and complete IF-THEN rules and related thresholds need to be defined according to laws, protocols and best practices including also socio-political and environmental conditions.

3   The DRA Application to a Mass Gathering Event: An Example

3.1   The DRA Practical Implementation

DRA methodology has been applied to a scenario representing a mass gathering event managed by a Law Enforcement Agency (LEA). The sources of WSs are:

- Normal citizens calling 112 emergency services;
- Stewards recruited to manage the event;
- Human-Centred Computer Vision (HCCV) tools able to semi-automatically recognise car plates, identify vehicles and suspicious behaviours of vehicles and individuals;
- Intelligence services.

The sequence of WS detection, SP generation and DRA is described in Fig. 1:

1. On the basis of the received WS, the corresponding values of sensor's credibility and reliability and the time distance from the event are identified.
2. The Significance is then computed using the formulas in Sect. 2 (with α, β and γ set to 1 for the sake of simplicity) and normalised to get values in the [0; 1] range.

Time	Signal/Pattern	Sensor	Description	Reliability R	TD	Significance	Norm. Significance	Risk Level
T01	WS01	Citizen	Suspicious Vehicle	4	1	8	0,06	
T02								
T03	WS02	HCCV	Suspicious Behaviour	3	1	6	0,05	
T04	WS03	Citizen	Suspicious Vehicle	4	1	8	0,06	
T05	SP01	DRA Rule	Suspicious Vehicle	WS01 & WS02 & WS03			0,17	
T06	Patrol sent to check							
T07	SP01 deleted after operator's check							1
T08	IA01	Intelligence	Possible terrorist attack	5	2	50	0,40	3
T09	WS04	HCCV	Red truck	5	2	40	0,32	
T10	IA02	Intelligence	Stolen yellow van	5	2	50	0,40	
T11	WS05	HCCV	Suspicious plate detected	5	2	50	0,40	
T12	SP02	DRA Rule	Suspicious Vehicle	IA02 & WS05			0,64	
T13	IA03	Intelligence	Terrorist presence	5	3	75	0,60	
T14	Reaction due to IA03							
T15	WS06	HCCV	Brown truck	5	3	60	0,48	
T16	WS07	HCCV	Red van	5	3	60	0,48	
T17	WS08	HCCV	Suspicious plate detected	5	3	75	0,60	
T18	WS09	HCCV	Blue car	5	3	60	0,48	
T19	WS10	HCCV	Suspicious plate detected	5	3	75	0,60	
T20	WS11	Steward	Suspicious person	5	3	75	0,60	
T21	WS12	HCCV	Suspicious plate detected	5	3	75	0,60	
T22	SP03	DRA Rule	Suspicious Vehicle	WS08 & WS10 & WS12			0,94	
T23	Reaction due to SP03							
T24	WS13	Steward	Suspicious person	5	3	75	0,60	
T25	SP04	DRA Rule	Probing security	WS11 & WS 13			0,84	4
T26	WS14	HCCV	Quite dense crowd	4	5	80	0,64	
T27	WS15	HCCV	Yellow van	5	5	100	0,80	
T28	SP05	DRA Rule	Ramming vehicle	SP02 & WS15			0,93	5
T29	Reaction due to SP05							

Fig. 1. DRA applied to a mass gathering event

Through the application of the DRA rules the Precursors are created and, if necessary, Risk Level is modified.

3.2 A Possible Architectural Approach for DRA Implementation

DRA has been implemented in the framework of the H2020 LETSCROWD project[2] in a Web-server GIS-based architecture receiving WSs from CCTV-based crowd density estimators, Web-crawling and semantic intelligence on social media, crowd behaviour modelling and humans-as-sensors. SPs above a selected Significance threshold are brought to the attention of an operator to allow a risk-aware decision-making process.

3.3 First Experimental Results

First experimental results have confirmed the validity and effectiveness of the approach, as confirmed by the involved LEAs and that DRA helps distinguishing irrelevant alerts, thereby reporting only significant threats to operators. The proposed DRA approach is going to be further validated on real scenarios (mass gathering events) from Law Enforcement Agencies (LEAs). The main problem of the DRA application lies in the identification of sources of WSs apart from human-as-a-sensors and (semantic) intelligence: most of the CCTV-based tools are either not sufficiently reliable or facing serious privacy issues.

---

[2] https://www.letscrowd.eu.

4   Conclusions

The proposed DRA methodology has the following advantages over more traditional approaches: it searches for out-of-the-ordinary behaviours, reduces the number of false alarms, does not require large statistical samples and is sufficiently simple to run in real-time. Further research should confirm the first promising experimental results focusing on identifying suitable WSs sources, characterising them in terms of reliability and credibility and evaluating the feedback from LEAs' operators.

Acknowledgements. This paper is based on the work carried out in the LETSCROWD project that has received funding from the European Union's Horizon 2020 research and innovation programme under Grant Agreement number 740466.

References

1. UK Government Office for Science: Blackett Review of High Impact Low Probability Risks, London (2011)
2. Ezell, B., Bennet, S., von Winterfeldt, D., Sokolowski, J., Collins, A.: Probabilistic risk analysis and terrorism risk. Risk Anal. **30**(4), 575–589 (2010)
3. Brynielsson, J., Horndahl, A., Johansson, F., Kaati, L., Martenson, C., Svenson, P.: Analysis of weak signals for detecting lone wolf terrorists. In: 2012 IEEE European Intelligence and Security Informatics Conference (2012)
4. Paté-Cornell, M.L.: Fusion of intelligence information: a Bayesian approach. Risk Anal. **22**(3), 445–454 (2002)
5. Holopainen, M., Toivonen, M.: Weak signals: ansoff today. Futures **44**, 198–205 (2012)
6. Chakir, E., Moughit, M., Khamlichi, Y.: A real-time risk assessment model for intrusion detection systems. In: 2017 IEEE International Symposium on Networks, Computers and Communications (ISNCC) (2017)
7. North Atlantic Treaty Organization (NATO) Information Handling Services: Annex to STANAG 2022 (Edition 8) (1992)
8. Vu, H.: Deep Abnormality Detection in Video Data, Melbourne (2017)
9. Xu, D., Ricci, E., Yan, Y., Song, J., Sebe, N.: Learning deep representations of appearance and motion for anomalous event detection (2015)
10. Hasan, M., Choi, J., Neumann, J., Roy-Chowdhury, A.K., Davis, L.S.: Learning temporal regularity in video sequences, Las Vegas (2016)
11. Strom, K.J., Hollywood, J.P.M.: Using 911 calls to detect terrorism threats, June 2009. https://www.nij.gov/journals/263/pages/911-calls.aspx
12. Lucas, P.J.F.: Certainty-factor-like structures in Bayesian belief networks. Knowl.-Based Syst. **14**, 327–335 (2001)
13. UK HM Treasury: Orange Book: Management of risk - Principles and Concepts, London (2004)
14. Schoemaker, P.J.H., Day, G.S.: How to make sense of weak signals. MIT Sloan Manag. Rev. **50**(3), 80–89 (2009)

On Actuator Security Indices

Jezdimir Milošević$^{(\boxtimes)}$, Sebin Gracy, and Henrik Sandberg

KTH Royal Institute of Technology, 10044 Stockholm, Sweden
{jezdimir,gracy,hsan}@kth.se

Abstract. Actuator security indices are developed for risk assessment purposes. Particularly, these indices can tell a system operator which of the actuators in a critical infrastructure network are the most vulnerable to cyber-attacks. Once the operator has this information, he/she can focus the security budget to protect these actuators. In this short paper, we first revisit one existing definition of an actuator security index, and then discuss possible directions for future research.

Keywords: Risk assessment · Cyber-attacks · Cyber-physical systems

1 Introduction

Actuators are one of the crucial components in controlling critical infrastructure networks. For example, generators in a power grid enable us to use electricity, and pumps in a water distribution network ensure that we have a stable supply of drinkable water. Due to their importance, one should ensure that actuators are secured. Namely, the problem of security of critical infrastructure networks is well recognized [1], and attacks against these networks have already been documented [2,5]. Hence, one should be able to characterize if the actuators are vulnerable, and if they are, build an effective defence strategy to protect them.

A possible way to characterize the security level of network components is by using security indices. The first security index was introduced to characterize the vulnerability of sensors monitoring a power network [7]. This sensor security index was further analyzed in [4,10], where it was discussed how to calculate it efficiently. Motivated by the research on sensor security indices, the work [6] proposed a security index that can be used to characterize vulnerability of actuators in a network. In this short paper, we first revisit the actuator security index from [6] in some detail, and illustrate with an example how the index can be used to characterize vulnerability of actuators. We then outline some open problems suitable for future work.

2 Actuator Security Index δ

In this section, we start off by listing the notations, then introduce the model setup, define an actuator security index, and finally conclude by illustrating on an example how to use the index for risk assessment purposes.

© Springer Nature Switzerland AG 2020
S. Nadjm-Tehrani (Ed.): CRITIS 2019, LNCS 11777, pp. 182–187, 2020.
https://doi.org/10.1007/978-3-030-37670-3_16

Notations

$\mathbb{R}$, $\mathbb{Z}$, $\mathbb{Z}_+$ and $\mathbb{Z}_{\geq 0}$ denote the set of real numbers, integers, positive integers, and non-negative integers, respectively. I_N indicates an identity matrix of size N. $|\mathcal{X}|$ indicates cardinality of a set $\mathcal{X}$. Given two matrices A and B, let $A \odot B$ denote the entrywise product. $[A]_{ij}$ denotes the element corresponding to the ith row and j^{th} column of matrix A.

Model Setup

·We first model dynamics of a critical infrastructure network. We use the linear time-invariant model

$$\begin{aligned} x(k+1) &= Wx(k) + B_a a(k), \\ y(k) &= Cx(k) + D_a a(k), \end{aligned} \tag{1}$$

where: $k \in \mathbb{Z}_{\geq 0}$ is a time step; $x(k) \in \mathbb{R}^{n_x}$ is the vector of physical states of the network (such as pressures, temperatures, or power flows); $y(k) \in \mathbb{R}^{n_y}$ is the vector containing measurements collected from the process; $a(k) \in \mathbb{R}^{n_u + n_y}$ is the attack vector. The first n_u elements of a model attacks against the actuators, while the last n_y model attacks against the sensors. Hence, the matrices B_a and D_a have the form $B_a = [B \ \mathbf{0}_{n_x \times n_y}]$, $D_a = [\mathbf{0}_{n_y \times n_u} \ \mathbf{I}_{n_y}]$, where $B \in \mathbb{R}^{n_x \times n_u}$ is assumed to have a full column rank. Note that the matrix W models interaction in between the system states and that the matrix C maps the system states to the sensor measurements.

Let $\mathcal{I} = \{1, \ldots, n_u + n_y\}$ be the set of sensors and actuators, and $\mathcal{I}_a \subseteq \mathcal{I}$ be the set of sensors and actuators controlled by the attacker. The attacker can arbitrarily select the values of the elements of a with the indices from $\mathcal{I}_a$. The elements of a that correspond to non-attacked components $\mathcal{I} \setminus \mathcal{I}_a$ are always equal to zero. Additionally, the attacker possesses full model knowledge, that is, knows the matrices W, B, C. Finally, we assume that the attacker wants to: (i) Attack one of the actuators; (ii) Remain undetected by the operator. To model the second goal, we need a suitable definition of undetectability. In this work, we use the definition of perfect undetectability [13].

Definition 1. *Let* $x(0) = 0$. *The attack* $a \neq 0$ *is perfectly undetectable if* $y = 0$.

In simple words, the measurements under the attack appear to be the same as in the steady state $x(0) = 0$, that is, $y = 0$. For this reason, perfectly undetectable attacks are potentially very dangerous.

Problem Formulation

We now introduce an actuator security index δ from [8]. By $\delta(i)$, we denote the security index of an actuator $i \in \mathcal{I}$. We define this index to be equal to the minimum number of sensors and actuators that need to be compromised to enable the attacker to conduct a perfectly undetectable attack. Additionally, we

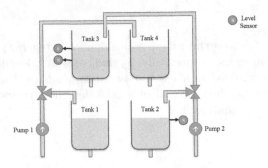

Fig. 1. Quadruple tank process.

impose the constraint that actuator i has to be used in the attack. In this way, we capture a goal or intent by the attacker.

Note that actuators that have small values of δ are considered to be more vulnerable compared to those with high values. Hence, one can use the security index in a risk assessment as a likelihood score of an actuator being attacked [11]. From the defender's perspective, the worst case that can happen is to have $\delta(i) = 1$. In this case, an attacker can attack i while remaining perfectly undetectable without compromising any other component.

Let $||a||_0 = |\cup_{k \in \mathbb{Z}_{\geq 0}} \mathrm{supp}(a(k))|$, where $\mathrm{supp}(a(k)) = \{i \in \mathcal{I} : a^{(i)}(k) \neq 0\}$. The problem of calculating security index $\delta(i)$ for an actuator i can then be defined in the following way.

Problem 1. Calculating δ

$$\delta(i) := \underset{a}{\text{minimize}} \quad ||a||_0$$
$$\text{subject to} \quad x(k+1) = Wx(k) + B_a a(k),$$
$$0 = Cx(k) + D_a a(k),$$
$$x(0) = 0,$$
$$a^{(i)} \neq 0.$$

Here, we have as the objective to find the minimum number of sensors and actuators to conduct a perfectly undetectable attack. The first two constraints are introduced to ensure that the physical dynamics is according to the model we introduced. The second and the third constraint ensure that the attack signal a is perfectly undetectable. The last constraint implies that actuator i for which we are calculating the security index is actively used in the attack. We now introduce an example to clarify the index.

Example

Consider a quadruple tank process shown in Fig. 1. The plant states x_1–x_4 are the levels in four tanks. There are two actuators in the system: Pump 1 (P_1)

and Pump 2 (P_2). From [12], we know that this process can be modeled by

$$x(k+1) = \begin{bmatrix} 0.975 & 0 & 0.0042 & 0 \\ 0 & 0.977 & 0 & 0.0044 \\ 0 & 0 & 0.958 & 0 \\ 0 & 0 & 0 & 0.956 \end{bmatrix} x(k) + \begin{bmatrix} 0.05155 & 0.0016 & 0 & 0 & 0 \\ 0.0019 & 0.0447 & 0 & 0 & 0 \\ 0 & 0.0737 & 0 & 0 & 0 \\ 0.0850 & 0 & 0 & 0 & 0 \end{bmatrix} a(k),$$

$$y(k) = \begin{bmatrix} 0 & 1 & 0 & 0 \\ 0 & 0 & 1 & 0 \\ 0 & 0 & 1 & 0 \end{bmatrix} x(k) + \begin{bmatrix} 0 & 0 & 1 & 0 & 0 \\ 0 & 0 & 0 & 1 & 0 \\ 0 & 0 & 0 & 0 & 1 \end{bmatrix} a(k).$$

By manipulating P_1, the attacker influences levels in Tank 1, Tank 2, and Tank 4. Since the level in Tank 2 is measured, the attacker needs to attack the corresponding sensor to stay perfectly undetectable. The levels in Tank 1 and Tank 4 are not measured, so the attacker does not need to attack additional components. Hence, the attacker needs to attack only P_1 and the sensor measuring level in Tank 2, so the security index for this actuator is $\delta(P_1) = 2$.

Attacking P_2 is more complex. Namely, this pump influences the levels in Tank 1, Tank 2, and Tank 3. Since the level in Tank 2 is measured by one, and the level in Tank 3 by two sensors, the attacker needs to attack three sensor to ensure perfect undetectability. Thus, the attacker needs to attack P_2 and three sensors, so the security index for this pump is $\delta(P_2) = 4$.

We now move to the next section, where we outline possible extensions of the work on security indices.

3 Actuator Indices Independent of System Parameters

Critical infrastructure networks are complex systems that can change configuration over time. Take for example power grids. There, micro-grids can detach from the grid to form separate grid [9] or power lines may be turned of due to maintenance or due to damage [3]. Hence, the matrices W, B_a, C, and D_a can change over time. Note that changing the coefficients in the system matrices might result in a change in the value of $\delta(i)$. To overcome this limitation, one could take recourse to structured systems theory. More specifically, the objective in such a setting would be to obtain a lower bound on $\delta(i)$ that is impervious to variations in system parameters. In some sense, if this lower bound is sufficiently high, then one can be certain that the system is secure for almost all realizations. In the rest of this section, we will focus on introducing this idea.

Problem Statement

Let $\mathcal{W}$ (resp. $\mathcal{B}_a$, $\mathcal{C}$, $\mathcal{D}_a$) denote structured matrices that obey the pattern of imposed zeros of W (resp. B_a, C, D_a). That is, fixed zeros in W (resp. B_a, C, D_a) would be denoted by zeros in $\mathcal{W}$ (resp. $\mathcal{B}_a$, $\mathcal{C}$, $\mathcal{D}_a$), while positions that are not fixed to zero in W (resp. B_a, C, D_a) would be represented by a parameter in $\mathcal{W}$ (resp. $\mathcal{B}_a$, $\mathcal{C}$, $\mathcal{D}_a$). Note that all such parameters are *free* parameters (i.e., real-valued parameters that can be chosen arbitrarily). The interpretation is as follows: the fixed zero positions denote interactions that are prohibited, while parameters represent the intensity of existing interactions. With respect to the Example depicted in Fig. 1, $\mathcal{W}$ and $\mathcal{B}_a$ are given by

$$
\mathcal{W} = \begin{bmatrix} w_{11} & 0 & w_{13} & 0 \\ 0 & w_{22} & 0 & w_{24} \\ 0 & 0 & w_{33} & 0 \\ 0 & 0 & 0 & w_{44} \end{bmatrix}, \qquad \mathcal{B}_a = \begin{bmatrix} b_{a_{11}} & b_{a_{12}} & 0 & 0 & 0 \\ b_{a_{21}} & b_{a_{22}} & 0 & 0 & 0 \\ 0 & b_{a_{32}} & 0 & 0 & 0 \\ b_{a_{41}} & 0 & 0 & 0 & 0 \end{bmatrix}.
$$

The matrices $\mathcal{C}$ and $\mathcal{D}_a$ can be written analogously.

Each numerical choice of free parameters yields a realization $\{W, B_a, C, D_a\}$. Let $\{\mathcal{W}, \mathcal{B}_a, \mathcal{C}, \mathcal{D}_a\}$ denote the family of all linear time-invariant (LTI) systems $\{W, B_a, C, D_a\}$ having dynamics as given in (1). The main objective is to provide a bound on $\delta(i)$, say γ (where $\gamma \in \mathbb{Z}_{>0}$) such that for *almost all*[1] realizations $\{W, B_a, C, D_a\} \in \{\mathcal{W}, \mathcal{B}_a, \mathcal{C}, \mathcal{D}_a\}$, $\delta(i) \geq \gamma$. A secondary objective is to seek strategies so as to increase γ. The rationale being the following: the higher the value of γ, the more secure actuator i is, since $\delta(i)$ becomes larger.

Note that addressing our main objective essentially translates to solving Problem 1 for almost all realizations $\{W, B_a, C, D_a\} \in \{\mathcal{W}, \mathcal{B}_a, \mathcal{C}, \mathcal{D}_a\}$, as opposed to a specific realization. However, this might be a rather cumbersome route towards achieving our goals, since for large-scale networks Problem 1 is NP-hard (see, Theorem 1 in [6]). This motivates us to seek alternative approaches.

Alternative Approach: Graph Theory

Structured system (1) can be described by a graph as explained in the following. Let $X = \{x_1, x_2, \ldots, x_{n_x}\}$, $Y = \{y_1, y_2, \ldots, y_{n_y}\}$, and $A = \{a_1, a_2, \ldots, a_{n_u+n_y}\}$ denote the set of state vertices, actuator vertices, output vertices, and attack vertices, respectively. We define by: $\mathcal{E}_W = \{(x_j, x_i) \mid \mathcal{W}_{ij} \neq 0\}$ the edges in between the state nodes; $\mathcal{E}_{B_a} = \{(a_j, x_i) \mid \mathcal{B}_{a_{ij}} \neq 0\}$ the edges in between the attack and state nodes; $\mathcal{E}_C = \{(x_j, y_i) \mid \mathcal{C}_{ij} \neq 0\}$ the edges in between the states and measurements; $\mathcal{E}_{D_a} = \{(a_j, y_i) \mid \mathcal{D}_{a_{ij}} \neq 0\}$ the edges in between the attack and measurement nodes. The graph associated with the system (1) can then be defined as $\mathcal{G} = (\mathcal{V}, \mathcal{E})$, where $\mathcal{V} = X \cup A \cup Y$ and $\mathcal{E} = \mathcal{E}_W \cup \mathcal{E}_{B_a} \cup \mathcal{E}_C \cup \mathcal{E}_{D_a}$.

Our approach towards addressing the aforementioned problem can be crystallized as follows. Given that we have knowledge of the underlying graph $\mathcal{G}$ and also of the set of attacked actuators and sensors $\mathcal{I}$: (i) Find graph-theoretic conditions which ensure that, for actuator i, for almost all choices of edge weights in $\mathcal{G}$, $\delta(i) \geq \gamma$; (ii) If possible, modify the graph $\mathcal{G}$ (for instance, by adding or deleting suitable edges) such that γ is increased.

---

[1] There might exist realizations $\{W^1, B_a^1, C^1, D_a^1\} \in \{\mathcal{W}, \mathcal{B}_a, \mathcal{C}, \mathcal{D}_a\}$, for which $\delta(i) < \gamma$. However, all such realizations would lie on a set of Lebesgue measure zero in the space of free parameters in $\mathcal{W}$, $\mathcal{B}_a$, $\mathcal{C}$ and $\mathcal{D}_a$. Hence, instead of ensuring that for *every* realization $\delta(i) \geq \gamma$, we seek to ensure for almost all realizations, $\delta(i) \geq \gamma$.

4   Conclusions

This work revisited the security index that can be used to measure vulnerability of actuators in a network, and illustrated in an example how this index can be used for risk assessment purposes. We then outlined possible directions for future research. Namely, since critical infrastructure networks are changing over time, and the security indices are fragile in terms of system variations, we plan to define novel security indices that are not fragile with respect to the aforementioned changes. Particularly, structured system theory seems to be a promising approach to analyze and efficiently calculate novel types of security indices.

Acknowledgments. This work was supported by the Swedish Civil Contingencies Agency through the CERCES project, the Swedish Research Council (grant 2016-0861), and the EU-project LarGo!

References

1. Guide to increased security in industrial information and control systems. Swedish Civil Contingencies Agency (MSB) (2014)
2. Analysis of the cyber attack on the Ukrainian power grid. Electricity Information Sharing and Analysis Center (2016)
3. Amin, M., Schewe, P.F.: Preventing blackouts. Sci. Am. **296**(5), 60 (2007)
4. Hendrickx, J.M., Johansson, K.H., Jungers, R.M., Sandberg, H., Sou, K.C.: Efficient computations of a security index for false data attacks in power networks. IEEE Trans. Autom. Control **59**(12), 3194–3208 (2014)
5. Kushner, D.: The real story of STUXNET. IEEE Spectr. **50**(3), 48–53 (2013)
6. Milosevic, J., Texeira, A., Johansson, K.H., Sandberg, H.: Actuator security indices based on perfect undetectability: computation, robustness, and sensor placement. CoRR abs/1807.04069 (2019). http://arxiv.org/abs/1807.04069
7. Sandberg, H., Teixeira, A., Johansson, K.: On security indices for state estimators in power networks. In: Proceedings of the First Workshop on Secure Control Systems (2010)
8. Sandberg, H., Teixeira, A.M.H.: From control system security indices to attack identifiability. In: Proceedings of the Science of Security for Cyber-Physical Systems Workshop (2016)
9. Simpson-Porco, J.W., Dörfler, F., Bullo, F.: Synchronization and power sharing for droop-controlled inverters in islanded microgrids. Automatica **49**(9), 2603–2611 (2013)
10. Sou, K.C., Sandberg, H., Johansson, K.H.: Computing critical k-tuples in power networks. IEEE Trans. Power Syst. **27**(3), 1511–1520 (2012)
11. Teixeira, A., Sou, K., Sandberg, H., Johansson, K.: Secure control systems: a quantitative risk management approach. IEEE Control Syst. **35**(1), 24–45 (2015)
12. Teixeira, A.: Toward cyber-secure and resilient networked control systems. Ph.D. thesis, KTH Royal Institute of Technology (2014)
13. Weerakkody, S., Liu, X., Son, S.H., Sinopoli, B.: A graph-theoretic characterization of perfect attackability for secure design of distributed control systems. IEEE Trans. Control Network Syst. **4**(1), 60–70 (2017)

Testbed Evaluation of DoS Attacks on PID-Controllers

(Short Paper)

Viktor Tuul and Henrik Sandberg$^{(\boxtimes)}$

KTH Royal Institute of Technology, Stockholm, Sweden
{tuul,hsan}@kth.se

Abstract. We present ongoing work in evaluating the performance of PID-controllers under DoS attacks. The experiments are conducted in a recently developed virtual testbed, which is openly available. An important observation is that also benign physical processes may exhibit potentially dangerous oscillations under DoS attacks unless care is taken in the control implementation. An event-based PID-controller with adaptive gain shows promising performance under DoS attack.

Keywords: Cyber-physical attack · PID-control · DoS attacks

1 Introduction

Cyberattacks on Industrial Control Systems (ICS) and other cyber-physical critical infrastructures is a growing concern in society [1]. Often these infrastructures have lagging cyber-defenses and successful cyberattacks may have devastating physical consequences. As complement to traditional IT-security solutions in these infrastructures, researchers have worked on security solutions tailored towards the cyber-physical nature of these systems. See [8], and references therein. In this vein, we will in this short paper present ongoing work in a virtual testbed for evaluation of cyberattacks and defenses in continuously controlled physical infrastructures.

The testbed has been developed in C# with the purpose of evaluating cyber-physical impact of attacks and defences in controlled critical infrastructures. The testbed uses five main software modules: (1) `Control Center`, (2) `Controller`, (3) `Plant`, (4) `Anomaly Detector`, and (5) `Channel`. Two instantiations of the `Channel` module are the *Supervisory control network* and the *Field communications network*) in Fig. 1. Due to the modular framework and use of UDP/IP-networking, the testbed is simple to deploy on standard computer architectures. The virtual testbed software can be downloaded from GitHub [7].

A contribution of this paper is to highlight the importance of the implementation of low-level controllers with respect to cyberattacks. We focus the tests on DoS attacks [4] in the field communications network, see Fig. 1 (right),

---

Work funded by the Swedish Civil Contingencies Agency (project CERCES).

S. Nadjm-Tehrani (Ed.): CRITIS 2019, LNCS 11777, pp. 188–194, 2020.
https://doi.org/10.1007/978-3-030-37670-3_17

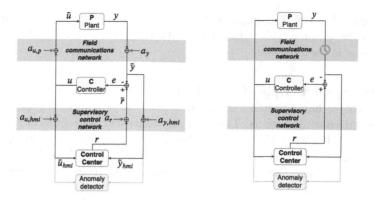

Fig. 1. Block diagrams illustrating the modules of the testbed, data-injection attacks in all channels (left), and DoS attacks on the sensor channel (right, see Sect. 3).

and propose a novel event-based PID-controller. Event-based control is not new, see [2,6], for example, but our design uses an adaptive gain (suppress factor) that explains its improved performance under DoS attacks.

2 Three PID-Controllers

The testbed `Control` module currently supports three PID-controller implementations: PID-, PIDplus-, and PIDsuppress-control. The testbed has been used for evaluating these controllers in various attack scenarios, see Sect. 3. In particular, the PIDsuppress-controller shows promising results under DoS attacks.

The ideal PID-controller [3] in continuous time is given by

$$u(t) = K_P e(t) + K_I \int_0^t e(\tau) \, d\tau + K_D \frac{de(t)}{dt}, \qquad (1)$$

where $e(t) = r(t) - y(t)$ is the control error, $r(t)$ the setpoint, and $y(t)$ is the measured process variable at time t. The parameters K_P, K_I, and K_D are the proportional, integral, and derivative gains, respectively. In the testbed, the signals and controllers are sampled with period $\Delta t_k := t_k - t_{k-1}$, where k is sample number, and e_k denotes the sample $e(t_k)$, for instance.

Time-Triggered PID-Control. In the time-triggered PID-controller, the integral term is discretized with *uniform* sampling intervals $\Delta t_k = \Delta t$, yielding $\sum_{i=1}^k e_i \Delta t$. Backward finite-difference approximation is used to approximate the derivative, $de/dt|_{t_k} \approx (e_k - e_{k-1})/\Delta t$. The sampled controller takes the form

$$u_k = K_P e_k + K_I \sum_{i=1}^k e_i \Delta t + K_D \frac{e_k - e_{k-1}}{\Delta t}, \qquad (2)$$

and the controller (2) is executed at time instants $t_k = k\Delta t$. If a measurement does not arrive at time t_k, because of DoS attacks, for instance, the last received measurement is used instead.

Event-Triggered PIDplus-Control. The PIDplus-controller [6] was introduced to better handle packet drops and time-varying sampling periods Δt_k in networked control systems. The PIDplus-controller acts (almost) as a normal PID-controller when there is no packet loss. The proportional, integral, and derivative terms are event based and only updated upon the arrival of a new packet $e_k = r_k - y_k$. The integral term is computed recursively using a filter state F_k,

$$F_k = F_{k-1} + (U - F_{k-1})(1 - \exp(-\Delta t_k/T_{\text{res}})). \tag{3}$$

Here U is the last confirmed actuator setting, and T_{res} is a tuning parameter for the integral action, which can be set as $T_{\text{res}} = K_P/K_I$. The derivative term is given by $D_k = K_D(e_k - e_{k-1})/\Delta t_k$, and the proportional term is $P_k = K_p e_k$. This yields the controller $u_k = P_k + F_k + D_k$.

An advantage with (3) is that after a long communication outage (Δt_k large), $F_k \approx U$, which avoids potentially dangerous wind-up phenomenon and harmful control commands. For comparison, in (2) the integral will increase at rate $e_i \Delta t$ per sample under packet drops.

Event-Triggered PIDsuppress-Control. The PIDsuppress-controller is a new event-based PID-implementation [7], which adapts *both* the proportional and integral gains depending on sampling period Δt_k. This is achieved using the *suppress*-factor $\gamma_k \in (0, 1]$. The control at time k is

$$u_k = K_P \gamma_k e_k + K_I \sum_{i=1}^{k} \gamma_i e_i \Delta t_i + K_D \frac{e_k - e_{k-1}}{\Delta t_k}. \tag{4}$$

The suppress factor γ_k changes the control characteristics depending on the communication quality (the sampling period). The derivative term does not include γ_k since it is already small for large Δt_k. The factor γ_k is updated using Algorithm 1. The tuning parameter T_{supp} is an order of magnitude larger than the nominal Δt_k, and $\beta \in (0, 1]$ is a low-pass filter constant. In case sampling time increases, Algorithm 1 makes γ_k small immediately. Conversely, γ_k is only slowly increased to ensure a sustained small suppress factor if packets arrive in bursts.

Algorithm 1. Suppress factor γ_k

1: **function** $\gamma_k(\gamma_{k-1}, \beta, \Delta t_k, T_{\text{supp}})$
2:     $\hat{\gamma}_k \leftarrow \exp(-\Delta t_k/T_{\text{supp}})$
3:     **if** $\hat{\gamma}_k \leq \gamma_{k-1}$ **then return** $\hat{\gamma}_k$
4:     **else return** $(1 - \beta)\gamma_{k-1} + \beta\hat{\gamma}_k$

To better understand the role of γ_k, please note that a sampling period Δt_k approximately introduces a time delay $\Delta t_k/2$ in the loop gain transfer function L (assuming zero-order hold sampling). To avoid an unstable or oscillatory feedback system for large Δt_k, one should decrease the system bandwidth (to increase the phase margin). The bandwidth is approximately given by the cross-over frequency ω_c, satisfying $|L(i\omega_c)| = 1$. Around the nominal cross-over frequency $\omega_{c,nom}$, we have $|L(i\omega)| \approx (\omega_{c,nom}/\omega)^\alpha$, $\alpha \approx 1.5$, for well-tuned systems. If we include the suppress factor $\gamma_k \leq 1$, we obtain an updated $\omega_c = \omega_{c,nom}\gamma_k^{1/\alpha}$, which implies a decreased bandwidth in response to large Δt_k and reduced risk for instability.

3   Testbed Evaluation of DoS Attack

In the following testbed experiments, the plant is a simulated nonlinear cascade of fluid tanks. The measurement y is a fluid level, and the input u controls the fluid inflow by means of a pump. The exact model is available in [7]. The performance of the three control algorithms, PID-, PIDplus-, and PIDsuppress-control, are compared by conducting experiments where the communication between the plant and controller is subject to packet-drop/DoS attacks, see Fig. 1 (right). The DoS attack model and three experiments are described next.

DoS Attack Model. A realistic DoS attack model should include long periods of communication outage. For this, we use a simple two-state Markov chain, namely the Gilbert-Elliott model [5]. The channel state X_k at sample k is dependent on the previous state X_{k-1} according the state transition probabilities $P_d^p = P(X_k = \text{pass}|X_{k-1} = \text{drop})$, and $P_p^d = P(X_n = \text{drop}|X_{k-1} = \text{pass})$. A topic for future work is to implement more realistic DoS attack models in the testbed, such as the ones listed in [4].

Change in Setpoint. The first experiment is conducted along the following procedure: (1) The setpoint r is changed from 0 to 6 (at Time ≈ 2 s). (2) A DoS attack starts, with the channel state transition probabilities set to $P_d^p = 0.9$ and $P_p^d = 0.1$ (at Time ≈ 5 s). (3) r is changed from 6 to 12 (at Time ≈ 6 s). Figure 2 shows the step responses. The results show that the three controllers exhibit similar nominal performance when there is no DoS attack (Time $\in [2,5]$ s). This is not the case when packet-drop starts (Time $\in [5,15]$ s). The time-triggered PID-controller exhibits very undesirable non-decaying oscillations in this phase, potentially causing physical damage. In contrast, in the PIDplus-controller the oscillations are more damped. In the PIDsuppress-controller, the oscillations are almost removed, indicating that this is a promising implementation under both nominal and attack conditions. The explanation is that the PIDsuppress-controller automatically decreases the bandwidth, making the step response slightly slower during attack, and thus significantly decreases the oscillations.

Table 1. Average time spent in the *pass* and *drop* channel states before switching.

Drop-out setting [%]	100–0	20–80	15–85	10–90	7–93	5–95
Average pass time [sec]	–	0.25	0.24	0.22	0.22	0.21
Average drop time [sec]	–	1.00	1.34	2.00	2.86	4.00

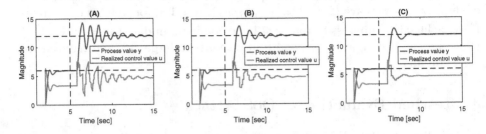

Fig. 2. (A) Time-triggered PID-control. (B) PIDplus-control. (C) PIDsuppress-control. The DoS attack starts at 5 s and causes various degree of oscillations following a setpoint change.

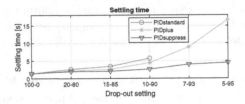

Fig. 3. Average settling time using time-triggered PID-, PIDplus-, and PIDsuppress-control with varying packet drop-out.

Varying DoS Attack Intensity. Step-response trials as in Sect. 3 are also conducted with varying attack intensity. For each drop-out setting, five trials are conducted. The results are summarized in Fig. 3 where average step-response settling time under attack is plotted against the drop-out setting (the state transition probabilities P_d^p and P_p^d in %). The average time spent in each channel state before switching, is reported in Table 1.

The time-triggered PID-controller did not manage to settle the system in any trial with the *7–93* and *5–95* drop-out. It is also seen that the PIDsuppress ensures faster settling time than PIDplus and time-triggered PID-control for all drop-out settings.

Influence of Measurement Noise. An experiment in steady state (no setpoint change) but in the presence of measurement noise is also conducted. Figure 4 shows a case where noise of standard deviation 0.2 is applied to the measured process value. The DoS attack starts at 6.5 s and the *5–95* drop-out setting is used.

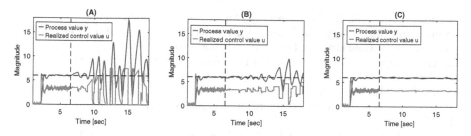

Fig. 4. (A) Time-triggered PID-control. (B) PIDplus-control. (C) PIDsuppress-control. The DoS attack starts at 6.5 s and causes various degree of oscillations, as triggered by natural measurement noise.

As before, the three controllers exhibit similar performance when there is no DoS attack (Time $\in [1, 6.5]$ s). When the attack is active (Time $\in [6.5, 18]$ s), the time-triggered PID and PIDplus-controller both exhibit non-diminishing oscillations, which is not the case for PIDsuppress. The occurrence of oscillations is because the received measurement varies quickly around the correct value due to noise and gets randomly "stuck" above, or below, the setpoint under attack, and the controller reacts accordingly. In the PIDsuppress case, the bandwidth is decreased to the extent that this noise is filtered out. The cost is a slower control system, as already illustrated in the first experiment.

4 Conclusions

We compared the performance of three different PID-controllers under DoS attack using experiments in a recently developed virtual testbed [7]. An event-based implementation (PIDsuppress) with adaptive gain outperformed the other implementations under attack. An important observation is that even a benign physical process (fluid tanks), exhibits potentially dangerous oscillations under DoS attack unless care is taken in the implementation of these low-level controllers.

For future work, the proposed implementations could be evaluated under more realistic DoS attack models [4]. Also more advanced attacks, such as data-injection attacks, Fig. 1 (left), could be similarly evaluated in the virtual test bed.

References

1. Guide to increased security in industrial information and control systems. Swedish Civil Contingencies Agency (MSB) (2014)
2. Årzén, K.E.: A simple event-based PID controller. IFAC Proc. Vol. **32**(2), 8687–8692 (1999). 14th IFAC World Congress 1999, Beijing, China, 5–9 July
3. Åström, K.J., Hägglund, T.: Advanced PID control. The Instrumentation Systems, and Automation Society (2006)

4. Cetinkaya, A., Ishii, H., Hayakawa, T.: An overview on denial-of-service attacks in control systems: Attack models and security analyses. Entropy **21**(2), 210 (2019)
5. Haßlinger, G., Hohlfeld, O.: The Gilbert-Elliott model for packet loss in real time services on the internet. In: 14th GI/ITG Conference-Measurement, Modelling and Evalutation of Computer and Communication Systems, pp. 1–15. VDE (2008)
6. Song, J., Mok, A.K., Chen, D., Nixon, M., Blevins, T., Wojsznis, W.: Improving PID control with unreliable communications. In: ISA EXPO Technical Conference (2006)
7. Tuul, V.: https://github.com/viktortuul/Modular_Control_System (2019)
8. Urbina, D.I., Giraldo, J.A., et al.: Limiting the impact of stealthy attacks on industrial control systems. In: Proceedings of the 2016 ACM SIGSAC Conference on Computer and Communications Security, CCS 2016, pp. 1092–1105. ACM, New York (2016)

Industry and Practical Experience Reports

White Paper on Industry Experiences in Critical Information Infrastructure Security: A Special Session at CRITIS 2019

Giacomo Assenza[1], Valerio Cozzani[2], Francesco Flammini[3]([⊠]),
Nadezhda Gotcheva[4], Tommy Gustafsson[5], Anders Hansson[6], Jouko Heikkila[4],
Matteo Iaiani[2], Sokratis Katsikas[9], Minna Nissilä[4], Gabriele Oliva[1],
Eleni Richter[7], Maaike Roelofs[8], Mehdi Saman Azari[3], Roberto Setola[1],
Wouter Stejin[8], Alessandro Tugnoli[2], Dolf Vanderbeek[8], Lars Westerdahl[5],
Marja Ylönen[4], and Heather Young[8]

[1] University Campus Biomedico of Rome, Rome, Italy
[2] University of Bologna, Bologna, Italy
[3] Linnaeus University, Växjö, Sweden
francesco.flammini@lnu.se
[4] VTT Technical Research Centre of Finland, Espoo, Finland
[5] Swedish Defence Research Agency, Linköping, Sweden
[6] Sectra Communications AB, Teknikringen 20, 58330 Linköping, Sweden
[7] EnBW Energie Baden-Württemberg AG,
Durlacher Allee 93, 76131 Karlsruhe, Germany
[8] TNO, Netherlands Organisation for Applied Scientific Research, Delft, Netherlands
[9] Norwegian University of Science and Technology, Gjøvik, Norway

Abstract. The security of critical infrastructures is of paramount importance nowadays due to the growing complexity of components and applications. This paper collects the contributions to the industry dissemination session within the 14th International Conference on Critical Information Infrastructures Security (CRITIS 2019). As such, it provides an overview of recent practical experience reports in the field of critical infrastructure protection (CIP), involving major industry players. The set of cases reported in this paper includes the usage of serious gaming for training infrastructure operators, integrated safety and security management in the chemical/process industry, risks related to the cyber-economy for energy suppliers, smart troubleshooting in the Internet of Things (IoT), as well as intrusion detection in power distribution Supervisory Control And Data Acquisition (SCADA). The session has been organized to stimulate an open scientific discussion about industry challenges, open issues and future opportunities in CIP research.

© Springer Nature Switzerland AG 2020
S. Nadjm-Tehrani (Ed.): CRITIS 2019, LNCS 11777, pp. 197–207, 2020.
https://doi.org/10.1007/978-3-030-37670-3_18

1   Introduction

Critical infrastructures must fulfil dependability requirements that impose the use of rigorous techniques during procurement, development, commissioning and training/preparedness, as well as in regulatory audits of the operational systems.

In this CRITIS special session we have solicited short presentations from an industrial perspective addressing any aspect of such processes and of the supervision of critical operations. Reports of actual cases were welcome including success stories or failure/emergency management operations with the aim of sharing lessons learnt. Contributions to this session were welcome by academics working on research projects with industrial partners who have driven experimental evaluations of research outcomes and prototypes with the help of real-world data, or have validated hypotheses by performing surveys and interviews.

For this special session, we finally accepted five contributions involving four universities together with six different companies and research centers. Each of the following sections will address a specific contribution for the special session.

More specifically, the rest of this paper is organized as follows: Sect. 2 provides an experience report on the usage of serious gaming for training infrastructure operators; Sect. 3 describes an experience of integrated safety and security management in the chemical and process industry; Sect. 4 addresses risks related to the cyber-economy for energy suppliers; Sect. 5 addresses an experience report related to intrusions in power distribution SCADA systems; Sect. 6 describes a novel industry concept known as smart troubleshooting with interesting IoT applications; and, finally, Sect. 7 draws conclusions.

2   Using Serious Gaming to Train Operators of Critical Infrastructure

This section presents the development of a serious game component used to train operators of critical infrastructure. It describes the basic operation of the game and how an iterative development process ensured that the pedagogical objectives were met. Lessons learned while developing and testing the game are also presented.

2.1   Introduction

When a new course to train operators of critical infrastructure to use security controls was developed at the Swedish Defence Research Agency (FOI), a serious gaming component was integrated into the course schedule. The purpose was to create a story-living experience, as described by Perla and McGrady [1], which enhances the learning process by allowing the course participants to work with the knowledge gained during the lectures and the laboratory sessions. In the game, the participants have to protect an IT environment of a fictitious company.

Here, the term *serious gaming* is used to describe *a game in which education is the primary goal, rather than entertainment*, as defined by Michaels and Chen in 2006 [2]. The decision to develop the game was made during the overall design of the training course. The game runs as short sessions throughout the course where each session focuses on the security controls presented in the foregoing lectures and labs.

During the development, a board game form factor was used which allowed the design team to focus on the game play rather than on technical solutions. An iterative development process was used with four test runs involving two groups of FOI personnel and two groups consisting of the intended target groups of the training course. After each test run, feedback was collected upon which the design team made relevant adjustments prior to the next test.

2.2   The Narrated Scenarios and the Game Play

During the game, the participants are divided into teams of three or four. To create a relevant narrative as described by Perla and McGrady [1], each team constitutes a group of consultants hired by a fictitious company operating a critical infrastructure. The board of executives of the company recently identified that their business falls under the EU directive on the security of network and information systems (NIS Directive) [3]. The task of the team is to ensure that the level of protection of the IT environment meets the requirements of the legislation. Each company has different needs of availability and confidentiality, which means that the groups need to prioritize different security controls.

During each session, the participants must choose a set of security controls to implement in order to handle vulnerabilities and to protect their systems. They can alter the overall design of the IT environment by changing the structure of the network as well as by moving critical systems. The participants also have to manage a series of vulnerabilities. The actions are performed and tracked on a game board having icons that represent the systems. The security controls are represented by playing cards of which only a limited set can be used in each session. Even though the game is not a competition against the other teams, a monetary measurement is used to motivate the teams as described by Sullivan et al. in 2018 [4]. At the end of each session, one or more incidents are played against the IT environments, and if the severity of the incidents surpasses the level of protection, the company will lose some of its revenue.

2.3   Lessons Learned

The feedback from the four test groups confirms that the use of serious gaming is a relevant way to train operators of critical infrastructure on cyber security. This conclusion is also supported by observations made by the design team during the tests, where the game engaged all of the course participants. The board game form factor supported vivid discussions within the teams.

During the first three test runs, the narrative was observed to be too weak to be engaging. This issue was solved by adding the NIS directive and the consultant perspective to the narrated scenarios. Another observation was that the initial amount of information early in the first two sessions was too large for the teams to manage. This was solved partly by simplifying the game play and partly by distributing the information more evenly between the sessions.

Future development will add better support for calculating the security levels of the IT environments and to visualize the performance of each team. The tests indicate that the security controls and the cyber incidents are relevant, but further effort is needed to ensure that the game remains relevant.

3　SAFeRA 4STER: Integrated Management of Safety and Security Synergies in Seveso Plants

The Chemical and Process Industry, due to the use of hazardous materials and to the role it plays in the economy, is vastly deemed to be a vital sector and thus considered as a Critical Infrastructure. In order to reduce the risk of failures and minimize the consequences of possible events, the European community created and implemented safety policies and standards such as the Seveso Directives [5,6]. However, security measures fall outside the scope of the previous version of such regulations and only in the Seveso III Directive they have been partially included. As highlighted in the SAFeRA 2018 call for proposals [7], the security of Seveso sites has become a matter of increasing concern due to growing threats stemming from terrorism, internal malevolence and cyberspace.

3.1　Objective

The objective of the 4STER project [8] is to suggest solutions for managing safety and security in a coordinated manner, as well as to examine how the threats stemming from digitalization are understood and identified. The following three Research hypotheses are defined: (1) Despite tensions, significant synergies between safety and security management exist; (2) Security-related scenarios concerning intentional acts are not adequately considered in documentation following up the Seveso Directive; (3) Many companies in the European process industry lack adequate cyber security awareness. The project will analyze how safety and security can be combined in an integrated approach for securing plants; it will investigate how cyber-physical threats are perceived; and it will suggest methodologies for identifying the indicators of imminent major accidents.

3.2　Relevance and Impact

The project will have three main contributions: (1) drawing an integrated safety and security management framework for Seveso sites; (2) providing deeper insights into attitudes, awareness and preparedness of European process industries in relation to cyber-physical security threats, which are not adequately dealt in Seveso Directives and safety reports; (3) Producing guidelines for the early identification of accident scenarios with intentional causes that allows an easier integration of the safety reports with security-related scenarios. These results will serve for significantly improving safety and security in the 12.000 Seveso III sites of the European Union (http://ec.europa.eu/environment/seveso/). Moreover, regulators, senior managers, safety/ security experts, shop-floor workers in companies, and policy makers benefits from the results, which will be disseminated via seminars, blogs and events by the SAFERA platform.

4 Recent Trends in Cyber Economy and Their Impact on Operational Technology

The experience report included in this section addresses the recent trends in cyber economy, summarized under the term "digital transformation", from the perspective of an energy supplier. An overview of changes, impacts and some ideas on how to survive in a multicloud universe are given.

The typical functioning of an energy supplier requires the production, transport, supply, trading and sales of energy. These five main parts of one company need to work together but they have widely different characteristics. Energy production, transport and supply are typical parts of the critical infrastructure. For energy transport and supply a grid is needed; the business of an energy distributor is more decentralized. The business of energy trading and sales is depending on data and information technology (IT). While trading operating at stock markets is regulated like banking business, energy sales has a distributed character. Sales agents, partners and being close to their customers dominate this business.

In the last few years some fundamental changes hit the energy suppliers: the liberalization of the energy market. They had to take out the energy transport section due to unbundling reasons. The end of nuclear power usage in Germany took out another stabilization factor. The grow of renewable energies spread our business all over the country. Energy production on the consumer side added more distributed micro-scenarios.

Low market prices for energy forces us to look for new business opportunities. In this segment they meet web companies and start-ups as aggressive competitors.

Due to the changes in the energy market and the impacts of the digital transformation[1] we are urged to move into a future digital market. This urge did not occur solely in our IT department but in any part of our company. Looking for a digital solution in the age of omnipresent easy-to-rent cloud services any part of our company will find something suitable. As outcome our landscape is covered with a lot of cloud solutions. Since most parts of our business cannot be done in isolation - things are interconnected and need to exchange data - we get into a complex interlinked meshed situation, a grid of data and control, spanning

---

[1] The term is quite modern in economy, widely used in business and especially in consulting. A number of diverse definitions exist in the literature [9], but a widely accepted one is still to be found.

through a public shared medium called "internet"[2]. Further, this expansion of the existence of our company over the internet and clouds is not only virtual. The internet of things (IoT) is offering even more opportunities. Just get some interoperable IT-gadgets, implement the solution, adapt operational technology (OT) and manage your identities and relations. The IoT, smart devices and any kind of smart technology act as a bridge between the virtual internet and the physical world, thus enlarging the IT network. Many of these new business ideas start as a small proof of concept and there is not enough time to or maybe not the will to waste time in things like enhanced security, administration or compliance. Having real start-ups as competitors a short time to market often dominates the action. At least we cannot slow down to a speed we were used to since the electrification took place[3].

To have a meaningful example for digital transformation at an energy supplier we will take a closer look at the maintenance of wind power stations. Wind farms are under permanent physical stress, so they need maintenance on a regular base. In the past we did the necessary registration of the inventory, checks and maintenance work locally. Operational information technology and office information technology where clearly separated. Today remote checks and control of power plants is common. External and internal staff is using a mixture of office IT and OT to do their job. Manufacturers of OT equipment modernize their technologies and adapt or enable IT network protocols to be used as transport layers in OT environments. Office IT technologies get partly mixed into operational IT. Tomorrow we will use IoT-devices in each wind station to measure and check the OT. We will collect a lot of data in real time and send it via internet to big data analytic services in the cloud. Leveraging artificial intelligence techniques on this data and on the results will allow improved predictive maintenance better then before. Our maintenance staff will be automatically managed by a Cloud-IT-System which controls and supports the work forces via smart gadgets via internet. Operational IT, office IT and cloud IT will be interlinked and mixed.

The Digital Transformation shifts our well known conflict situation "IT versus OT" into a three-party-problem: "OT versus on premise IT versus cloud IT". While the gaps between the technologies are closing, the differences regarding the understanding of risks, the handling of failures and consequences and the understanding that staff have of their job are still there. We are addressing these with cross-functional work groups, overall architectural approaches and a group wide program for a cultural shift which is strongly enforced by the top management.

---

[2] Anything which uses internet as transport layer can be considered as somehow shared and public. Even if a VPN is used, it will still have the public internet as a base layer.

[3] For example, it took from 1922 up to 1925 to build the Schwarzenbach Dam.

5   Intrusion Attempt on the Power Distribution Grid

Digitalization transforms energy companies to IT constellations within the energy sector. The increased level of system-to-system connectivity enables automation and increases efficiency. New business models are being developed that use the inter-connectivity between such systems. Technologies like virtual local area networks, virtualization and cloud platforms are increasingly utilized to reduce hardware, administrative and maintenance costs. This technology change introduces new dependencies into SCADA systems. As availability of these systems is often critical, such dependencies add new risks. SCADA systems now share both computing and network resources with less critical systems. This experience report addresses a real world intrusion attempt utilizing dependencies that in this case would not have been detected without the visibility provided by network monitoring.

5.1   Digitalization

Digitalization means IT-systems, network domains and connected things (IoT) are being connected with each other and thus enabling exchange of data between these entities. The driving forces for this digital transformation are an increased level of automation, improved efficiency and the enabling of new digital services. Out of this transformation new business models are being developed. Traditional energy companies will in the future become IT-cooperation's within the energy sector. Digital systems with different purposes and requirements, like information technology (IT) and operational technology (OT) systems are interconnected. Applications and services that solve a broad range of different tasks share the same computing resources, but also in some cases the same network assets. The security implication of resource sharing is that less trusted applications, services and networks may share the same computing or network resources. This fact may be used to attack critical systems like SCADA networks for power distribution.

Great efforts are being made at many organizations to reduce the burden related to administration of the ever increasing complexity of IT systems. This has introduced virtualization and cloud platforms, which now is common in many origination's IT environments. A typical IT environment today is a hybrid, consisting of a mix of on-site and outsourced IT infrastructures. Sharing resources reduces costs for administration and maintenance. As soon as there is a potential for cost savings or increased profits, a transformation to a new technology cannot be stopped.

5.2   Sharing Resources

The security implications due to the evolution of IT infrastructures into hybrid systems has not been fully addressed in real world systems. Sharing resources in such systems applies to both servers and network appliances. As an example, core functions in our society like our broadband infrastructures share is some cases network assets with SCADA systems for power distribution. The reason for sharing network resources is simple - It's all about cost savings. If we can use the same network switches for a geographically distributed SCADA system with for example a broad-band management network, there is a possibility for significant cost savings. However, shared resources like network assets may increase the attack surface. In the case presented here, sharing network resources increased the attack surface for a SCADA system that is used for power distribution.

5.3   An Intrusion Attempt

Proactive security and the ability to detect threats related to shared infrastructure resources as early as possible is essential. The earlier a threat can be detected, the less risk for serious and costly incidents.

In this experience report, we describe a real-world intrusion attempt and demonstrate the importance of visibility into shared network resources. By monitoring both SCADA and broad-band management network traffic segments in a shared network switch, the attack could be mitigated before it became a direct threat to the SCADA power distribution network.

6   Smart-Troubleshooting in the Connected Society

Today's digital world and evolving technology have improved the quality of our lives but they have also come with a number of new threats. In the society of smart cities and Industry 4.0, where many cyber-physical devices connect and exchange data through the Internet of Things, the need for addressing information security and solving system failures becomes inevitable. System failures can occur because of hardware failures, software bugs or interoperability issues. In cooperation with Sigma Technology AB[4] (Sweden), we introduced the industry-originated concept of "smart troubleshooting", that is the set of activities and tools needed to gather failure information generated by heterogeneous connected devices, analyze them, and match them with troubleshooting instructions and software fixes.

6.1   Introduction and Objective

Most of the components in modern computer systems are based on interconnected devices which are manufactured by different vendors. Though many failures within an individual component may be taken care of by their respective manufacturers; it is likely that any other failure between different components in modern computer systems, such as a simple connectivity problem will not be supported by the manufacturers, as it is generally not covered under the warranty. Therefore, due to interoperability issues, it will not be possible to troubleshoot all system failures based on single product information.

---

[4] https://www.sigmatechnology.se/news/sigmas-notes-disruptive-innovations-in-the-world-around-us/.

Instead, a large amount of information sources should be explored to build knowledge about failure modes, causes (intentional and unintentional), consequences, as well as how to diagnose them and finally repair the system. Also, if performed manually, such a process can be highly time consuming and error-prone.

All the above discussion leads us to believe that diagnosing and troubleshooting failures in an IoT system will be a huge problem in the near future which may not be covered by any manufacturer, unless all the entities within the system are manufactured by the same company. In [10] we look through and analyze previous works in the field of diagnosing and troubleshooting IoT systems. Other related concepts such as error prevention also were looked at. Furthermore, we take a step ahead and look for ways through which the IoT system, in case of a failure, can automatically diagnose itself and possibly, also compute a viable antidote which can be applied to the system to fix the problem in real time. This phenomenon of predicting and preventing a fault, or automatically diagnosing and repairing the system in case of an error, and simultaneously learning so that the same error does not occur twice, is termed Smart Troubleshooting. Smart troubleshooting can be categorized into four primary phases, namely:

- Prevention
- Detection & Diagnosis
- Recovery
- Evolution.

As can be intuitively inferred, these phases are sequential and recurrent in a connected cyber-physical system. Prevention, as the name suggests, is the ability of a system to prevent a fault before it happens. However, if the fault is somehow activated resulting in an error, the virtue of the system to detect the same and diagnose it so that an appropriate fix can be applied is termed as Detection and Diagnosis. Further, the process of applying the fix is dubbed as Recovery. Moreover, the system should also be able to learn so that the same error could be prevented from happening again. We call this process "Evolution".

Based on the discussion and motivation above, we can formulate our research question as *How can we promptly recognize anomalies in heterogeneous connected devices (including Embedded Systems, Cyber-Physical Systems and the Internet of Things), and (semi)automatically apply appropriate troubleshooting solutions based on available information, in order to restore correct system operation, reduce the time-to-repair and the probability of maintenance mistakes?*

6.2   Challenges and Opportunities

It is evident that the problem of smart troubleshooting - although relatively easy to specify - is highly challenging due to its multifaceted and cross-discipline nature, entailing aspects of artificial intelligence, formal modeling and data analytics, in order to support online identification of failure patterns, mine troubleshooting information based on a combination of natural language and machine readable sources, match appropriate solutions to recognized failures, apply those solutions through structured workflow management models and procedures.

This project shows that while there are numerous approaches to tackle issues like Error Prevention, Detection and Diagnosis, Recovery and Evolution for specific domains in IoT, there is no concrete solution or framework for Smart Troubleshooting that can handle all these issues at once, plausibly in the form of a feedback loop [11]. Moreover, as different components in an IoT system fabricate their own event logs, comprehending event logs with diverse formats is an ambitious problem to solve. Even in case of log format standardization, the events and states recorded could differ in each device.

Digital twins is an important concept that can play a pivotal role in troubleshooting IoT systems in the future. It is essentially a virtual representation, or a virtual doppelganger, as termed by IBM, of a cyber-physical asset. It enables the interaction of the application with devices in a consistent manner by providing an appropriate abstraction layer. Digital twins are conceptualized to follow the life-cycle of a device and its associated data. It can also be used to simulate system operation in a specific scenario without actually running the system, in order to anticipate any faults-errors-failures that might occur over time. The simulations can also be "fast-forwarded" to foresee the effects of updates, repairs, preventive maintenance, and even future threats. Apart from avoiding a failure in an IoT system, using digital twins can also help predict the future, increase the accuracy and reduce costs. Despite those initiatives, digital twins for IoT can still be considered as a "concept", and future efforts will be needed to make IoT digital twins a reality. Therefore, we believe IoT digital twins can be a promising research area which is destined to generate key technologies which can effectively support smart troubleshooting.

7   Conclusion

This paper has provided a brief summary of practical experience reports presented at the industry dissemination session of the 14th International Conference on Critical Information Infrastructures Security (CRITIS 2019). Such a session is very important to stimulate discussion about real-world industry needs and how recent research developments can be leveraged in order to tackle current industry challenges in the CIIP area. We believe the diversity of applications included in this session is also essential to foster comparison and facilitate both knowledge and technology transfer across multiple security-critical domains [12].

Acknowledgement. The work reported in Sect. 3 was supported by INAIL via the European Safera project "Management of Safety and Security Synergies in Seveso Plants" (4STER).

References

1. Perla, P., McGrady, E.: Why wargaming works. Nav. War Collage Rev. **64**(3), 111–130 (2011)
2. Michael, D., Chen, S.: Serious Games - Games that Educate, Train and Inform. Thomson Course Technology, Boston (2016)
3. Directive (EU) 2016/1148 of the European Parliament and of the Council of 6 July 2016 concerning measures for a high common level of security of network and information systems across the Union, OJ L 194, 19.7.2016, pp. 1–30
4. Sullivan, D., Colbert, E., Hoffman, E., Kott, A.: Best practices for designing and conducting cyber physical system war games. Computational and information sciences directorate, U.S. Army Research Laboratory, Adelphi, MD, USA (2018)
5. Council Directive 82/501/EEC of 24 June 1982 on the major-accident hazards of certain industrial activities, OJ L 230, 5.8.1982, pp. 1–18
6. Directive 2012/18/EU of the European Parliament and of the Council of 4 July 2012 on the control of major-accident hazards involving dangerous substances, amending and subsequently repealing Council Directive 96/82/EC, OJ L 197, 24.7.2012, pp. 1–37
7. https://www.safera.eu/
8. Integrated Management of Safety and Security Synergies in Seveso Plants (SAF€RA 4STER) project. https://projects.safera.eu/project/21
9. Reis, J., Amorim, M., Melão, N., Matos, P.: Digital transformation: a literature review and guidelines for future research. In: Rocha, Á., Adeli, H., Reis, L.P., Costanzo, S. (eds.) WorldCIST'18 2018. AISC, vol. 745, pp. 411–421. Springer, Cham (2018). https://doi.org/10.1007/978-3-319-77703-0_41
10. Caporuscio, M., Flammini, F., Khakpour, N., Singh, P., Thornadtsson, J.: Smart-troubleshooting connected devices: concept, challenges and opportunities. J. Future Gener. Comput. Syst. (2019, in press). https://doi.org/10.1016/j.future.2019.09.004
11. Fortino, G., Russo, W., Savaglio, C., Shen, W., Zhou, M.: Agent-oriented cooperative smart objects: from IoT system design to implementation. IEEE Trans. Syst. Man Cybern. Syst. **48**(11), 1939–1956 (2018)
12. Tokody, D., et al.: Complex, resilient and smart systems. In: Flammini, F. (ed.) Resilience of Cyber-Physical Systems: From Risk Modelling to Threat Counteraction, pp. 3–24. Springer, Cham (2019). https://doi.org/10.1007/978-3-319-95597-1_1

Correction to: A Comparison Between SWIFT and Blockchain from a Cyber Resiliency Perspective

Luisa Franchina and Guido Carlomagno(iD)

Correction to:
Chapter "A Comparison Between SWIFT and Blockchain from a Cyber Resiliency Perspective"
in: S. Nadjm-Tehrani (Ed.): *Critical Information Infrastructures Security*, **LNCS 11777,**
https://doi.org/10.1007/978-3-030-37670-3_12

Reference 26 of this paper has been updated. The authors were unaware that [1] had almost fully plagiarized [2] and wish to give full credit to the original authors.

[1] RETRACTED ARTICLE: Dheeraj, J., Gurhubaran, S.: DDoS mitigation using blockchain. Int. J. Res. Eng. Sci. Manag. **1**(10) (2018).

[2] Rodrigues, B., Bocek, T., Lareida, A., Hausheer, D., Rafati, S., Stiller, B.: A blockchain-based architecture for collaborative DDoS mitigation with smart contracts. In: Tuncer, D., Koch, R., Badonnel, R., Stiller, B. (eds.) AIMS 2017. LNCS, vol. 10356, pp. 16–29. Springer, Cham (2017). https://doi.org/10.1007/978-3-319-60774-0_2.

The updated version of this chapter can be found at
https://doi.org/10.1007/978-3-030-37670-3_12

Author Index

Printed in the United States
By Bookmasters